White House Operations

THE JOHNSON PRESIDENCY

An Administrative History of the Johnson Presidency Series

White House Operations

THE JOHNSON PRESIDENCY

By Emmette S. Redford and Richard T. McCulley

University of Texas Press, Austin

Printed in the United States of America

First edition, 1986

Requests for permission to reproduce material from this work should be sent to:
Permissions
University of Texas Press
Box 7819
Austin, Texas 78713

Library of Congress Cataloging-in-Publication Data

Redford, Emmette Shelburn, 1904–
White House operations.

(An Administrative history of the Johnson presidency)
Bibliography: p.
Includes index.
1. Presidents—United States—Staff. 2. United States—Politics and government—1963–1969. 3. Johnson, Lyndon B. (Lyndon Baines), 1908–1973. I. McCulley, Richard T., 1946– II. Title. III. Series.
JK518.R43 1986 353.03'1'0924 85-26437
ISBN 0-292-79033-3

Contents

Tables

Foreword

This is the fifth in a series of publications that will form An Administrative History of the Johnson Presidency. Ten to twelve special studies like this one and an overall volume are planned.

Our objective is to provide a comprehensive view of how a president and those who assisted him managed the White House and the executive branch to achieve the objectives of law and presidential policy. Administration will be studied as part of the responsibility of a president—in this case, President Lyndon B. Johnson.

The view taken of administration is comprehensive. It includes the interrelations among policy, administration, and program development. It encompasses administration in its various aspects: development of the infrastructure, including structuring and staffing the executive branch and budgeting for its operations; implementation of policy; and presidential management of the executive branch.

We aim for an authentic and adequate historical record based primarily on the documentary materials in the Lyndon B. Johnson Library and on interviews with many people who assisted President Johnson. We hope the historical record as presented from a social science perspective will amplify knowledge of administrative processes and of the tasks and problems of the presidency.

The series is being financed primarily by a grant from the National Endowment for the Humanities, with additional aid from the Lyndon Baines Johnson Foundation, the Hoblizelle Foundation, and the Lyndon B. Johnson School of Public Affairs of the University of Texas at Austin.

The findings and conclusions in publications resulting from this study do not necessarily represent the view of any donor.

Emmette S. Redford, project director

James E. Anderson, deputy project director

Preface

Writing a book on White House operations has been a challenging task. Since ours was the first effort to treat this subject in one administration comprehensively, we have had to develop an organization through which the diverse aspects of the subject could be included in a balanced treatment. We had to penetrate an arena clouded from outside view and, with difficulty, define precisely what that arena was and who the participants were. Moreover, many papers of President Lyndon B. Johnson are not open to researchers until fifty years beyond his death.

We have tried to present a systematic view on the basis of information gleaned primarily from the Lyndon B. Johnson archival library. This often gives not only fragmentary but conflicting views of reality, but cumulatively illustrates and substantiates the picture we present.

We have also benefited by the other studies in this series, either published or with the publisher or yet to be completed. We realize that the incomplete studies will further illustrate White House operations and we hope they will enrich and not substantially qualify the conclusions drawn here on the Johnson presidency.

We are grateful to those with specialized competence who have read and commented on our drafts of this book. Harry Middleton, speechwriter for President Johnson and now director of the Lyndon B. Johnson Library, read the first draft. Nancy Smith, the expert on the Library staff on task forces, read chapter 5. Elspeth Rostow, teacher of courses on the presidency at the University of Texas at Austin and close observer of the Johnson presidency, read the first draft and gave us many suggestions for alteration. Her husband, Walt W. Rostow, White House assistant in the Johnson presidency, read sections and offered his comments. Writers of other volumes in the Johnson administrative history series assisted us: James E. Anderson by reading the entire manuscript and Paul Y. Hammond and David M. Welborn by reading parts of it. Finally, the penultimate draft was read by

Richard E. Neustadt and Harvey C. Mansfield, Sr., political scientists with preeminent qualifications for evaluation and advice on improvements. Both gave us many suggestions which were of value to us in final revision of the book. We would like to express our appreciation for assistance to the highly professional and responsive staff of the Lyndon B. Johnson Presidential Library. We alone, of course, take responsibility for the product but acknowledge that its defects are less and its merits greater because of the assistance generously and carefully given by these persons.

The collaboration between a political scientist and a historian on this book has been complete. It has extended to development of structure, sharing of writing, agreement on interpretation and conclusions, and editorial revision. We hope the book will be valuable and interesting to both political scientists and historians and to a larger number of persons who are neither.

Emmette S. Redford

Richard T. McCulley

White House Operations

THE JOHNSON PRESIDENCY

1. Introduction

The operating presidency at any time is composed of a person and a large group of other persons who assist him. The president not only needs "help," as the famous Brownlow Committee said, he requires it.[1] His performance depends largely upon the sufficiency, quality, and organization of assistance available to him and upon his ability to assimilate this assistance and use it for his purposes. This book deals with the crucial presidential function of obtaining and using White House assistants.

To describe all the assistance to a president we use the term "subpresidency." This concept includes all those who serve the president, on a continuing or an ad hoc basis, in an institutional capacity or otherwise in the exercise of his responsibilities.[2] The subpresidency includes institutional components such as the organizations within the executive office of the president, including the White House itself. The concept is, however, basically a functional rather than structural one: it includes those persons who by virtue of position or personal association with the president are able to help him in the discharge of his responsibilities. This may include at a specific time and with respect to specific problems or areas of responsibility Cabinet officers and agency heads and subordinates of theirs, task forces or presidential commissions, and individuals without official position who have come to have the president's confidence. Since these are all people, the concept, regarded functionally, includes the networks of cross-communications, friendships, rivalries, and tensions that exist (or are perceived) among them. Also, because they are people, most of them have individually their own private or official worlds and goals. Single-minded devotion to the president's wants and needs to the exclusion of all else cannot realistically characterize very many of them.

White House Assistants

Nevertheless, within the subpresidency there is an inner circle of White House aides constituted ideally of just such people. It is characterized by formal or institutional position, in contrast to task forces or personal advisers without official position. Yet it differs in its service to the president from every other public institution. It includes persons expected to have a single loyalty—loyalty to the president alone, not impaired or contradicted by any personal legal obligations or structural affinities. It is the ever-present servant and extension of the president himself.

As extensions of the president their relations with him are peculiarly personal. They are his day-to-day official intimates, in whom he places his trust and from whom he expects confidentiality. He normally expects from them secrecy on office information and deliberations. He also expects submergence of personal ambition or desire for public notice—"a passion for anonymity," as phrased in a famous report.[3] They are subject to his command and control of their time and are expected to give full service to his purposes.

These qualities of White House loyalty assume legality and rectitude in presidential direction—that the president is loyal to the ideals of the office he holds. Moreover, they may in practice be vitiated by a White House aide's affiliations of external interest, his ambition, or his personal zeal beyond or for objectives different from those of the president. But they are the normal expectancies of conduct and attitude of those in the inner circle (however threatening they may be to the personal lives of incumbents).

To safeguard their service to the president alone Congress has abstained from prescription of qualifications for White House aides or requirement of senatorial confirmation of their appointments, or indeed even of defining positions to be included or duties to be performed.[4] They are the president's people, those he includes and appoints.

Working in the same directions are legal prohibitions against vesting official authority in White House assistants. The authorization of the McCormack Act of 1951 to the president to delegate statutory functions to the heads of a department or agency, or any other official of the executive branch whose appointment is confirmed by the Senate, carries the implication that delegation should not be made to White House assistants.[5] Moreover, an executive order issued in 1939 specified that assistants not be "interposed between the president and the head of any department or agency or between the president and any of the divisions of the Executive Office of the President," a standard that may be violated in practice.[6] Whether the president may delegate constitutional responsibilities to assistants is not determined. Nor, despite frequent congressional prodding, has it been determined to what extent they may claim executive privilege with respect to confidentiality of communications.[7] It has been suggested, also, that they may not even have the constitutional status of "inferior officers."[8]

While law does not prescribe duties or status, there is much constancy from president to president in roles of White House aides. In general, every president needs similar kinds of service as he operates as chief of state and chief of government, in the wide span of foreign and domestic affairs, in policy deliberation and political strategy, and in regular events or crisis situations. He needs eyes and ears, brains and voices in all these arenas. Yet balances among these roles may vary and new roles become important as conditions change or the purposes of presidents develop. This may be true even within the space of a single presidency. President Franklin D. Roosevelt began with domestic crisis and ended in international conflict, and President Lyndon B. Johnson began with legislative programming and ended in war and domestic protest. Despite the elements of constancy, flexibility in roles of White House aides may be expected.

Concerns about the Role of White House Assistants

The role of White House aides in the conduct of the affairs of the presidency has been, and undoubtedly will continue to be, the subject of much discussion and some disagreement. Frequently the size of the White House staff disturbs observers. It has "grown in four decades from . . . 37 to over 500."[9] *"The trend toward enlargement of the immediate White House staff should be reversed."*[10] "The White House Staff should be limited to not more than 15 top aides to the president and should not exceed 50 supporting professional employees. . . ."[11] This anxiety about size reflects the much larger concern that presidents may overextend, or may already have overextended, the role of White House assistants, thereby weakening other parts of the subpresidency and the ability of the president himself to discharge his responsibilities.

The three studies from which the above quotations are taken encompass the main apprehensions about the scope of the White House staff role that have troubled informed observers. Stephen Hess of Brookings Institution argues that "the centralization of responsibilities in the person of the president has lessened his ability to perform the duties of the office."[12] White House growth has both reflected and encouraged this centralization. Hess proposed that the role of White House assistants should be diminished by "creating more nearly collegial administrations in which presidents rely on their cabinet officers as the principal sources of advice" and as "personally accountable" for "the operation of the different segments of the government."[13]

Instead of looking toward the Cabinet, a panel of the National Academy of Public Administration in *A Presidency for the 1980s* believed "the place to begin is at the institution of the presidency," where "the forces of cohesion and integration" can be strengthened. The objective of its recommendations was "to ensure that every President inherits an Executive Office equipped for the challenge of governing in the 1980s."[14] While this line of development would be viewed adversely by some because it would enlarge the "presidential establishment," it would be a means of reversing the trend toward expansion of White House assistance.[15]

Another panel of the Academy seeking answers for the problems presented by the Watergate experience was concerned with the moral tone of the White House and with inappropriate extension of the role of White House aides. It saw Watergate as arising from a political and administrative climate in which the motivating drive was presidential *power,* and it was concerned that public virtue exist in the White House with sanctions to maintain it. But it saw also "centralization of power in the White House and the concomitant confusion of roles and responsibilities by placing operating authority in personal and advisory staff." "The role of the principal assistants to the president has been virtually transformed to one of 'assistant presidents.'" It recommended strengthening legal prohibitions against delegation to White House aides and the "essential distinction between staff serving the president and staff serving the presidency." It suggested also that the president "should look outside the White House and the government for legitimate campaign assistance."[16]

Cumulatively, these studies reflect many of the prevailing concerns about the role of White House aides: that the Cabinet will not be used sufficiently, that the institutionalized structure for presidential aid will not be adequate, that presidential assistants will have operative responsibilities or be interposed between the president and the departments and the agencies, and that they may be overinvolved in the politicization of the presidency.

All of the studies recognize the need of the president for White House assistants. Yet none of them survey *the roles that White*

House assistants have performed in the presidential subsystem and the extent of the president's need for these roles to be performed in the White House. The period of expansion of the White House is the period of expansion of the national government. Foreign and domestic policy burdens on the president have increased enormously. The complexity of the government that has developed with its increased functions has made it necessary for the president to have assistance in dealing with its parts and in providing him with a more comprehensive view of its problems than will exist in the departments or agencies or executive office units. Moreover, he holds a political office and must have assistance in linking policy to politics and maintaining liaison with the Congress, the media, and beyond to the public. In view of the position of the president today it is important to have a view of the roles that a president may regard as necessary or convenient for a White House staff to perform. To this end we need an intimate look into practice for clues.

Strategies of White House Management

More attention has been given to the ways presidents have structured and operated their White Houses than to the role of White House assistants. Almost all commentators on presidential management distinguish two models of presidential use of White House aid. One emphasizes institutionalization, the other personalization. Structure and regularized process are characteristic of one; personal effort and fluidity in relationships mark the other. Frequently the first is termed formal and the second informal. The models grow out of a distinction between the methods of presidents Dwight D. Eisenhower and Franklin D. Roosevelt. Eisenhower's White House was tightly organized, "with straight lines and tidy boxes," peaked to a chief of staff, with structure and process both charted, minor decisions decentralized, and major ones guided by "completed staff work."[17] Roosevelt's White House structure was undefined and fluid, his supervision over individuals direct, with decisions centralized in him and based on competing advice and personal analysis.

Authors often locate other presidents with respect to these models. One, for example, arranging presidents on a continuum of "Formalization of Staffing Arrangements," places them in this order: FDR, John F. Kennedy, Johnson, Harry S. Truman, Nixon, and Eisenhower, and marks Johnson and Truman as "mixed."[18] Yet another concludes that "The Johnson White House moved closer to approximating the FDR model than at any time since the death of the founder of the modern presidency."[19] Still another contends that "While LBJ tended toward the formalistic approach, his personality simply overshadowed it."[20]

The distinction between institutionalization and personalization, formal and informal, has been supplemented by specific attention to decision-making processes. Characterizing the two models just discussed as "adhocracy" and "centralized management" and building on earlier discussion, Roger B. Porter presents a third model, called "multiple advocacy," whose design is "to expose the President to competing arguments and viewpoints made by advocates themselves rather than having viewpoints filtered through a staff to a presidency."[21] He advocates for the president a decision-making process where White House assistants would be only "honest brokers" (i.e., neutral) in transmitting proposals to the president. A means of achieving a decentralized process of multiple advocacy would be a conciliar structure in which agencies and other advisers in broad policy areas—such as economic policy, foreign affairs, and social policy—would be brought together in councils, with a White House assistant and his staff serving in each case as honest brokers among them and in representation to the president. The process would differ from adhocracy in its continuity and from centralized management in its openness to departmental resources and expertise. It would differ, we observe, from plans for decentralization to the Cabinet in that it would preserve the responsibility of the president personally.

"Multiple advocacy maximizes the use of and participation by departments and agencies and [it is suggested] minimizes the role played by White House staff."[22] The proposal for use of the model therefore relates to the role of White House staff as well as to presidential strategy. We must add, also, that Porter concludes, "The president should not opt exclusively for only one of these models; rather, he should be versatile and adaptive in making intelligent use of all three from time to time."[23]

Although models of presidential operations have been advanced—personalized versus institutionalized, centralized versus decentralized (open, participative, competitive)—it would be admitted generally by scholars of the presidency that analysis of the behavior of presidents in White House management and decision making has been less intensive than is merited by the importance of the subject. This reflects a general deficiency in studies of the presidency. In an analysis for the Ford Foundation in 1976, Hugh Heclo concluded that while "provocative interpretations" are written and "important questions" asked, "in terms of original empirical research to test these interpretations and help answer the important questions, the field [of presidential studies] is an overwritten wasteland."[24] And although there is attention to "court politics and crisis decision making in the White House," there has been far less interest in studying the work flow and everyday operations of presidential institutions and staff.[25] As a specific example of "lack of basic research," Heclo refers to comments about a "swollen," "bloated," and "bureaucraticized" White House without empirical data on growth and size that would be the base for such attributions.[26] Similarly, Thomas E. Cronin had criticized earlier the lack of empirical focus in studies of presidential advisory systems.[27] A recent study of Eisenhower's style provides an example of how empirical study of one presidency can challenge traditional views and lead to a reassessment of presidential performance.[28]

What is needed in the case of both institutionalization versus personalization and centralization versus decentralization is understanding of the constraints in both directions and of the possibilities revealed by experience for combinations of, perhaps more than choices among, methods.

Purpose of This Book

We will not in this book address issues about the correctness of the decisions of the framers of the Constitution to create the presidency or those about the alleged aggrandizement of the presidency with respect to Congress.[29] We are interested rather in the uses the president makes of White House assistance in the performance of such functions—legal or political—as accrue to him.

Since the work of White House assistants is done behind a heavy curtain of secrecy, responsible authors have found it difficult to discern the influences that operate within and from outside, the relative roles of president and staff, and even the purposes and scope of presidential interventions in public action. While eye witnesses and journalists have offered numerous insights and anecdotes on the inner workings of the Johnson White House, they have contributed little toward understanding these and other aspects of presidential management of the White House. The dominant view of the Johnson White House that has emerged is one of instability, ineffectuality, and internal conflict. A leading journalist wrote that "ceaseless turnover" plagued the White House and that Johnson's "over-large" staff created "confusion" throughout the government.[30] One former staff member wrote that the White House became "a shifting band of individuals and groups moving in mutual suspicion around the commanding, demanding figure of Lyndon Johnson."[31] George E. Reedy, one of Johnson's press secretaries, wrote of the "unhealthy environment" and the "mass of intrigue" beneath the president.[32] More important, Reedy believed that the power and prestige of the office, as well as Johnson's personality, overpowered the assistants and prevented them from offering frank advice or realistic alternatives. The result, according to Reedy, was that Johnson lost "contact with reality."[33]

One purpose of this book is to provide an accurate and more detailed understanding of the actual nature of White House operations under one president. The curtain will not be fully lifted, for staff work is recorded in pieces and much of the president's thinking is not revealed. Our primary sources are the memorandums of staff members located in the Lyndon B. Johnson Library and the subsequent reports of these aides in oral histories, interviews, books, and articles. These are sufficient to provide a more accurate and intimate view than has hitherto been presented.

Definite answers cannot be given to the concerns that have developed in recent years about White House operations. These relate to balance and degree. What is effective and safe in the governmental system may depend largely on time and circumstances, not least of which are the aims, abilities, and preferred means of individual presidents. Nevertheless, the penetration into the experience of one presidency may illuminate the consideration of the questions that are ever present. This will be particularly true if the presentation is based on a positive view of what White House aides really do, and perhaps must do.

The presidency of Lyndon B. Johnson is a good one for analysis. While distinctive features of the time and the qualities of the man produced peculiarities in White House operations, the presidency had arrived at a position of twentieth-century maturity where essential White House staff roles were rather clearly delineated and issues concerning them apparent.

One influence on White House operation in the Johnson presidency had special significance then and reveals problems that could recur. The unanticipated transition in the presidency caused by death of the occupant created special problems for the successor, some but not all similar to those associated with presidents Truman's and Gerald R. Ford's successions to this office. It will be necessary therefore to insert discussion of the effects of the tragic event that brought a new president to power.

The primary purpose of the seven chapters that follow this one is a descriptive and analytical portrayal of White House operations during one presidency. A final chapter will summarize and evaluate elements in Johnson's White House operations; it will in addition return to the arguments about scope and strategy in our samples of recent literature, and from the perspective of the Johnson presidency evaluate the approaches suggested in them with respect to presidential use of the White House.

2. Duality, Change, and Stabilization

Sometimes the course of history is understandable only against the backdrop of the drama of a moment and the constraints that flow from it. Lyndon B. Johnson's administration was born in an event that dominated his choices, including the composition and management of his White House. In the first phase of a transition, there was a Kennedy-Johnson White House staff. In time the transition would move gradually through a second phase, and a Johnson White House staff would come into being. The evolution of the White House staff and the circumstances influencing this evolution are examined in this chapter.

Johnson's Accession

The sharp sound of a shot—12:30 P.M., 22 November 1963. Thirty minutes later, the report—John F. Kennedy was dead. Two hours later, Lyndon B. Johnson had taken the oath.

Occupancy, the personal endowment of power, is transitory; office, the responsibility of position, is enduring. Succession to office marks the essence of a polity—the political character of a nation. Most often it has been done by council of an elite or seizure by force, with sanction from tradition, religion, or police and military might. In this country it was declared in a constitution nearly two hundred years before and assured by practice since the friendly passing of the torch from George Washington to John Adams and the transition from Adams to his political enemy, Thomas Jefferson. It is a glorious torch of constitutionalism and democracy, a fixed, accepted transition of power. It was for President Johnson assurance of universal acceptance of his occupancy.[1]

Most presidential transitions are preceded by election and are typically marked by cooperation and assistance of the outgoing administration. But Johnson was the eighth president to succeed to office unexpectedly and suddenly by the death of his predecessor, the fourth in the midst of the complexities of twentieth-century government.

The President's Response

The transition presented Johnson with an immediate challenge. He had no elective mandate of his own, his place on the ticket and his campaign participation in 1960 being only to strengthen the candidacy of his predecessor. He was distrusted and his accession resented by many who had supported his party in the election. He succeeded a president who, although narrowly elected in 1960, had won hearts and lifted visions of multitudes in his nation and now in death had acquired a halo. While the people of the nation would wish the new president success vital to their welfare and national security, there would be no joy and enthusiasm such as reign when elected presidents are inaugurated. And in the nations of the world uncertainty prevailed, based on unfamiliarity with Johnson and his untested qualities in defense policy and diplomacy. As in the case of Harry S. Truman following Franklin D. Roosevelt, a quagmire of doubt and suspense mixed with grief was present.

The theme of Johnson's response was continuity. In a meeting after ex-President Kennedy's funeral he said, "I think continuity without confusion has got to be our password and has to be the key to our system."[2] In an address to Congress two days later he proclaimed, "Let us continue."[3] Bill D. Moyers has said that he "was dominated by the idea of continuity," first because "the stability of the American government was at stake in the eyes of its beholders, both internally and internationally," and second because he knew he was "untrusted."[4]

The continuity proclaimed in addresses was reflected in his activities. He met promptly with Kennedy aides who could be assembled. New relationships were initially ambiguous. George E. Reedy has reported on the "strained and strange" atmosphere at Johnson's first meeting with the Cabinet and the Kennedy staff:

> The Kennedy people knew the realities of power and they were looking to him for a cue to their future conduct. *He, on the other hand, was looking to them for a cue as to what Kennedy would have done.* His lifetime in politics had taught him that what counted was the opinion *of the man who had been elected.* He did not want to take off on his own until he had been elected.[5]

He engaged at once in efforts to promote the legislative program of his predecessor. He requested occupants of top executive positions to remain in their posts and in some cases he implored their continuance with strong emphasis on his need for their service.

In addition to maintaining continuity, the new president needed to establish confidence in his own capability for leadership. He knew that the American system concentrates and personalizes the responsibility for leadership and that confidence in his personal leadership was at stake at home and abroad. Later he would write, "I had no mandate from the voters. . . . I knew it was imperative that I grasp the reins of power and do so without delay."[6] He was well known in the Washington community and particularly in the Congress, where he had served for 26 years, successively as congressman, senator, senate minority and majority leader, and presiding officer of the Senate. His abilities for leadership in that forum were recognized in the nation and indeed thought by many to be equaled by few among his predecessors. Yet he needed confidence from the Washington community and the populace in his capability for various new responsibilities and from the constituency of world leaders in his ability to conduct foreign affairs. To establish his own position in the world he held a succession of conferences with the leaders of other countries who had come to Washington for President Kennedy's funeral. He spoke to the General Assembly of the United Nations on 17 December. He spoke to Congress, to the nation, and to numerous groups within and outside of government. He presented an image of an active, forceful, competent leader for domestic and foreign affairs.

The Kennedy-Johnson White House

Johnson's desire for continuity was achieved in the major units of the executive branch. The Cabinet remained—the first resignation, that of Attorney General Robert F. Kennedy, occurred nine months after Johnson's accession; all others served through their term. Some served longer, and three—Dean Rusk, secretary of state, Stewart L. Udall, secretary of interior, and Orville L. Freeman, secretary of agriculture—remained until the end of Johnson's presidency. Continuity prevailed in certain other positions which were important for the president. The director of the Bureau of the Budget (BOB) remained until August 1965, the chairman of the Council of Economic Advisers (CEA) until November 1964. For another executive office position, director of the Office of Science and Technology, President Kennedy had selected a man to fill a vacancy; Johnson approved the selection and the man served until the end of the Johnson presidency.[7] The chairman of the Civil Service Commission remained to the end of the Johnson presidency and became one of the president's most important aides.

In the White House, too, effectiveness in the transition and beyond and the appearance and reality of continuation of President Kennedy's program would be served by continuity in staff. Johnson has said:

> I needed that White House staff. Without them I would have lost my link to John Kennedy, and without that I would have had absolutely no chance of gaining the support of the media or the Easterners or the intellectuals. And without that support I would have had absolutely no chance of governing the country.[8]

But the president would also need men in whom he could place his full trust and on whom he could depend for a wide variety of activities, ranging from errand service to confidential advice. As Moyers has said, he respected and needed the Kennedy staff, but he needed also "a band of brothers."[9] In short, the circumstances of transition led toward duality in presidential service.

The duality that was to occur, in response to the requirements for continuity and personal responsibility, was foretold in the service and presence of both Kennedy and Johnson aides in the most immediate events of the transition. Even before the oath of office was taken Johnson was in telephone communication with Attorney General Robert Kennedy, brother of the fallen president, who was painfully acting as instrument of official transition and giving Johnson legal advice on taking the oath; with McGeorge Bundy, who held responsibility in the Kennedy White House for advice to the president on national security matters; and also with Walter W. Jenkins, aide to Senator and Vice President Johnson. Johnson, seemingly conscious of historical significance, dictated,

> McGeorge Bundy and Walter called me—thought we should come to Washington as soon as could. Told them I was waiting for the body and Mrs. Kennedy. The attorney general interrupted the conversation to say that I ought to have a judicial officer administer the oath here.[10]

On the president's plane were Lawrence F. O'Brien, P. Kenneth O'Donnell, Dave Powers, Malcolm M. Kilduff, and Evelyn Lincoln from the ex-president's staff, and Moyers, Jack J. Valenti, Cliff Carter, and Elizabeth Carpenter, to be aides to the new incumbent. To this latter group the president gave his first directive: prepare a statement for him to make on the landing in Washington.

Promptly, the Johnson group was at his side, ready for whatever service he required. Upon hearing of the assassination, Moyers rushed to Dallas from Austin and arrived in time to board the president's plane. Moyers had helped Johnson direct the vice presidential campaign and had subsequently become deputy director of the Peace Corps. In Washington, where Johnson had only a small staff as vice president, three men—Jenkins, Horace Busby, Jr., and Reedy, who had rendered long-time service to Johnson—were on hand. Jenkins had joined Johnson's staff in 1939 and during Johnson's Senate years had been general office manager, personnel chief, private secretary, and administrative assistant. Busby served as a legislative assistant on Senator Johnson's staff from 1949 to 1951, when he left to organize a management consulting and advertising firm. During the vice presidential years Busby accompanied Johnson on numerous foreign missions. Reedy had met Johnson in 1951 and under his guidance served as staff counsel to the Senate Armed Services Preparedness Subcommittee and as staff director of the majority policy committee. When Johnson became vice president in 1961 Reedy was named his special assistant to coordinate speechwriting and press relations. These three men had been on Johnson's staff for a total of forty-one years; thus, continuity in personal service to the new president contributed another factor in continuity of government.

Jack J. Valenti was another confidant who assisted the president immediately. Although Valenti had never served on Johnson's staff, they had become close friends after meeting in 1957. Johnson selected Valenti's advertising firm to handle the Democratic party's advertising throughout Texas during the 1960 presidential campaign. Valenti was in Dallas at the time of the assassination because Johnson had asked him to help develop the plans for the Kennedy-Johnson trip to Texas. After returning to Washington with the president, Valenti resided in the White House for several months before moving his family to the capital.[11]

There were other long-time trusted associates of President Johnson who gave him counsel in the transition but who held no official position in the White House, among them Abe Fortas, Clark M. Clifford, James Rowe, Edwin Weisl, Robert Anderson, and Congressman Homer Thornberry.[12] But the five named in the preceding two paragraphs became members of the White House staff where they formed an inner circle of fully dedicated Johnson aides.[13]

While close associates immediately surrounded Johnson, men of the Kennedy staff remained to provide the continuity of White

House operations that he desired. Only four of the top White House officials left the White House at an early date: Theodore C. Sorensen, Pierre E. G. Salinger, Arthur Schlesinger, Jr., and Andrew T. Hatcher. These had been among President Kennedy's most intimate and dedicated associates. Salinger, press secretary to the president, left the White House in March 1964 to become a candidate for the United States Senate. Schlesinger and Sorensen undoubtedly found the transition difficult and their opportunity for service less than in the Kennedy White House. Sorensen left 29 February and Schlesinger 1 March 1964. Hatcher and Schlesinger had been special assistants to the president and Sorensen had the title of special counsel, but a White House memorandum defined his assignments to include almost all types of White House duties: preparing the president's legislative program, assisting with the budget and fiscal and economic policy, drafting speeches and assisting in preparation for press conferences for the national convention and campaign, advising the president on administrative matters, serving on the National Security Council (NSC) Executive Committee, and others.[14] No one in the Johnson presidency would succeed to this combination of duties or come as close to being a chief of staff.[15]

One area in which continuity was most significant was in the conduct of foreign affairs. The special assistant to the president in this area was Bundy, who served in that capacity from the beginning of the Kennedy administration to 26 February 1966 and who continued as special consultant after that date. A strong tradition of public service motivated Bundy and complemented Johnson's desire to maintain continuity in foreign policy. Bundy was born into a prominent Boston family noted for a long history of public service. Although a Republican, Bundy gave up the deanship of a college of arts and sciences at Harvard to become Kennedy's national security adviser. Moreover, Bundy had worked closely with Secretary of State Rusk and with Secretary of Defense Robert S. McNamara during Kennedy's presidency and Johnson was determined to retain the triumvirate. They formed the president's advisory core on foreign affairs until Bundy resigned to become president of the Ford Foundation. Not only did Bundy perform his primary functions, but he sent the president reports on various other matters of presidential concern such as representations to the academic community, appointment of the special counsel in the White House, and recommendations of a vice presidential candidate.

Another area of distinctive continuity was that of congressional liaison. O'Brien, long-time friend and political aide of Kennedy in his senatorial and presidential campaigns, had performed the congressional liaison function for President Kennedy, primarily with the aid of two assistants—Mike N. Manatos for the Senate and Henry Hall Wilson for the House of Representatives. Even before the departure from Dallas after the assassination, President Johnson said to O'Brien: "I want to urge you to stay and stand shoulder to shoulder with me. I need you more than you need me—and more than Jack Kennedy needed you." O'Brien was pressed again to remain during the trip to Washington and repeatedly in following days, and he ultimately agreed with Johnson that he could honor Kennedy's memory by continuing to work on his program. He was importuned further after the 1964 elections to stay and help pass the legislative program. He agreed, conditional on Johnson's promise not to press him to stay beyond the 1965 legislative session. Johnson obliged, and at the end of the period appointed O'Brien postmaster general.[16] But an office was retained for O'Brien in the White House and he continued to assist President Johnson in obtaining congressional passage of bills. O'Brien's top assistants likewise remained, Wilson until the middle of 1967 and Manatos until the end of the Johnson presidency.

Despite Sorensen's departure, a wide range of duties assigned to the special counsel's office remained under holdover staff assistants. Myer Feldman, deputy special counsel, became counsel to the president, and Lee C. White, assistant special counsel, became associate counsel and later special counsel. Feldman remained until November 1965 and White until March 1966. Feldman and White placed their extensive administrative and legislative experience at the president's disposal. Feldman had been an executive assistant to the chairman of the Securities and Exchange Commission and White had worked in the legal division of the Tennessee Valley Authority. Both had served on Senator Kennedy's staff during the 1950s.

In addition to their legal duties, Feldman and White were the president's chief advisers in many important policy areas. White's area of responsibility for presidential assistance included civil rights. He had worked with the vice president on the Committee on Equal Employment Opportunity and gave immediate assistance to President Johnson as he arranged for conferences with civil rights leaders in the ten days following the assassination.[17] His presence assured President Johnson of experienced aid on important civil rights issues for the first two and one-half years of his administration, as did his and Feldman's presence on many other policy questions.

These retentions in the areas of foreign policy, congressional liaison, and policy aid—supplemented in the last case by the loyal assistance of holdovers in the CEA and BOB—supported the continuity President Johnson strongly desired in foreign affairs and legislative programs. Yet there were additional continuities in staff. Special Assistant O'Donnell had been especially close to Kennedy and was so grief-stricken by the assassination that he remained away from the White House for days. With the help of Jenkins, Johnson persuaded him to make the effort to serve another leader. The new president was especially interested in enlisting O'Donnell's considerable political talents since he, like O'Brien, had been among the leading figures in the Kennedy rise to power. He had been campaign aide during Kennedy's first race for Congress in 1946 and served as Kennedy's chief political tactician in the 1960 presidential campaign. O'Donnell yielded the work of appointments secretary to Valenti, but the two shared an office in the White House. During 1964 O'Donnell spent most of his time at the Democratic National Committee and became one of Johnson's chief liaisons to the national party. He remained on the White House staff until January 1965.

Like other Kennedy holdovers, Ralph A. Dungan had extensive executive and congressional experience since he had worked at BOB and as a Kennedy legislative aide during the 1950s. Dungan continued as advisor on presidental appointments, although he felt that his relations were more formal and less influential with the new president than with his predecessor.[18] Jenkins particularly, but also Valenti, Moyers, and others among the new entrants to the White House, became important in recruitment and advice on presidential appointments. Dungan too remained until after the 1964 election, when he was appointed by Johnson as ambassador to Chile. Finally, service functions for the White House continued to be performed during the transition under the same direction from the president's military aide and the executive clerk of the White House as in the Kennedy administration.

In contrast to these continuities, changes in two essential areas of staff services were particularly significant. On Salinger's departure in March 1964 Johnson designated Reedy as his press secretary. The two top assistants were Hatcher and Kilduff; the first departed in March 1964, but the latter remained to July 1965. For the speechwriting function, initially old and new members of the White House staff cooperated. Notes in the president's diary and diary backup show that Johnson discussed the speech to the joint session of Congress on 27 November separately at least with Busby, Dungan, and Sorensen and that Moyers, Jenkins, Valenti, Busby, and O'Brien participated in the drafting conferences.[19] But other speeches were being written by the small group that came in with Johnson, and Moyers, Busby, and Valenti soon formed the center of the speechwriting operation. Fortuitously, however, Johnson inherited from Kennedy co-workers a valuable addition to the White House speechwriting group. Richard N. Goodwin, appointed by Kennedy to a position in the State Department and later transferred to the Peace Corps, had been speechwriter for Kennedy and had created for him the famous policy term "Alliance for Progress." Goodwin had accepted an invitation from Kennedy to come into the White House only to withdraw after the assassination. But Moyers, himself from the Peace Corps, immediately tapped Goodwin for assistance in speechwriting; Johnson asked for his further help and made use of Goodwin's phrase "The Great Society."[20] Goodwin became an official member of the White House staff in April 1964.

Press and speech were the two means for representation of the president to the public, and Johnson's own men dominated the staff operations in both. Yet the new president's personal brand was being placed on the White House office in other ways. Moyers, who had been designated as Johnson's liaison with the Kennedy campaign staff in 1960 and who had developed friendships with that group, now had the responsibility of maintaining harmonious relations with them.[21] Reedy, prior to becoming press secretary, prepared statements of the president's position in reply to numerous inquiries and assisted in speechwriting.

Jenkins, moving from his position in the vice president's office, became the central person in administration of the White House. Immediately he became a utility man when Johnson called him from Dallas and asked him to get information about the oath, locate from Washington Federal District Judge Sarah T. Hughes, and arrange three meetings—with the Cabinet, the NSC, and congressional leaders—in Washington upon the president's arrival. His role as an administrative chief of staff developed from such assignments. Indeed, the knowledge throughout the White House of his long years of staff work for Johnson led to the channeling of communications through him. He assembled papers and placed them in order of priority for the president's attention, he disposed of details that did not require presidential attention, and he followed up on numerous assignments from the president. In addition to these managerial tasks Jenkins assisted Johnson on congressional liaison. He was in frequent contact with the Texas congressional delegation and with friends of the president in Congress. With Dungan's assistance he compiled lists of candidates for presidential appointment, solicited advice concerning appointments, and secured FBI clearances.[22]

Managing the president's schedule took more of Jenkins' time than anything else. But he did not stand between the president and anyone who wanted to communicate with him, and he took no part in speechwriting or press relations and recognized the direct relations of Bundy with the president. One staffer has said that "everything went through Walter," but Jenkins himself says that was because he saw the president earlier and stayed with him longer than anyone else. He said also that numerous telephone calls and referrals were made to him because people had known him and his work with Johnson through previous years. He occupied the office close to the president that Sherman Adams had occupied when assistant to President Dwight D. Eisenhower, but a staff aide says he was pushed into it by Dungan's insistence that he must be close to the president.[23]

Valenti took a desk in O'Donnell's office and soon became appointments secretary. He, Moyers, and Busby were generalist aides to the president. These men promptly began to sit in on important meetings, including those of the Cabinet and the NSC. They were on the telephone with the president or in his office constantly, and they assumed tasks as they recognized them and worked whatever hours were required.[24]

To this nuclear group Johnson added others, including S. Douglass Cater, Jr. During the 1950s Cater came to know Johnson through articles he wrote while a journalist for the *Reporter*. In 1963 he was national affairs editor, a visiting professor at Wesleyan University, and associate director for the Center for Advanced Studies. In 1961 the vice president asked Cater to join his staff, at least on a part-time basis, but Cater refused, since writing about and working for a political figure posed a conflict of interest. After talking with Moyers, Bundy, and the president during February 1964, Cater agreed to join the staff at the end of the spring semester at Wesleyan.[25]

The appointment of Roger L. Stevens as special assistant for the arts was another White House appointment that Johnson made during his first few months in office. Stevens was both a producer of Broadway shows and a highly successful businessman. Moreover, he was an active Democrat who had participated in fund raising from 1956 to 1960. Johnson appointed the first black to his White House staff when he named Hobart Taylor, Jr., associate special counsel in April 1964. Taylor was a Texan who had participated in Johnson's 1960 presidential campaign and worked under Vice President Johnson as executive vice chairman of the President's Commission on Equal Employment Opportunity.

As two new tasks arose for Johnson in 1964 he was able to find help he needed within the existing White House staff. For one, the campaign for election, the Kennedy holdovers and the Johnson jacks-of-all-trades each supplied needed competence. Three of several operating teams that made up the highly successful 1964 campaign organization were White House centered. One was Jenkins, Moyers, and Valenti, assisted by Goodwin, Busby, Cater, and Secretary of Labor Willard W. Wirtz. An all-purpose team, they wrote the speeches and controlled the media campaign, with Wirtz becoming coordinator of speechwriting. Another was O'Brien and O'Donnell—the old "Kennedy team minus Robert Kennedy." They were campaign directors, O'Brien reporting from the field and O'Donnell planning the president's traveling schedule. Still another centered in Feldman, who reported to the president on plans developed in daily conferences with bright Washington thinkers on counter-offensive tactics against speeches of his Republican opponent, Barry Goldwater.[26] The additions to the White House staff by Johnson, the flexibility in White House assignments, and the capacity of old and new staff to absorb additional workload made it possible to conduct a successful campaign from the White House and ensure a second phase in the transition, the phase in which Johnson's personal occupancy was founded on electoral victory.

The second new task was the development of a legislative program for the new phase. The enactment of the tax reduction, civil rights, and educational programs proposed by Kennedy and the passage of the anti-poverty programs grasped by Johnson from Kennedy staff proposals in 1964 would complete the immediate obligation of Johnson to the Kennedy legacy. Also, it would create the need for new program proposals to satisfy the ambition of the president for a large legislative program. Goodwin had supplied the phrase to characterize the purpose of new policy moves. To fill in the content for "The Great Society" legislation, Johnson's famous task force operation came into being (see chapter 5). The commission to direct this operation and come forward with a legislative program was given to Moyers. Assistance in developing the new domestic program was given by both carry-over staffers—such as O'Brien, White, and Feldman from the Kennedy period and Johnson appointees, notably Cater, whose place in the Johnson presidency was to be established in legislative program development.

Comments on the Kennedy-Johnson White House

The foregoing story is one of a sudden intra-party transition in occupancy of the presidency where the incoming president used for White House staffing a mix of the persons in place upon his accession and persons brought into service by him personally. Both contributed to the continuity of government, while the latter guaranteed the president's confidence.

Staff service of high responsibility was provided by both groups. Significantly, the Kennedy staff was left in place for two of the most important areas of White House assistance to the president: foreign affairs and congressional liaison. Significant also was the assignment to his "own" men of the task of representing the president to the people. But in other tasks—legislative programming, presidential appointments, legal advice, and assistance on a variety of special tasks—a merger of the old and new staff was achieved. These differences may have been due in large part to chance circumstances of competence, availability, and loyalty of particular persons. Thus Bundy and O'Brien and White and Feldman were present with the attributes needed, and Jenkins, Moyers, Valenti, Busby, and Reedy brought their own qualities to the White House.

The circumstance of prior service to Johnson of the men in this latter group was significant for their utilization and performance. Jenkins, Busby, Reedy, and Moyers had served Johnson in previous positions, the first three for protracted periods. The president knew their strengths and could depend on their loyalty and willingness to give unstintingly to his service. While none of them, except Moyers in the Peace Corps, had served in an executive position, they were knowledgeable about government in Washington and had learned how to work with Johnson.

The two groups in the staff worked together with more effectiveness and smoothness than might have been anticipated. Many factors contributed to this result. There was, first, a continuance of party responsibility and a mutual desire to renew the party's tenure in the election of 1964. Second, there were various motivations for the carry-over group. There was loyalty to the government and the party. There was pride in performance at the highest level of government. Moreover, as O'Brien said, they could be convinced that they were contributing to the fulfillment of President Kennedy's program. By the time this program was enacted they found the Johnson philosophy and program acceptable and leadership stimulating. There were elements of strain in a situation in which staff members continued to attend Washington parties where reverence for Kennedy and disdain of Johnson were sometimes conversation topics, but loyalty was given to Johnson nevertheless.

A third factor was Johnson's personal actions to make the mix work. He directed his staff to be considerate of the feelings of those who had suffered the loss of their esteemed chief, and some of the holdovers have reported that Jenkins particularly and the Johnson appointees in general reflected no impressions of superiority in staff relationships. His reliance on the key holdovers was evident and in some cases this was supplemented by personal attentions that were unusual.[27] They were able, in fact, to act generally in the spirit of the new president's instructions. The new aides were adaptable. Moyers had moved upward as a Kennedy appointee in the Peace Corps and had links with the Kennedy staff; Valenti apparently held them in awe; and Jenkins, Busby, and Reedy had acquired ability to work with others in their long years of congressional service. The experience in the Johnson presidency shows that it is practicable to make smooth and effective use of a mixed staff, but that the result is largely dependent upon concurrence in objective, mutual trust and the presidential fostering of cordiality.

The nature of the White House operation and the relationships within it during this period cannot be readily characterized. Some have described it as a two-layer operation, with the new Johnson men serving as a second layer above the Kennedy carry-overs.[28] This explanation is too simple for accuracy. Johnson's appointees were not superimposed above Bundy, O'Brien, O'Donnell, or perhaps Feldman and White. There was some parallelism between areas occupied by the carry-over staff and the new staff, some union of activity of both in other areas, and undoubtedly some elements of hierarchy in the patterns that developed. It is sufficient at this point to say that Johnson consciously built his operation on a mix of personnel. His White House operation—during and after the transition—cannot be explained purely, or mainly, in hierarchical terms. The general nature of White House operations, and the particular Johnson qualities, will be portrayed in the succeeding discussion.

A Johnson White House

An amalgam of Kennedy holdovers and close personal associates formed the staff for the first two years of the Johnson presidency. By the spring of 1966, however, the staff was largely shorn of Kennedy-appointed aides as well as the original circle of Johnson confidantes. No precipitating event or single cause underlay this transformation, nor are there sharp temporal boundaries. Yet phases of the transformation from a dual staff to a Johnson-appointed staff are evident. They are portrayed on Figures 1 and 2 and explained in the following discussion.

The first phase began with the resignation of Dungan, Jenkins, and O'Donnell near the end of or shortly after the 1964 presidential campaign. The second phase is marked by the concurrence of two groups of terminations of staff service. Between November 1965 and March 1966, the four top Kennedy holdovers departed. Between July 1965 and April 1966, Reedy, Busby, and Valenti left, leaving only Moyers from the original Johnson appointees. With new appointments, the transition to a Johnson White House was substantially completed. In a third phase marked by the departure of Moyers and a few other staff changes, the Johnson White House was completed and stabilized. The key White House posts were staffed almost entirely by aides who had no connection with the Kennedy White House or intimacy with Johnson prior to his presidency, and in most cases the occupants remained until the end of the period.

The Personnel Changes

The resignations of Dungan, Jenkins, and O'Donnell and Johnson's selection of John W. Macy, Jr., and Marvin Watson to perform many of their duties marked the first phase of the transformation of the staff. By the last half of 1964 Dungan found his influence on the appointments process diminished. When an ambassadorial post in Chile became vacant, he got Valenti to communicate his interest to the president, who appointed Dungan in November 1964. The president did not recruit a special assistant who specialized in appointments, but, following the election, he asked Macy, chairman of the Civil Service Commission, to serve as his adviser on executive appointments. Thus much of Dungan's appointment work was shifted to Macy, who was not officially on the White House staff.[29]

A more significant staff change occurred with the resignation of Jenkins on 14 October 1964. The Jenkins departure was occasioned by a personal scandal that had no relation to his White House service. Consequently, Johnson suddenly found himself without an aide who by lengthy experience was attuned to Johnson's peculiar work habits and was thoroughly familiar with the broad range of Johnson's associates. As Reedy noted, Jenkins was a loss that was never completely repaired: "The only thing that counts where a White House assistant is concerned is his closeness to the President. . . . Walter Jenkins had been *the key* staff member for at least twenty-five years."[30]

Valenti and Moyers began picking up many of Jenkins' duties, but when Johnson appointed Marvin Watson on 1 February 1965, a process of reconsolidating management functions in a single aide began. When Watson first joined the staff he worked closely with Valenti and was soon making the president's daily appointments, controlling the flow of memos and documents to the president, and tending to the administrative details of White House management. Watson's appointment was especially timely because of the departure of O'Don-

Figure 1. *Tenure of Kennedy-Appointed White House Aides and Original Johnson Inner Circle*

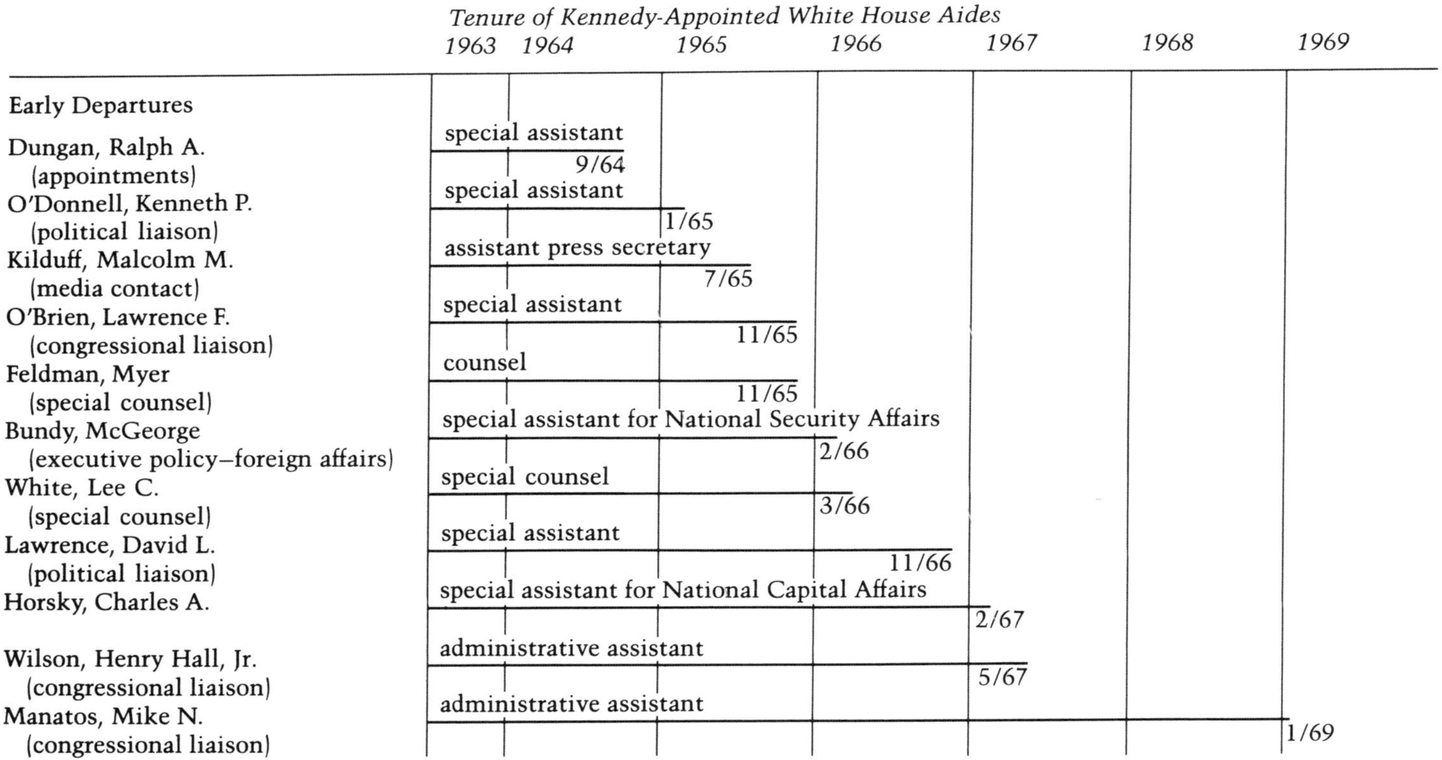

Tenure of Kennedy-Appointed White House Aides

1963 1964 1965 1966 1967 1968 1969

Early Departures	Position	Departure
Dungan, Ralph A. (appointments)	special assistant	9/64
O'Donnell, Kenneth P. (political liaison)	special assistant	1/65
Kilduff, Malcolm M. (media contact)	assistant press secretary	7/65
O'Brien, Lawrence F. (congressional liaison)	special assistant	11/65
Feldman, Myer (special counsel)	counsel	11/65
Bundy, McGeorge (executive policy–foreign affairs)	special assistant for National Security Affairs	2/66
White, Lee C. (special counsel)	special counsel	3/66
Lawrence, David L. (political liaison)	special assistant	11/66
Horsky, Charles A.	special assistant for National Capital Affairs	2/67
Wilson, Henry Hall, Jr. (congressional liaison)	administrative assistant	5/67
Manatos, Mike N. (congressional liaison)	administrative assistant	1/69

Tenure of Original Johnson Inner Circle

	1963	*1964*	*1965*	*1966*	*1967*	*1968*	*1969*
Jenkins, Walter W. (management service)	special assistant	10/64					
Reedy, George E. (media contact)	special assistant	3/64	9/65				
Busby, Horace, Jr. (management service)	special assistant		10/65				
Valenti, Jack J. (management service, speech preparation)	special assistant			4/66			
Moyers, Bill D. (executive policy, legislative program, media contact)	special assistant			12/66			

nell the previous month. Johnson's retention of O'Donnell was of great symbolic and practical importance because of his close identification with the slain president, his unusual political talents, and his links with big-city Democratic leaders. Since Watson had been active in Democratic party politics and had efficiently coordinated the Democratic National Convention of 1964, he absorbed many of O'Donnell's political duties, including liaison with the Democratic National Committee.

The appointment of Jake Jacobsen as legislative counsel was an additional staff change that occurred during 1965. He is significant because he was a confidant of Johnson who was on the staff after all of the original inner circle departed. Johnson knew Jacobsen because the latter was on the staff of Price Daniel while Daniel was state attorney general, U.S. senator, and governor of Texas. While on Daniel's staff Jacobsen came to know and work closely with Jenkins, Reedy, and Busby. After Jacobsen entered private law practice in 1958 he became a leading figure in organizing Texas Democrats solidly behind the Johnson presidential drive in 1960.[31]

The second phase of the transformation of the Johnson staff is especially marked by the exodus of four important Kennedy holdovers between November 1965 and March 1966. On 3 November 1965, Johnson swore in O'Brien as postmaster general. While the post was a reward for loyal service as congressional liaison, the appointment was a means of keeping him in the administration and available to work with the White House on congressional matters. O'Brien continued to maintain an office in the White House and spent several hours a day on congressional liaison work. Nevertheless, his official and full-time service as a White House aide ended in November 1965.[32]

Since O'Brien continued in an unofficial capacity as a Johnson aide and his top assistants—Wilson and Manatos—remained, a replacement was not necessary. This was not the case when Bundy resigned effective February 1966. On 31 March 1966, Johnson appointed Walt W. Rostow to succeed Bundy. Rostow had been a deputy special assistant to President Kennedy before joining the State Department as chairman of the Policy Planning Council in November 1961.[33] Rostow was the president's top White House foreign policy adviser for the remainder of the administration.

Two of Johnson's policy advisers who carried legal titles, both Kennedy holdovers, resigned shortly after the Bundy resignation. Both, like O'Brien and Bundy, had served from the beginning of the Kennedy administration. Feldman, who was counsel to the president, resigned in November 1965 and White, special counsel to the president, resigned 2 March 1966 as he moved by presidential appointment to chairmanship of the Federal Power Commission. To succeed Feldman, Johnson on 23 February 1966 appointed Milton P. Semer. Semer resigned on 23 November 1966, and Johnson never appointed another person with the title of counsel. He did name two deputy special counsels, Lawrence E. Levinson and W. DeVier Pierson, shortly after Semer's resignation, and named Larry E. Temple, appointed 26 October 1967, special counsel even though that title was already held by another person.

White's replacement as special counsel was appointed on 11 February 1966 as White was preparing to leave. With this title Harry C. McPherson, Jr., would become, with Semer's departure, Johnson's chief legal adviser. Johnson had observed McPherson closely when he was assistant counsel for the Senate Democratic Policy Committee, which Johnson had headed. After becoming the committee's general counsel in 1961 he moved in 1963 to the Department of Defense as deputy under secretary of the army for international affairs. The following year Johnson appointed him assistant secretary of state for educational and cultural affairs. McPherson took on many of Feldman's and White's responsibilities, such as processing enrolled bills en route to the president and liaison with the Department of Justice. While he did not succeed to the various policy responsibilities of Feldman and White, he took an active role in civil rights, foreign trade, and immigration and gained influence in the White House because he eventually acquired major responsibility for speechwriting.[34]

Paralleling these changes around the turn into the year 1966 was the departure of Johnson's own appointees. On 8 July 1965 Reedy resigned as press secretary and took an indefinite leave of absence for treatment of a serious foot ailment. Following an operation Reedy returned to the White House in September as special consultant to the president for special projects. As a consultant Reedy was far from the center of White House activity and was assigned an office in the East Wing of the White House where he had less access to the president. He served as a consultant until 25 April 1966 when he left the administration to become a vice president of a New York engineering firm. At the time of his departure Reedy had served Johnson in various capacities for fifteen years.[35]

The only staff member who had worked with Johnson longer than Reedy was Busby. On 15 September 1965, Busby submitted his resignation effective 1 October and returned to his management consulting business in Washington, D.C. On 25 April 1966 Valenti left the White House to become president of the Motion Picture Association of America. Although Johnson had not known Valenti as long as he had known Jenkins, Reedy, or Busby, Valenti's work made him no less an intimate of the president during Johnson's first two years in office. Thus, Reedy, Busby, and Valenti departed within the space of eight months.

A limited number of changes would complete the transformation to a complete Johnson White House. The most important changes were the departure of Moyers and the recruitment of Joseph A. Califano, Jr., George E. Christian, and H. Barefoot Sanders. Moyers was the only member of the original inner circle remaining by the end of April 1966. The most rewarding experience of Moyers' White House service had been his management of the task force operations and his direction of the legislative program. When Johnson designated him press secretary following Reedy's resignation, a less happy phase of his White House tenure began. By 1966, according to McPherson, Moyers had become "very troubled by the President . . . troubled about the war, troubled about his [Johnson's] moods."[36] Relations between Johnson and Moyers became strained and during December 1966 Moyers resigned to become publisher of the Long Island newspaper *Newsday*.

Moyers' appointment as press secretary and his subsequent resignation precipitated Califano's and Christian's assumption of key roles in the second Johnson White House staff. Johnson appointed Califano special assistant on 26 July 1965. Califano had joined the Defense Department in 1961 and became a special assistant to Secretary of Defense McNamara. Califano first came to the attention of the White House through Moyers, who was impressed with Califano's abilities during the course of his liaison work with the department. Johnson placed Califano in charge of legislative program development just nineteen days after he designated Moyers his press secretary. Califano quickly won the president's confidence. After placing the aide in charge of the legislative drive to establish a Department of Transportation, Johnson told the Cabinet, "When Joe speaks, that's my voice you hear."[37] Califano's responsibilities widened, especially after Moyers' departure. He not only continued to coordinate legislative program activities but was given responsibility for coordinating executive economic policy. Additionally, he exercised some oversight of the most important Great Society programs that the departments administered. By the end of the administration Califano had acquired a support staff of five assistants.

Following Moyers' resignation Johnson designated Christian press secretary, and he served until the end of the Johnson presidency. Since Christian was a newcomer to Washington and did not have the breadth of experience of his predecessor, his duties were limited to press relations. Nor was Christian a long-time acquaintance of Johnson, as was Reedy. Nevertheless, Johnson reposed great confidence in Christian, whose tenure as press secretary was longer than either Salinger's, Reedy's, or Moyers'.

When Wilson, who had assisted O'Brien in liaison with the House of Representatives, left the White House in May 1967, H. Barefoot Sanders, Jr., came in to replace him. Sanders, experienced in the legislature of Texas and the U.S. Department of Justice, stayed with Johnson until the end of his administration.

Stabilization in the Johnson White House

Figure 2 lists the names and dates of service of top White House aides who were neither Kennedy holdovers nor part of Johnson's original inner circle and who were the stable core of Johnson's White House staff after 1965. William J. Hopkins, executive assistant, Donald F. Hornig, special assistant for science and technology, and Douglass Cater are included on the list because, while they served Johnson during the early transition, they fall in neither of the two essential categories of the dual staff: Kennedy appointed or Johnson intimate. Yet they were part of the transformed White House.

The significant thing about the chart is that it reveals the stabilization of personnel in major White House roles during, in rough terms, the second half of the Johnson presidency. Management operations and party liaison settled into the hands of Watson, while Macy took on executive appointments. Coordination of domestic policy aid moved to Califano in July 1965 and foreign policy assistance to Rostow in April 1966. Health and education continued to be Cater's domain. The functions of legal counsel were shared by McPherson and Semer until the latter's departure in November 1966. By January 1967 Christian was in place as press secretary. By that time also one other change had occurred. Robert E. Kintner had been appointed in April 1966 with functions in media contact, as Cabinet secretary, and for some functions in staff coordination. He found no significant role to perform in the last of these, except that he did accomplish an integration of the speechwriting function under McPherson's clearance, thus unifying that operation by the beginning of 1967. Hence, by January 1967, except for Sanders' later entry and Cater's departure to join the Hubert H. Humphrey presidential campaign, all the major roles had become responsibilities of persons who would perform them or coordinate their performance until the end of the Johnson presidency. The continuity in the transition to the Johnson presi-

Figure 2. ***Tenure of Top Johnson-Appointed White House Aides***

Aide	Title	Start	End
Hopkins, William J. (routine service activities)	executive assistant		
Hornig, Donald F. (executive policy–science and technology)	special assistant for science and technology	1/64	
Cater, Douglass, Jr. (executive guidance and control)	special assistant	5/64	10/68
Macy, John W., Jr. (appointments)	no official White House title	11/64	
Watson, W. Marvin, Jr. (management service)	special assistant	2/65	4/68
Califano, Joseph A., Jr. (executive policy, legislative program development)	special assistant	7/65	
McPherson, Harry C., Jr. (special counsel, speech preparation)	special counsel	2/66	
Rostow, Walt W. (executive policy–foreign policy)	special assistant	4/66	
Christian, George E. (media contact)	special assistant	5/66	
Sanders, H. Barefoot, Jr. (congressional liaison)	special assistant	5/67	

Timeline axis: 1963, 1964, 1965, 1966, 1967, 1968, 1969

dency was followed by stabilization after the transformation from the Kennedy-Johnson to the Johnson White House.

Concluding Comments

Several significant conclusions emerge from the preceding discussion. Various students of the Johnson presidency have written that the salient feature of the staff was its "ceaseless turnover." Such judgments require careful qualification. No data exist for comparison with other presidents.[38] Moreover, such characterizations do not take account of the fact that Johnson assumed that he had little choice but to retain the Kennedy staff *in toto* and reach for support during the transition to a handful of close associates who were available. The result was a dual White House staff, the creature of the unique circumstances that brought Johnson to the presidency. It was an assemblage of staff support that had two goals: the election of Johnson and the passage of a legislative program that built upon Kennedy's. After these goals were attained, the incentive to remain in the White House was diminished; some staff members apparently regarded the period following the epochal congressional session of 1965 as an appropriate interval to make a departure.

Johnson's ability to retain the services of top Kennedy-appointed aides was impressive. The retention of the professional, experienced, and policy oriented Kennedy appointees over a period averaging nearly three years may have served Johnson's need as much as the personal services and, except for Moyers, less policy-oriented assistance of his "band of brothers." Figure 1 reveals that O'Brien, Feldman, Bundy, White, Wilson, and Manatos remained with Johnson for an average of thirty-five months. Notably, the average length of service of the Kennedy holdovers exceeded the average length of service (twenty-four months) of the inner circle Johnson brought into the White House when he became president. With the exception of Hopkins and Hornig (who were in fact inherited from Kennedy but who were technically appointed by Johnson) the average tenure of the second wave of Johnson appointees was thirty-eight months.

The notion that excessive turnover plagued the Johnson White House not only ignores the circumstances that accounted for the dual staff, but disregards the very substantial stability in the most important administrative and policy areas to which Johnson made assignments. This stability, already noted for the transformed White House, was notable even for the entire Johnson presidency. Jenkins' role as administrative chief of staff was taken over by Watson. After Feldman and White resigned, McPherson clearly became the dominant legal adviser to the president. Hopkins maintained continuous control of all routine service activities. Rostow succeeded Bundy in directing foreign policy and remained until the end of the administration. Califano succeeded Moyers in the coordination of the legislative program and consolidated his role as the president's chief aide for economic policy. Hornig became special assistant in science and technology matters after the second month of Johnson's presidency. Macy was the top White House adviser on appointments after the election of 1964.

There was remarkable stability in congressional liaison. Manatos served Kennedy and Johnson the full eight years of their presidencies. Wilson served for six and a half years. O'Brien headed the effort until his appointment as postmaster general in November 1965 but worked part-time with Congress until he left the administration in April 1968. By that time Sanders and Manatos had consolidated control of congressional liaison activities. During the first three years of Johnson's presidency speechwriting had been widely dispersed but became centralized under McPherson during the last two years Johnson was in office. Only in the area of media contact was there notable discontinuity. Yet, as already noted, with the appointment of Christian, Johnson seemed to have finally found a press secretary with whom he was fully satisfied.

The evolution of Johnson's White House staff that we have traced suggests that there was sufficient continuity and stability of White House personnel for effective presidential governance. Equally significant was the number and quality of presidential assistants and how they assisted the president with making and executing policy and the associated managerial and political tasks. These topics will receive our attention in the following chapters.

3. The Johnson White House: An Overview

For an analysis of how Johnson's White House operated, it will be useful to present a general view of its dimensions, institutional features, tasks to be performed, and the size and qualities of personnel performing critical service to the president.

The Total Operation

Official budget summaries show that the average number of employees carried on White Houe rolls ranged during the Johnson presidency from 250 in 1966 to 263 in 1963 and 1964. This did not include those carried on the rolls for Special Projects under a separate appropriation of $1.5 million per annum. It did not include an undetermined number of persons detailed to the White House from departments and agencies, nor the White House police, Secret Service detail, and assigned military personnel performing protective, transportation, communication, and "mess" service.

Special statutory recognition had been given to the president's need for a top level group of advisers who would be the core of the White House operations. He was authorized to employ fourteen persons with basic compensation not to exceed Level II of the Federal Executive Salary Schedule. Most of these had the title of special assistant to the president, but there were variations such as administrative assistant to the president, special counsel to the president, or press secretary to the president. The Special Projects funds could be and were used for additional assistants with similar titles and similar levels of compensation.

Within the approximately 250 persons officially listed on White House rolls during the Johnson presidency approximately 60 percent were assigned to a service unit that handled documents and correspondence and supervised clerical services. Study of White House rolls led us to the conclusion that perhaps half the remainder of White House official personnel performed secretarial or other service activities. The institutionalization and continuity of personnel in the service unit contributed greatly to the smoothness of operations and, under the management of long-time civil servant William J. Hopkins, to relief of the president and his top staff from attention to detail.

The details concerning the total White House and the imprecision of figures on White House size are set forth in Appendix 1. We concentrate our attention in this study on the aid given to the president for his core functions of policy making and execution and the managerial and political tasks accompanying them.

Management, Policy, and Representation

From study of interoffice communications, we are able to discern the variety of things done for a president and to aggregate these in categories of functions that were performed for President Johnson and that almost certainly were or will be performed for his successors (see Figure 3). The first are management and legal services—the overall functions that enable a president to perform his varied tasks. The management function includes generally (1) control of the president's schedule: access to him and scheduling his personal and public appearances; (2) control of the flow of written communications to and from the president; (3) clearance of documents (with appropriate preliminary legal and other approvals) requiring the president's signature; and (4) preparation of plans and assembly of papers for Cabinet and other meetings or conferences in which the president is involved. Legal services include legal clearance of documents for the president's signature, assistance on legal problems not provided by the Department of Justice, and liaison between the president and the Department of Justice.

The second category of functions are those directly related to presidential decisions on government policy and execution and hence describable as core functions of White House staff. They include (1) identification and assessment of prospective presidential appointments to executive and judicial positions; (2) assistance on development and action on legislation; (3) assistance on executive policy making and application in foreign and domestic affairs, whether through general policy decisions or engaging in case work on particular policy or administrative matters officially within the president's responsibility or assumed by him for his attention; and (4) assistance in general executive management—departmental and agency liaison, oversight, and direction.

Figure 3. ***Functional Representation of White House Activities during the Johnson Presidency***

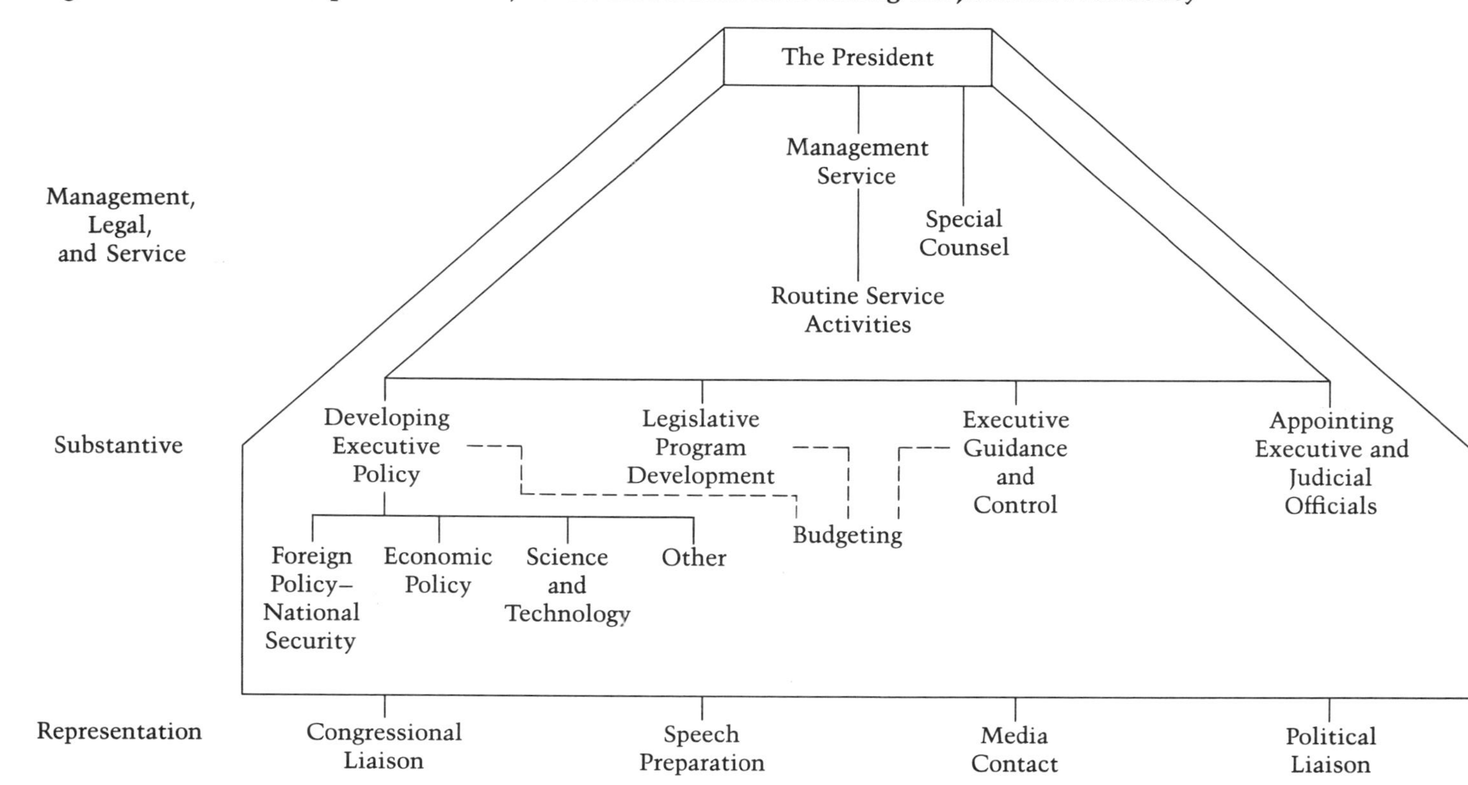

The third category of functions comprises those related to the representation of the president to obtain acceptance of his policies and actions and to maintain his policial influence. These include (1) assisting in congressional liaison; (2) preparation of presidential messages, speeches, remarks, and correspondence; (3) assisting the president in his communications to and other relationships with communication media; and (4) assisting the president in his relations with state and local officials, party officials, and private and quasi-public groups.

Some observations should accompany this analytical breakdown and aggregation of functions of White House aides. First, there is some overlap within or between the three categories. Substantive presidential policy may be made in the process of preparing a speech or through the negotiations that often characterize congressional liaison. Policy may be made through preparation of a Cabinet agenda or in the procedure of clearance of documents for presidential signature.

Second, White House structuring and personnel assignments within it may separate or combine the various functions in different ways. For example, management aid may be distributed among aides called by such titles as appointments secretary or Cabinet secretary or aggregated under a management chief of staff. Legal counsel may be assigned legal duties only or may, as in the Johnson presidency, engage in a wide range of other functions. Further, White House assignments may be made on other bases than type of functions, such as area of interest or special competence. Seldom in complex organizations are assignments made or developed on a single basis, and the variations in the Johnson presidency will be described more fully in chapter 4. Moreover, whatever structural arrangements are made, cooperation across lines will be regularly needed. At a given time (e.g., the preparation of the State of the Union Message or response to a crisis situation) coordination of structures or individuals engaged in work on such diverse tasks as foreign policy advice, domestic policy advice, congressional liaison, speechwriting, media presentations, or other matters will be required. The rapid movement of events within the White House creates a problem of coordination.

Third, the extent to which these presidential functions that require sizeable staff are performed within the White House will be dependent upon the degree and nature of the president's use of aid from outside the White House. By the time of the Johnson presidency the need for White House aid in several functions or types of policy had been greatly reduced by the development of institutional aid in the executive office of the president. This was true of budgeting and managerial aid and of national security, economic, trade, science and technology, marine resources, and space policy, for each of which an executive office staff had been established. In addition, the president may reach for help to officials directing or within executive departments and agencies, groups within congress, commissions and task forces, and political and personal associates outside the government. The White House is only the inner circle within a larger subpresidency composed of regular or occasional components, and its size and activities will be determined in large measure by the habits of the president in use of other resources.

Fourth, the "work" of the president and his staff is not limited to categories of activities of intrinsic importance. Matters that interest people, however transiently, may also interest the president at a given moment. So a great deal of his time and attention is inevitably devoted to amenities and symbolic, ceremonial occasions. Much staff time is similarly absorbed.

Varieties of Staff Activities

In the discharge of these functions White House aides engaged in a variety of activities. A certain amount of errand service characterized the activities of even the top White House aides that we have identified. Whoever happened to be in the president's company might be asked or told to make a telephone call, fetch a report, or make arrangements for a trip. Such service gives a personal quality to the White House and eclipses boundaries between functional areas of responsibility.

While errand service was especially typical of aides whose primary responsibility lay in management service, a great variety of incidental chores was indispensable to performance of major White House responsibilities. Walt W. Rostow, who was Johnson's national security adviser from 1966 to 1969, noted that "in-house foreign policy business" required much of his time. This assistance to the president included "Rose Garden speeches" not requiring "full consultation" with the State and Defense departments, "informal meetings with the press," "planning of visits by foreign dignitaries and of presidential trips abroad," and "drafting of letters to congressmen and others; etc." Rostow considered these activities so numerous that he warned his successor to budget a large amount of time for them.[1]

The most important activities of assistants revolved around the process of facilitating presidential decision making. Both Rostow and Joseph A. Califano, Jr., have summarized their most important activities. Rostow believed that "to lay before the president the widest possible range of options" was his first responsibility. This included the role of generating the material needed by the president for decision and analyzing the alternatives. Associated with this task was Rostow's practice of keeping "a wide range of intelligence flowing to Johnson" from cables and intelligence items so that "he could develop an independent feel for the situation."[2] Similarly, Califano said that "The most important thing is to get the alternatives clearly laid out."[3]

Mediation was also involved in presidential decision making. The government is composed of numerous actors with defined duties, views on desirable policy, and personal motivations. Information to the president may not be sufficient for the president's decision or his communication for its execution; reconciliation of agency viewpoints may be necessary for the former and consensus for the latter. Much of the work of the staff aide will be toward lightening the president's load and making possible his decisions and their execution by search for agreement in line with presidential purpose among those in strategic positions. Thus, Califano has commented on the "time-consuming process" of organizing "a number of meetings and consultations to get agreement on one or two of the alternatives."[4]

Among important activities of presidential assistants is the offering of advice. Rostow, however, noted that "I would rate the role of adviser as the least important among the NSC special assistant's functions."[5] Similarly, in the formulation of economic policy, Califano spent much more time on the activities enumerated above than on offering substantive policy advice to the president.[6]

Finally, Rostow noted that another "major task is to help assure that a president's decision is executed."[7] This could include transmission of information and instructions to executive officials and further follow-up activity. Califano noted that his final responsibility in the process of presidential decision making was "to write or coordinate the writing of the President's message announcing his policy decision."[8]

While these activities could be grouped or classified differently, it is significant—and sufficient for the purposes of this brief overview of the White House—that Johnson's top foreign and domestic policy assistants concurred. We shall take a more detailed and critical look at some of the top assistants' facilitating, mediating, advising, and implementing activities in later chapters.

By rearrangement and extension of these two aides' description of their tasks we can delineate crucial elements of White House service. The first is the communication of information to the president for the making of his decisions. This includes selection and aggregation from the numerous sources from which communications are sent and shielding the president from overflow and disorganization of material and from excessive use of his time in oral communication by telephone or appointment. It includes also alertness to needs for additional information on present or anticipated problems. It includes analysis and concise and clear presentation of data. It may include, as Rostow thought was crucial, the sharpening of options. And while Rostow regarded it as less important, it may include communication of advice. The second task is mediation of viewpoints and positions among advisers and administrators, even including suggestions of additional alternatives and leadership toward concurrence with presidential objectives. The third task is communication of the president's decisions, desires, or motivations to those who can implement them. Finally, an aide must assist in service and representational functions.

Aides for White House Operations

Identification of Top Aides

We have developed a list of the top White House aides during Johnson's presidency. It is shown on Table 1, along with information to be used in our subsequent analysis. After laboring with various lists in library, newspaper, and journal sources, we decided to base a list on an official source—the annual listings under "White House Office" in the *United States Government Manual*. We deleted from these lists the president's physicians and military aides because they were not primarily engaged in the policy and managerial tasks of government. Also excluded from the list were Kennedy aides who left the Johnson administration within approximately four months. This included such top Kennedy aides as Theodore C. Sorensen, Pierre E. G. Salinger, and Arthur M. Schlesinger, Jr., as well as Carl Kaysen, Andrew T. Hatcher, and Brooks Hays. Another Kennedy aide excluded is Stafford Warren, an unpaid assistant on mental retardation who saw the president very infrequently.[9] Although the manual lists Timothy Reuter, we have excluded him because he was the executive director of the Food for Peace Program, an operating agency initially placed in the White House that was transferred to the Department of State by executive order on 20 October 1965.

Included on the list are two names that did not appear in the manual. John W. Macy, Jr., was added because he actually directed operations in an important White House function—appointments to executive positions—while he was the chairman of the Civil Service

Table 1. ***Top White House Aides during the Johnson Presidency***

	Who Appointed	Months of Service under LBJ	Age at Time of Appointment	Highest Degree	Regional Origin	Position prior to WH Appointment	Position after WH Service	Remained until End?
Alexander, Clifford L., Jr.	J	7	30	L.L.B.	MA (NY)	U.S. (Ex.)	U.S. (Ex.)	NO
Bator, Francis M.	J	32	40	Ph.D.	F	U.S. (Ex.)	A	NO
Bundy, McGeorge	K	27	44	A.B.	NE (MA)	Acad.	P	NO
Busby, Horace, Jr.	J	22	39	—*	WSC (TX)	Priv.	P	NO
Califano, Joseph A, Jr.	J	41	34	L.L.B.	MA (NY)	U.S. (Ex.)	P	YES
Cater, S. Douglass, Jr.	J	54	40	M.A.	ESC (AL)	P	P	NO
Christian, George E.	J	32	39	A.B.	WSC (TX)	State	P	YES
Dungan, Ralph A.	K	12	40	M.P.A.	MA (PA)	U.S. (Leg.)	U.S. (Ex.)	NO
Feldman, Myer	K	14	46	L.L.B.	MA (PA)	U.S. (Leg.)	P	NO
Fleming, Robert H.	J	31	54	B.A.	ENC (WI)	P	U.S. (Ex.)	NO
Furness, Betty	J	21	51	—*	MA (NY)	P	P	YES
Goldstein, E. Ernest	J	13	48	L.L.B.	MA (PA)	P	P	YES
Goodwin, Richard N.	J	22	31	L.L.B.	NE (MA)	U.S. (Leg.)	A	NO
Hopkins, William J.	J	62	—*	L.L.B.	—*	—*	—*	YES
Hornig, Donald F.	J	56	43	L.L.B. Ph.D.	ENC (WI)	A	P	NO
Horsky, Charles A.	K	38	53	L.L.B.	M (MT)	P	P	NO
Jacobsen, Jake	J	24	45	L.L.B.	MA (NJ)	P	P	NO
Jenkins, Walter W.	J	11	45	B.A.	WSC (TX)	U.S. (Ex.)	P	NO
Johnson, W. Thomas, Jr.	J	31	25	M.B.A.	SA (GA)	P	U.S. (Ex.)	YES
Jones, James R.	J	48	25	L.L.B.	WSC (OK)	U.S. (Leg.)	P	YES
Kilduff, Malcolm M.	K	20	36	L.L.B.	MA (NY)	U.S. (Ex.)	U.S. (Ex.)	NO

Kintner, Robert E.	J	14	56	B.A.	MA (PA)	P	P	NO
Komer, Robert W.	J	15	43	M.B.A.	ENC (IL)	U.S. (Ex.)	U.S. (Ex.)	NO
Lawrence, David L.	K	36	74	—*	—*	S	—*	NO
Levinson, Lawrence E.	J	25	36	L.L.B.	MA (NY)	U.S. (Ex.)	P	YES
Macy, John W., Jr.	J	61	46	B.A.	ENC (IL)	U.S. (Ex.)	U.S. (Ex.)	YES
Manatos, Mike N.	K	62	49	B.S.	M (UT)	U.S. (Leg.)	P	YES
McPherson, Harry C., Jr.	J	36	36	L.L.B.	WSC (TX)	U.S. (Ex.)	P	YES
Moyers, Bill D.	J	38	29	B.D.	WSC (OK)	U.S. (Ex.)	P	NO
Murphy, Charles S.	J	11	58	L.L.B.	SA (NC)	U.S. (Ex.)	P	NO
O'Brien, Lawrence F.	K	23	46	L.L.B.	NE (MA)	P	U.S. (Ex.)	NO
O'Donnell, Kenneth P.	K	14	39	B.A.	NE (MA)	P	P	NO
Peterson, Esther	J	29	58	M.A.	M (UT)	U.S. (Ex.)	P	NO
Pierson, W. DeVier	J	19	35	L.L.B.	WSC (OK)	U.S. (Leg.)	P	YES
Pollak, Stephen J.	J	8	38	L.L.B.	ENC (IL)	U.S. (Ex.)	U.S. (Ex.)	NO
Reedy, George E.	J	25	46	B.A.	ENC (IN)	U.S. (Ex.)	P	NO
Roche, John P.	J	24	44	Ph.D.	MA (NY)	A	A	NO
Rostow, Walt W.	J	34	49	Ph.D.	MA (NY)	U.S. (Ex.)	A	YES
Sanders, H. Barefoot, Jr.	J	20	42	L.L.B.	WSC (TX)	U.S. (Ex.)	P	YES
Semer, Milton P.	J	9	47	J.D.	NE (MI)	U.S. (Ex.)	P	NO
Stevens, Roger L.	J	57	54	—*	ENC (MI)	P	—*	NO
Taylor, Hobart, Jr.	J	10	43	L.L.B.	WSC (TX)	U.S. (Ex.)	U.S. (Ex.)	NO
Taylor, Maxwell D.	J	30	63	B.S.	ENC (MO)	U.S. (Ex.)	—*	YES
Temple, Larry E.	J	15	31	L.L.B.	WSC (TX)	S	P	YES
Valenti, Jack J.	J	28	42	M.B.A.	WSC (TX)	P	P	NO
Watson, W. Marvin, Jr.	J	39	40	M.B.A.	WSC (TX)	P	U.S. (Ex.)	NO
White, Lee C.	K	14	40	L.L.B.	WNC (NE)	U.S. (Leg.)	U.S. (Ex.)	NO
Wilson, Henry Hall, Jr.	K	41	42	L.L.B.	SA (NC)	S	P	NO

*Information unavailable in the Macy files or other sources at the LBJ Library.

Commission. Esther Peterson, special assistant for consumer affairs, has been included because her successor was listed in the manual.

We have not included the names of some persons whose assistance to the president may have been as or more significant than that of persons officially on the White House rolls. It was generally known among informed persons that the president's wife was his constant and valued counselor and that she assisted him particularly in representational activities. Elizabeth Carpenter, her press secretary, was an active participant in preparation of speeches and press-related activities. Vice President Hubert H. Humphrey is also not listed as a White House aide, though his role is referred to on occasions in the subsequent discussions. Nor have we included personal advisers to the president who held no official position or members of Congress or the judiciary.

We arrived at a list of forty-eight persons who formed the core of the president's managerial, policy, and representational aides during his term of five years, one month, and twenty-eight days. To supplement it we looked for the staffing of the White House on a typical date for the number of core staff and of backup staff; that is, the total number of people serving the president in his managerial, policy, and representational functions.

On 18 October 1967 seventeen people were on a list of "Principal Assistants (holding Presidential Commissions)" and twelve others on a list of "Other Assistants (not holding Presidential Commissions)," making a total of twenty-nine.[10] At the same time we looked at a listing of all employees working in each division of the White House on 21 October 1967. From our analysis of similar documents, this appeared to be a typical listing. Leaving off those who appeared to be engaged in secretarial, routine, or semiroutine activities (e.g., making photographs, arranging tours, or answering correspondence under guidance), we counted sixty-two persons, including Hopkins and a group of eight in a special office under Ambassador William Leonhart.[11] Making allowance for some error in inclusion or exclusion, we concluded that President Johnson's White House professional staff for his primary functions of governance—including White House management, policy making, and representation—was composed of from sixty to sixty-five persons. The figure would be somewhat higher if some persons officially in NSC but linked to White House operations were included. Yet the totals are consistent with Hopkins' estimate that 60 percent of the White House worked for him and our estimate from numerous listings that perhaps one-half of the remainder performed routine services.[12]

The conclusions are significant for those interested in the size of

White House operations. President Johnson operated at a given time with a White House staff for nonroutine matters of about fifteen principal assistants, about an equal number of other top assistants, and back-up aides for these that produced a total of between sixty and seventy-five. This was lean staffing for the range of functions on which assistance was needed. President Johnson was interested in keeping the staff as small as possible and on various occasions asked for comparisons of the size of the staff with that on the date when he came to office. The effects on the lean staff had important consequences noted in the next chapter—maintenance of a personalized operation, heavy workload on the staff, and staff interrelationships.

Profiles of the Top Aides

Because of the small size of the staff Johnson could afford no excess baggage. He exercised the caution and care in the selection of White House aides that characterized his executive appointments.[13] He continuously employed his mastery of detail and power of recall to draw talent into the White House. One staff member reported, "I can't remember the President when he is not sizing people up. He has an antenna; he has a radar that goes twenty-four hours a day on sizing people up."[14] As his presidency progressed a distinct recruitment pattern emerged.[15]

As discussed in the preceding chapter, Johnson retained as many Kennedy assistants as possible and drew into the White House a core of personal associates that he had known for years and whose work habits he had observed first hand. This group included Walter W. Jenkins, Horace Busby, Jr., Jack J. Valenti, George E. Reedy, and Bill D. Moyers, all of whom became White House aides immediately upon Johnson's accession to the presidency. Four months after becoming president, Johnson designated Reedy press secretary. By April 1965, this circle expanded to include Jake Jacobsen and W. Marvin Watson but no longer included Jenkins.

As Johnson made other appointments he relied upon the judgment of this inner circle of aides who in turn had first-hand knowledge of potential aides' abilities. For example, Busby through Macy called the president's attention to E. Ernest Goldstein. "This is about the best recruit my net has caught in a long time," Busby wrote of Goldstein. Busby regarded Goldstein as a "heavyweight" and urged the president to consider him "for positions of appropriate heft."[16] Within four months Johnson called Goldstein to the White House and asked him to join the staff. In addition to relying upon the evaluation of trusted aides, Johnson also depended upon the judgment of personal friends and political allies outside the White House. For example, the president recruited Larry E. Temple and George E. Christian through Texas governor John B. Connally, for whom they had been working.

When Johnson had no first-hand knowledge of the new staff members' work habits, he watched their performance closely. Various staff aides report that they experienced a "testing" process before their positions were fully established. For example, Johnson was vague concerning Christian's duties when he joined the staff. After Christian worked two or three months with Rostow, Johnson assigned him to the press office. By the time Moyers resigned in January 1967, Johnson was convinced that Christian could handle the job and appointed him press secretary.[17] Similarly, when Temple joined the staff as a special counsel in October 1967, liaison with the Justice Department was the only responsibility that Johnson designated. After six months on the staff Temple began to perform many of Watson's duties following the latter's appointment as postmaster general, succeeding Lawrence F. O'Brien.[18]

Another category of aides consisted of those who were linked to groups outside the government. These aides included Roger L. Stevens, special assistant for the arts, Donald F. Hornig, special assistant for science and technology, and Esther Peterson and Betty Furness, who were special assistants for consumer affairs. These aides did not know Johnson well before their appointments nor did they have a history of working with the other White House aides. Johnson had less personal contact with these aides, who were regarded as specialists and who did not perform the multiple tasks expected of the other aides. The elements of personal loyalty and service were much less important in the relation between these aides and the president. Indeed, Johnson appointed these members of the staff because of their ability to represent the presidency to distinct interest groups outside the government.

These recruitment practices account at least partially for many of the characteristics of the White House staff. The presence of the Kennedy holdovers and those that Johnson recruited yielded a White House that was overwhelmingly white and male. Only two blacks (Hobart Taylor, Jr., and Clifford L. Alexander, Jr.) and two women (Furness and Peterson) were members of the staff. Yet these were significant appointments that occurred at a time when the advantages of racial and sexual representation in the White House were less recognized than in later years.

The circumstances of Johnson's accession and the recruitment process he adopted also account for the geographic make-up of the staff.

Table 2. ***Regional Origins of White House Staff***

Region	Number
New England	5
Middle Atlantic	12
East North Central	7
West North Central	2
South Atlantic	3
East South Central	1
West South Central	12
Mountain	3
Pacific	0

While all regions except the Pacific Coast were represented, the New England, Middle Atlantic, and the West South Central states were heavily overrepresented (see Table 2). Of the twelve Kennedy hold-overs in the list eight were from the Middle Atlantic or New England states. The West South Central states are heavily represented because Johnson appointed eleven Texans and two Oklahomans as White House aides. Since there are only thirty-six Johnson appointees in our list, the presence of eleven aides from the president's native state is interesting, though it is doubtful that the division "between Texan and non-Texan" was significant in White House operations.[19]

Johnson was acutely aware of the high intellectual calibre of the Kennedy staff and actively sought aides who would meet that standard. Because he valued education and respected academic credentials, the educational level of his assistants was impressive. Of the forty-eight top advisers, forty-four held college degrees and thirty-three held graduate degrees. The degrees included twenty-one law degrees, five doctoral degrees, six master's degrees, and one divinity degree. Of the staff members who held graduate degrees, over half—nineteen—held degrees from Ivy League schools. For the thirty-six Johnson-appointed aides twenty-six held advanced degrees and fifteen graduated from Ivy League universities.

The aura of youth and activity that infused the Kennedy staff also characterized Johnson's. He was especially impressed by young men who quickly mastered the mechanics of government and who were adept at dealing with the departments and agencies of the executive branch. According to W. DeVier Pierson, Johnson had a "genuine interest in bringing along young men."[20] Two of Johnson's most important aides, Moyers and Califano, were ages twenty-nine and thirty-four, respectively, when they joined the White House staff. At the time Johnson appointed them Alexander was thirty, Richard N. Goodwin, thirty-one, Thomas W. Johnson, Jr., twenty-five, and James R. Jones, twenty-five. Yet the average age of the top staff was 43.5 years and the median was forty-three. Over half of the sample—twenty-five—were in their forties. Thus, when Johnson became president at the age of fifty-five, he relied upon a group of principal aides whose average age was only 11.5 years less than his own.

More important than any of the characteristics thus far considered were the occupational backgrounds of the staff members. Johnson looked for those with experience that equipped them for the White House tasks that he wished them to perform. As a result, he automatically turned to those with government experience and looked infrequently outside the government for aides. An examination of the positions of aides immediately preceding their White House appointment reveals the institutions that the president drew upon to assemble his staff. Of the forty-eight top aides, thirty came from government, fourteen from the private sector, and three from academia. Of those who came from government, twenty-one came from the executive and five from the legislative branches of the federal government. Four came from state government. Of the staff members from the private sector, the overwhelming majority were from the legal, public relations, journalism, and broadcasting professions. Only one had experience in industry.

Of the thirty-six staff members whom Johnson appointed, seventeen remained until the end of his presidency. Of the remaining nineteen, Johnson appointed six to other government posts.[21] Three resigned for health or personal reasons.[22] Three were lured from White House service by unusually attractive job offers outside the government.[23] At least two others had agreed to become aides for a definite time and departed upon the agreed date.[24] One returned to his academic position at the beginning of the school year of 1968–69 following Johnson's decision not to seek re-election.[25] Another left the administration to join the Hubert H. Humphrey presidential campaign.[26]

Summary

Within the vast and diversified apparatus serving the presidency officially and exclusively is a nuclear White House office. Its precise boundaries and size are difficult to determine. Use of any figures on size is meaningless unless founded on analysis of the relationships to other units of service and the tasks that were performed in the White House itself.

Much of the activity centered on and within the White House is purely service. While the amount of this activity is largely uncontrollable by the president, its institutionalization relieves him of burden. The primary tasks for which Johnson used White House assistance were varied and can be classified generally as managerial, policy, and representational. The activities ranged generally from errand service, through communication of information to and from the president, to consensus building and advice.

For performance of the primary tasks the Johnson White House staff was lean. It was composed initially of Kennedy holdovers and persons experienced in Johnson's service, and additions were made cautiously. The top staff came predominately from the Northeast and Texas, had high academic credentials, was experienced in government, included an overwhelming majority from legal and public relations professions, and served long enough to provide substantial continuity in White House operations.

4. Johnson's Management Style

We have noted in chapter 3 the kinds of functions performed in the White House for Lyndon B. Johnson and asserted that almost certainly these would be performed for other presidents. We have shown the size, qualifications, recruitment, continuity, and change in personnel performing these functions, and may assume there will be some similarities with other presidencies, especially those where presidents have succeeded to the office by death, removal, or resignation of a predecessor. Trends and uniformities in functions are, we believe, inherent in successive presidencies, and undoubtedly their constraints will force some similarities in size, qualities, and use of personnel.

Nonetheless, the White House will inevitably reflect presidents personally. The man who occupies thc office at a particular time will influcnce the extent to which tasks are readily embraced or sought for the White House or shifted to other locations; the kinds of men and women attracted as aides, the scope given to them, and the motivations and inspiration that infuse their efforts; and the ways the duties are allotted and recombined and supervision is provided. In sum, while constraints and tendencies will operate through successive presidencies, individual personality and interests will, if history indicates the future, produce large differences.

The climb to the presidency maintains and accentuates the differences in the qualities and methods of its occupants. They have not been socialized to the requirements of office as has a British cabinet member rising by stages to the premiership, an American corporate executive absorbed by experience in corporate relationships, or a congressional committee chairman schooled by service to committee habits. There is indeed no comparable position to train one for the multiple and vast responsibilities of the presidency, and no common route to it. Moveover, presidents are prima donnas, individualized by personal work experiences and rendered egocentric by the adulation of campaign followers, favor seekers, and sycophants.

What the Constitution personalizes in responsibility, the distinctiveness of the office and the ways of reaching it personalize in operation.

In Johnson the personalization of the White House operation was particularly evident. We have seen no evidence that Johnson sought to follow any pattern used by his predecessors or ever seriously deliberated about how he would handle White House operations, or that he was influenced by the dichotomies set forth by commentators, either on White House role or methods of directing its operations. We assume that he gave some thought to such matters, but the evidence indicates that management process resulted more from interactive personal response than deliberation and planning. Inheriting a White House already partially established, he directed a multicentered, semi-hierarchical, flexible system, adapted over time to personal changes and moved by his own unmitigated drive for accomplishment, pervasive and intimate involvement, personal work habits, and desire for unity and loyalty. Among the consequences were dependence for coordination on the energy and competence of the president personally, strain on personnel, and accompanying danger of lack of adequate analysis and deliberation.

The story in this chapter is of these and other features of Johnson's management of the White House and is built from reports from participants. Although Johnson's papers will not be released until fifty years after his death, numerous internal memorandums and oral histories of his staff provide intimate insight into White House structure, processes, and behavior beyond that available previously for any president.

The Personal Setting

Johnson's imprint on White House operations seems to have flowed from his experience, his strong desire for accomplishment, and his personal activism. No man has reached the presidency with more public experience. It was experience within government, not in private representation before it or in reporting about it. It was Washington experience: except for a short period as state director of an agency and a shorter period in military service in World War II, he had spent his public life on the banks of the Potomac. There it was legislative experience: twenty-four years in Congress before becoming vice president, eleven in the House of Representatives, and twelve in the Senate, including service as minority and majority leader. Johnson was by experience the public man, the Washington man, the legislative man.

Such experiences could be both restrictive and broadening. Harry C. McPherson, Jr., staff aide to Johnson in the Senate and the presidency, has said that he was not a "Texas provincial" but a "Washington provincial."[1] Certainly he was fully at home and competent in the ways of the Washington community.

Legislative experience had enhanced his opportunity for leadership from the White House. His role as majority leader made him unusually familiar with all the issues of public policy that had required votes or were being generated for later vote in Congress. It probably made him feel that great issues were public issues, also national issues, and that issues are resolved through a process of give and take. It had made him a master of the art of gaining consensus or compromise on a course of action among those representing conflicting interests and holding different views. It had made him knowledgeable about the centers of personal power in congress—who, as he put it, were the "whales" in the Senate and indeed in the House also. It had given him friendships and a sense of indebtedness from many of these. It had made him sensitive to the necessity for favorable constituency response in the behavior of members of Congress. In sum, service in Congress had given him much competence as a political man.

He came then to the White House with knowledge on public issues and practice in the political processes in Washington. With respect to the former, James C. Gaither, one of Joseph A. Califano, Jr.'s assistants, said, "He really knows what this government is doing."[2] And with relation to the latter, it could lead to the charge by *New York Times* columnist James Reston that he was "trying to run the Presidency as if it were a Senator's office on Capitol Hill."[3] This implied that the vast experience in political processes was still inadequate for or perhaps divergent from the management tasks of the president, which included White House management.

He brought to the presidency a strong desire for accomplishment and, as George E. Reedy said, "a determination to reach high goals."[4] There appeared to be a strong mixture of personal vanity in the drive for accomplishment, but it also reflected a deep sense of mission for government and for the presidency. It was in the beginning a sense of mission for the domestic presidency. Civil rights, tax reform, war on poverty, education, and then other areas engaged his commitment. Two of his aides caught the dual aspects of the philosophy that dominated the president. One was populism: the view that government could do things for the well-being of those who need help. McPherson said he had "a genuine populist feeling about poor people."[5] The other was the idea of opportunity. Gaither said it was giving people "a chance to help themselves," "not giving them handouts."[6] Reedy was more expansive about the dual aspects of Johnson's philosophy: "Lyndon Johnson was a man who thought that all of the world's problems could be solved by giving people greater access to electric power, by placing an adequate floor under wages, by placing an adequate floor under farm prices, by assuring everyone an equal right to a job, and by giving everyone an education."[7] Johnson's philosophy was further illustrated by a statement of Senator Johnson to one of the authors in 1956: "If we can give the Negro education and the vote, he will be able to take care of himself."[8] The sense of public mission was shared by and stimulated the creative legislative planners in the Johnson presidency: Bill D. Moyers, Douglass S. Cater, Jr., Califano, McPherson, and others. There was also a sense of American mission that dominated, as with other presidents, the course of foreign policy and was shared in the White House by those who worked with the president.

The intense desire for accomplishment was combined with personal activism. His tireless energy was expended almost completely in his official activities. The word "workaholic" would be particularly applicable to him. Absorption in work was a habit from early manhood. An associate when Johnson was state director of the National Youth Administration in the mid thirties said that Johnson would assert and demand, "I work seventeen hours a day and live on Ex-lax and aspirin, and I expect you to work fifteen."[9] In later life he knew how to avoid the need for stimulants by spacing rest, exercise, and relaxation in conversation. He needed less sleep than most people and could catch it quickly when time was available. His normal daily schedule included two periods of work: from 7:30 A.M. or earlier to after lunch, then after a nap a second period from midafternoon to dinner or later. And whether at his desk, the dinner table, or in the conversation that he relished, his interest seemed always to be concentrated on questions of public affairs and on his role, official or personal, in creating or maintaining some form of public action.

The desire for accomplishment and personal activism led to an activist presidency and to activism in the White House. Cater has said that he "energized the presidency more than any president in memory with the possible exception of Franklin D. Roosevelt."[10] And Califano said, "His staff system was frenetic, seeking a cure for every ill; his appearance one of indefatigable perpetual motion, in constant conversation and consultation."[11] In turn, McPherson said, "He consumes people, almost without knowing it."[12] They worked long hours, whatever hours were required, whatever days were required, kept their luggage packed at the White House for quick notice of trips to be taken, responded to his changing work demands, and were variously stimulated to share his desire for great accomplishment.

Matching Men to Tasks

Jake Jacobsen has said that he had read all the books about presidential assistants and "they're all wrong. They're just wrong because what they want to think is that you compartmentalize everything. Maybe this is their way of doing it. Johnson didn't compartmentalize his mind, and therefore he didn't subdivide the work in the office that way."[13]

Various aides have reported that Johnson asked different people to prepare organization charts, but that no chart was ever adopted. The president instructed Califano to draw up an organizational chart; Califano worked about a week on it with the aid of charts drawn up in the Department of Defense and presented it to the president, who rejected it.[14] Robert E. Kintner, whose responsibilities included tying together loose ends in staff operations, wrote to Moyers about preparation of an organization chart. Moyers' reply included the following comments:

> . . . let me briefly say such an exercise is a gross misuse of a good man's time; nothing useful can come of it, since the White House reflects the personal needs of the President rather [*sic*] a structural design. If there is a design, it is radial—like the spokes of a wheel radiating out from the hub. Each person has a special relationship to the President and does what the President needs done; you can define very briefly what each man does, but it is impossible to catch the full scope of his duties.
>
> In his own mind the president knows what each man does; he doesn't need an organization chart to show him. In our minds, we know what the president expects of us; a chart is irrelevant.[15]

Nonetheless, Johnson's White House was not unstructured. He certainly made some firm differentiations in task assignments; radial design need not indicate that all spokes were the same thickness or length or unsegmented hierarchically, and the complexities of White House operations may merely have overtaxed Califano's skills and ingenuity in such a matter. Although Johnson did not consciously apply organization theory or hold a preconceived organization plan, organizational logic flowing from natural differentiations of tasks is evident.

Undeterred by Califano's and Moyers' charting difficulties, we differentiated in the preceding chapter the tasks we had observed were performed by White House staff. We now show on Table 3 how the roles of persons corresponded in part with the basic task differentiations. Staff roles may have occurred by assignment or evolution and may reflect only concentrations, single or multiple, rather than any containment of activity. They reveal roles developed either on the basis of a type of function or policy area, either of which (or even the two in combination) would be recognized in organization theory as a legitimate basis for structuring personnel assignments. Certainly, the assignment of Lawrence F. O'Brien first and Barefoot Sanders later to congressional liaison, of Califano to legislative programming, of John W. Macy, Jr., to presidential appointments, and of a succession of people to the jobs of press secretary and speechwriting were allocations according to type of function. At the same time, the allocation of responsibility to Donald F. Hornig for advice on science and technology matters, to Roger L. Stevens on the arts, and to Esther Peterson and later Betty Furness on consumer policies was made on the basis of policy area. Assignments to McGeorge Bundy and Walt W. Rostow could be rationalized on either of the two bases. While the two are different and result in overlapping, they reflect logic in organization in response to the differentiation of duties. In White House operations irrespective of the occupant of the presidency and regardless of the use or nonuse of conscious planning and charts, differentiation in assignments to correspond to constant requirements for aid will determine major, though not necessarily all, allocations. The White House is in this respect like other organizations.

Centers of integration existed within the structure: Bundy, then Rostow, headed the foreign policy operation; Moyers and then Califano the legislative program development; Califano in a general way all domestic executive decision making; Macy appointments to the executive branch and, in the last part of the administration, Larry E. Temple judicial appointments; O'Brien and after him Sanders congressional liaison; Reedy and then Moyers and then George E. Christian the press; Myer Feldman and then Lee C. White and then McPherson the variety of things the special counsel did;[16] and at the end of the administration McPherson, John P. Roche, and Charles M. Maguire the speechwriting operation. These were kingpins whose uncharted positions in radial and hierarchical behavioral patterns were clearly established.

One center of integration and order was management service. After Walter W. Jenkins' service for a year as administrative chief of

Table 3. *Primary Task Assignments*

Management, Legal, and Service

MANAGEMENT SERVICE

Appointments secretary
Walter W. Jenkins, special assistant (11/63–10/64)
Jack J. Valenti, special assistant (11/63–4/66)
W. Marvin Watson, special assistant (2/65–4/68)
James R. Jones, assistant (2/65–1/68), deputy special assistant (1/68–1/69)

Cabinet secretary
Horace Busby, Jr., special assistant (11/63–10/65)
Robert E. Kintner, special assistant (4/66–6/67)

Other
Larry E. Temple, special counsel (10/67–1/69)
W. Thomas Johnson, Jr., special assistant (9/68–1/69)

SPECIAL COUNSEL

Myer Feldman, deputy special counsel (11/63–1/65)
Lee C. White, assistant special counsel (11/63–3/64), associate counsel (4/64–2/65), special counsel (3/65–3/66)
Hobart Taylor, Jr., associate special counsel (4/64–9/65)
Clifford Alexander, Jr., deputy special assistant (7/64–8/65), associate special counsel (9/65–8/67)
Harry C. McPherson, Jr., special counsel (2/66–1/69)
Milton P. Semer, counsel (3/66–11/66)
W. DeVier Pierson, special counsel (3/67–1/69)
Larry E. Temple, special counsel (10/67–1/69)

ROUTINE SERVICE ACTIVITIES

William J. Hopkins, executive clerk (11/63–1/69)

Representational

CONGRESSIONAL LIAISON

Lawrence F. O'Brien, special assistant (11/63–11/65)
Mike N. Manatos, administrative assistant (11/63–1/69)
Henry Hall Wilson, Jr., administrative assistant (11/63–5/67)
Jake Jacobsen, legislative counsel (4/65–5/67)
H. Barefoot Sanders, Jr., legislative counsel (5/67–1/69)
James R. Jones, assistant (2/65–1/68), deputy special assistant (1/68–1/69)

Speech Preparation

Bill D. Moyers, special assistant (11/63–7/65)
Jack J. Valenti, special assistant (11/63–4/66)
Richard N. Goodwin, special assistant (4/64–9/65)
Harry C. McPherson, Jr., special counsel (2/66–1/69)
John P. Roche, special consultant (9/66–9/68)

Media Contact

Press secretary
George E. Reedy, special assistant (3/64–7/65)
Bill D. Moyers, special assistant (7/65–1/67)
George E. Christian, administrative assistant (4/66–11/66), special assistant (12/66–1/69)

Assistant press secretary
Malcolm M. Kilduff, assistant press secretary (11/63–7/65)
Robert H. Fleming, deputy press secretary (2/66–9/68)

Other
Robert E. Kintner, special assistant (4/66–6/67)

Political Liaison

Jack J. Valenti, special assistant (11/63–4/66)
Lawrence F. O'Brien, special assistant (11/63–11/65)
David L. Lawrence, special assistant (11/63–11/66)
W. Marvin Watson, special assistant (2/65–4/68)
Joseph A. Califano, special assistant (7/65–1/69)

Substantive

Developing Executive Policy

Foreign Policy—National Security
McGeorge Bundy, special assistant for National Security Affairs (11/63–2/66)
Robert W. Komer, deputy special assistant (11/64–2/66), special assistant (3/66–1/67)
Maxwell D. Taylor, special consultant (7/65–1/69)
Walt W. Rostow, special assistant (4/66–1/69)
Francis M. Bator, deputy special assistant (6/66–9/67)

Economic Policy
Bill D. Moyers, special assistant (11/63–7/65)
Joseph A. Califano, Jr., special assistant (7/65–1/69)
E. Ernest Goldstein, special assistant (9/67–1/69)

Science and Technology

Donald F. Hornig, special assistant for Science and Technology (1/64–1/69)

Other

Charles A. Horsky, special assistant for National Capital Affairs (11/63–2/67)

Stephen J. Pollak, special assistant for National Capital Affairs (1/67–10/67)

Esther Peterson, special assistant for Consumer Affairs (12/64–4/67)

Betty Furness, special assistant for Consumer Affairs (5/67–1/69)

Roger L. Stevens, special assistant for the Arts (4/64–1/69)

LEGISLATIVE PROGRAM DEVELOPMENT

Bill D. Moyers, special assistant (11/63–7/65)

Joseph A. Califano, Jr., special assistant (7/65–1/69)

Lawrence E. Levinson, deputy special counsel (12/66–1/69)

EXECUTIVE GUIDANCE AND CONTROL

McGeorge Bundy, special assistant for National Security Affairs (11/63–2/65)

Bill D. Moyers, special assistant (11/63–7/65)

Lee C. White, assistant special counsel (11/63–3/64), associate counsel (4/64–2/65), special counsel (3/65–3/66)

S. Douglass Cater, Jr., special assistant (5/64–10/68)

Joseph A. Califano, Jr., special assistant (7/65–1/69)

Harry C. McPherson, Jr., special counsel (2/66–1/69)

Walt W. Rostow, special assistant (4/66–1/69)

E. Ernest Goldstein, special assistant (7/65–1/69)

APPOINTMENTS

Ralph A. Dungan, special assistant (11/63–9/64)

John W. Macy, Jr., no official White House title (11/64–1/69)

Larry E. Temple, special counsel (10/67–1/69)

---

staff, Johnson brought in W. Marvin Watson, who served both as political aide and management aide. For managerial operations "Johnson ordered a tight ship at the White House and Watson took him at his word."[17] Others—Jack J. Valenti, Jacobsen, James R. Jones, Temple, Sherwin J. Markham—shared these activities and sometimes appeared to operate with much independence, but they recognized Watson as chief of management service. He was the point of coordination for the services supplied by William J. Hopkins and the military, Secret Service, and police units. He, or others with him, took care of the president's calendar and his travel. Both were large responsibilities—one calling continuously for careful judgment, the other for managerial efficiency. He safeguarded the White House budget and handled White House service operations with an iron and impecunious hand, cutting newspaper or book expenditures or persistently notifying staff members of their inappropriate use of White House cars.[18]

Nevertheless, despite the structural unities and continuities in White House operations, Johnson allowed and even encouraged the development of role specializations by individual talent, choice, and initiative. While types of function fashioned personal allocations, men also determined their roles. When Cater came into the White House in April 1964, Johnson told him "to be his reporter, that he wanted me to keep my eye on all the government and bring the best ideas to him in a way that he could use them. Secondly, he said he wanted me to think ahead, to look down the road."[19] With only this general assignment Cater found an office in the basement and worked at odd jobs. He spent most of his first months writing commencement speeches and writing or editing campaign speeches and putting together statements for Johnson's book, *My Hope for America*. During the presidential campaign of 1964, however, he worked to make education a public policy priority; by the end of 1964 he was draftsman for the education message of the president. Thereafter, he came to be the White House special aide on education. Then, when Horace Busby, Jr., who had coordinated the first health message in 1965, left the White House, Cater, with his experience with Health, Education and Welfare (HEW), took over health matters. On health and education he was the liaison with HEW staff and prepared first drafts of messages to Congress and speeches to the public. At Johnson's request he became the White House representative on the highway beautification act, and either by assignment from the president or assumption he became active in such additional projects as the development of legislation for the Public Broadcasting Corporation and the arts and humanities endowments. Thus, Johnson's idea man became specialized program aide by evolution, as Hornig and some others by assignment.[20]

E. Ernest Goldstein reported that the only thing the president told him he would definitely do was to take care of the regulatory agencies. He began to pick up things that other people wanted to get rid of or that were free for assumption. He began to attend National Security Council (NSC) meetings and soon was involved in some tasks ancillary to Rostow's. He picked up, for example, liaison with a commission on travel and soon was involved in tourism, and that ultimately led to his participation in the major balance of payment problem. Thus, by initiative and accretion he established his position.[21]

Temple desired top status when he came into the White House; the president gave him the title of special counsel, despite the fact that it duplicated McPherson's. Temple's only assignment in the beginning was liaison with the Department of Justice, chiefly because of his acquaintances there. This included checking on recommendations for judicial appointments. He worked out arrangements with McPherson, but his duties were diverse. He handled tariffs, wrote speeches, and then was asked by the president to take on "bedroom duty," joining the president each morning as he sorted out the day's assignments. This led him into whatever activities the president chose to assign because he was the "nearest and the handiest."[22]

When McPherson came to the White House on loan from the State Department, he underwent a trial period of staff work before becoming a special assistant. "Months passed before I became fully employed at the White House," he recalled. "In time the paper flow started to move my way. I became a necessary part of the staff, as pale and tired as anybody."[23] He not only became special counsel but inherited various responsibilities that had been held by Feldman. When Richard N. Goodwin and Moyers left, he acquired the top role in speechwriting for the president.[24] With respect to organization, he said that what counts are the requirements of the job and the individual capacities of staff members.[25]

Markham was selected for White House service conditionally on how he performed over a six-month period in the State Department. Watson suggested him to the president and he took his place beside Jacobsen in Watson's office. But at times he was spending as much as 60 percent of his time working with Henry Hall Wilson in steering bills through the House of Representatives. Though he was third man in Watson's office he saw the president nearly every day and claims he had a significant part in getting the president to back certain bills. He took up Johnson's challenge to live a week in a ghetto and came back from a Chicago South Side ghetto with follow-up recommendations.[26]

Certain personnel specializations on the basis of type of policy had developed for staff members in the Kennedy administration and continued in substantial part for them or their successors even after Califano had been given an integrative responsibility with respect to domestic policy. Feldman had international air route cases, tariff and international trade matters, agricultural matters, textile industry matters, immigration, depressed areas, fuels policy, transportation matters, and a great variety of other matters. As Feldman prepared to leave the White House, he recommended the transfer of thirty-six listed, quite miscellaneous subject or functional responsibilities to five White House aides and the attorney general. He wrote that the Office of the Special Counsel could best be described as performing "whatever functions the president directs."[27] White had civil rights, minority matters, executive clemency, housing and urban affairs, natural resources conservation, veterans matters, TVA, and public power.[28] As further indication of the variety of factors that may influence the structure of assignments in the White House, Feldman (and McPherson after him) had responsibility for matters affecting the Jewish community and Valenti assumed responsibility for such consideration of Italian-related issues as seemed desirable to him. The responsibility areas of Feldman and White and those developed later for Cater and others segmented domestic policy advice and prevented a full responsibility for policy advice on domestic matters in Califano and his staff.

Certain kinds of responsibilities were shared broadly through the staff. Primary responsibilities were overlaid by others. Thus, responsibilities for day-to-day contacts with departments and agencies were divided among the various top staff assistants. A memo from Califano for the president on 21 October 1965 showed contact responsibilities for eleven departments divided among seven assistants. In some cases, two or more assistants dealt with the same department but on different subjects. Responsibilities with respect to forty-five agencies were similarly distributed.[29] On the whole the assignments paralleled the subject areas that had developed for the assistants, but the evolution of personal spheres influenced or modified the assignments. Thus, a memorandum to Hopkins clarifying assignments for the purpose of directing communications showed AEC matters handled by Rostow because these mingled with State-Defense matters; civil rights concerns generally handled by McPherson; selective service matters handled by Lawrence E. Levinson because he had emerged in that activity; and labor management items being such a hybrid that communications went to Califano but with copies to Roche and Jones because they had responsibility for Labor and Commerce department matters, respectively.[30]

For quite different reasons (to enlist additional help or to make use of developed contacts), various staff members were given delegations or groupings of members of Congress with whom they would maintain contact. Thus Maguire, while primarily engaged in speechwriting, had responsibility for contact with members from certain Midwestern states, and Valenti came to be a link with members who because of their strategic positions were in frequent contact with the president through the appointments office, which Valenti headed. Persons operating in separate policy areas, such as Cater in education and health, dealt both with the congressional liaison persons in departments and the strategic committee members handling related legislation in Congress. The staff sharing of these activities increased the administration's coverage in Congress and the information flowing to the president, but obviously also created overlapping in assignments and a consequent need for coordination on a day-to-day basis with O'Brien or others carrying the general responsibility for assisting the president in gaining congressional consent. Even more widely shared, as chapter 8 will show, was speechwriting. This function could not be separately compartmentalized, even though some persons were assigned exclusively to it. Those who worked in substantive areas of policy were of necessity collaborators in framing public statements of policy. There was thus only a partial structural differentiation of staffing for the congressional and public representational functions from that of other functions. And there was, overall, a quite considerable crisscrossing of activities of presidential assistants.

Temple regarded White House staff work as evolutionary.[31] Thus, when Busby left the White House in 1965 he detailed the varied matters that he had dealt with that others would need to assume: Cabinet secretary, deputy to Bundy, cost reduction, consumer affairs, science-space affairs, state visits, "Library and Institute," and the press.[32] Reedy has said that "as a general rule when you go to work for Johnson, you find yourself doing everything in the place, from writing speeches to carrying out the trash. And after awhile, he settles in his own mind on what you can do, and you start picking up things."[33] It is reported that Califano said: "There are vacuums everywhere, and if you do it, if you take it and seize it and run with it, it's yours, and you develop a certain right of adverse possession to responsibility."[34]

The president's own habits contributed to this process of personal accrual of responsibilities. He often made ad hoc assignments. For example, Gaither, on Califano's staff and normally reporting to the president through Califano, reports that the president asked him to write a report because he was unhappy with what he had received from McPherson and Califano.[35] Johnson's practice of planning his day's activities during early morning sessions in his bedroom resulted in special assignments, either to those attending or to others through them.

The president's constant push for more information often led him to make special assignments. Christian has said that he often gave several aides the same assignment without their knowledge. Also, he had a "bear pit technique" of testing people by giving the same assignment to more than one person.[36] And Gaither said that "He also plays people off against one another, so that he can get both sides of the picture."[37] Cater said he could tell "you to find out about something and then you'd pick up the phone" to "find he was on the other line finding it out for himself," and that he would reassign the draft of a speech prepared by an aide and that aide wouldn't know who had revised it.[38]

As a result of these processes there were aides with primary assigned roles, either on the basis of type of function or of substantive area, and others with dual, multiple, or even generalist roles. Valenti was appointments secretary, office manager, speechwriter, and for a time Cabinet secretary. Busby, Moyers, and Reedy, when the latter was not press secretary, were generalist aides. Watson's reach went into many corners. Many felt a general responsibility to report to the president on any matter within their knowledge and competence or to represent him before different constituencies as the opportunities came to them.

Some hierarchy was apparent in the operation of the staff system. With the president as the hub of a wheel, major spokes reached to persons who had directive and integrative responsibility over clusters of staff. The president had most frequent contacts with these persons. Nevertheless, other staff members frequently sent memos directly to the president and conferred with him on particular matters on which they were working. Matthew Nimetz, a member of Califano's staff, recalled that "We send innumerable memos in to him [the president], and Califano is very good about putting our names on the memos . . . which gives us quite a bit of visibility."[39] Largely because of Johnson's dislike of large staff meetings and his disposition to deal directly with those with integrative authority, however, Nimetz concluded that "We don't get to work with the President that much directly."[40]

Some Operational Aspects

Complexities in structure create complexities in operation. During the Johnson presidency structural disunities enhanced the tendencies toward a chaotic White House produced by his drive for action. Yet there is staff testimony that the operation was not frantic. While Cater conceded that his, Califano's, and Gaither's overlapping responsibilities for HEW "may have created a little confusion in the department," there was no misunderstanding at the White House, either by the president or the staff, over the division of duties.[41]

The usual administrative problems of coordinating activities and maintaining cooperative interpersonal relations, though ever present in such diverse operations, seem never to have been serious. Mutual awareness, the base for all interpersonal collaboration in organizations, may have been increased by the crisscrossing of responsibilities. Likewise, the sense of contribution may have been increased. The small size of the staff facilitated adjustments that were needed. Johnson's rigid requirements of secrecy on predecision processes and his close confinement of contacts with the press tended to push inward to his staff and upward to him decisions on the administration's position and avoid eruptions in the press of in-house differences that occur in some administrations. Collaboration was facilitated by the structural unifications that existed: integration of administrative chief-of-staff functions first in Jenkins and then in Watson and those working with him (Valenti, Jacobsen, Jones, Markham, Temple); unification of assistance in foreign affairs; partial unification of domestic policy assistance first in Moyers and then in Califano; leadership in congressional relations in O'Brien and then Sanders. The overlappings that existed may have enriched and diversified the help to the president more than it encumbered him with problems of coordination. Nevertheless, a few aspects of coordination and interpersonal behavior deserve consideration.

Staff Meetings

One method of collaboration—the staff meeting—was used less in the Johnson White House than in many organizations. Johnson himself garnered information and directed his staff chiefly through man-to-man contacts—by memorandum, telephone, or office visit. As will appear in chapter 6, he used group deliberations in foreign policy, but he did so less in domestic policy. Occasionally, he held a staff meeting, more frequently a meeting with a portion of the staff, and also occasionally suggested to some member of the staff that meetings be held on some topic or area of work. Variously, the top staff aides would arrange meetings on an occasional or regular basis with those working in their clusters or with all staff members who might collaborate.

In 1965 the president established staff meetings, without his presence, on a regular basis. On 1 February, Moyers communicated to ten people that the president had asked for weekly staff meetings to enable them to keep informed.[42] But such efforts tended to dissipate toward meetings of a few who needed to coordinate their efforts.[43]

There followed a year of the Kintner staff meetings. Kintner, a business executive in the media world, was expected by the president to improve staff coordination, and his chief instrument in trying to establish a position for himself was the staff meeting. He was instructed by the president "to meet regularly with the staff to discuss matters of mutual interest."[44] The meetings began on 6 May 1966. Invitations went initially to about eighteen people, including the vice president and Governor Ferris Bryant, director of the Office of Emergency Planning. The meetings were well attended and the topics ranged widely. The second meeting, on 13 May, included control of the volume of the president's night reading, labor relations, status of legislation, foreign policy issues, contacts with agencies, and the president's speeches. The third sought to improve the logging of congressional contacts, said to be one of "the most disorderly of our staff procedures and the easiest to correct."[45] By 10 June, the agenda was quite extended: McPherson reporting on a method of attracting professionals and intellectuals to the government, Bryant on a meeting of representatives of state government with the Cabinet, Rostow on three topics, Robert W. Komer on economic aid to Vietnam, Moyers on public opinion polls, O'Brien and Califano on legislative problems, Cater on a book on a presidential topic.[46]

Pressure for inclusion in these meetings came from various staff members and by 30 January Kintner's invitation list included thirty-five persons.[47] On 1 March 1967 Kintner asked the president whether he wanted to continue meetings of that size.[48] They were discontinued following Kintner's resignation three months later.[49]

Arrangements continued or followed for meetings for various functional activities. Jones held Friday afternoon meetings of a small group to plan presidential appearances.[50] Sanders, who had succeeded O'Brien, held weekly meetings of congressional liaison staff.[51] McPherson, or his aide Maguire, held weekly meetings of the writers' group.[52] Califano arranged meetings on the legislative program for the next session. At the president's request occasional meetings with him of people in particular work areas were called by the area chiefs—Sanders, Maguire, etc.[53] Yet the meetings of all the chief assistants for sharing of knowledge had been abandoned, except for an occasional call by the president to achieve coordination of staff activity in a particular area.

Tensions

Tension, more or less favorable or unfavorable in result, exists in all group activity. The extent of tension within the Johnson staff is difficult to evaluate, and the effects are probably imponderable. Reedy's service led him to strong conclusions: "The White House does not provide an atmosphere in which idealism and devotion can flourish. Below the president is a mass of intrigue, posturing, strutting, cringing, and pious 'commitment' to irrelevant wind-baggery."[54] Reedy thought this was not unique to any president's White House, but was associated with the "environment of deference" for an imperial presidency, combining the head of government and head of state functions.[55] He thought it resulted also from the fact that White House staffers had no base of support independent of the president.[56] Hardesty referred to the "shark-infested waters" of the White House,[57] although he didn't draw massive conclusions similar to Reedy's.

Christian believed that Reedy had overstated the amount of intrigue and in-fighting among the staff. While "vicious intrigue" existed, "most of the staff made a real effort to get along with the other staff members." He did view Johnson's methods as possibly contributing to tensions: his effort to draw out the best in everybody, to give a staff member an assignment beyond his experience and power to see how he would handle it; his habit of giving the same assignment to more than one staff member.[58] Problems were created because staff assignments led aides into other people's domains:

> He [Moyers] was involved in a lot of things. He was interested in a lot of things. He was interested in the domestic programs and in foreign policy. So he crossed into other people's areas, and he was controversial. Marvin was controversial because he touched everybody's life in the White House. Kintner moved in different areas, had to kind of create his own niche when the President brought him in, and when that happened he created some animosity. Califano was a controversial member of the White House staff because he was always churning something.

But tensions were also created because there were "strong people" in the White House and some wanted to expand their positions.[59]

The comments of other staff members on causes for tension are less extensive than those of Christian, but they indicate chiefly bitterness or resentment toward Watson, Moyers, and Califano. Watson was "a divisive influence within the staff," according to White.[60]

"Moyers was always undercutting somebody" and "Califano was an empire builder," were Jacobsen's ways of stating views that were extensive among staff.[61] Although other charges were made against Moyers,[62] the comments quoted above indicate that strong people with ambition and crisscrossing responsibilities were base causes of tensions.

Others saw nothing extraordinary about these conflicts and tensions. Cater, who served through most of the Johnson period, thought it "remarkable the degree to which there wasn't serious conflict. . . . The White House under Johnson was singularly free of prima donnas or people who suffered personality conflicts with one another or were trying to do the business of the President."[63] Another aide said that "It was a remarkably disciplined crowd who held their views in check."[64] Strains were inevitable in an operation where so many activities had to be coordinated in single actions, as when, for example, the scheduling officials and the writers believed that their failure to get timely information on a bill-signing ceremony was attributable to Califano's negligence or unconcern.[65] The president must have felt that the positive results he was getting from his people and his methods outweighed adverse effects of conflict within the system.

A Flexible Operation

Flexibility was the salient feature of Johnson's White House operation. Pivotal points of integration were fixed by the nature of the tasks to be performed. These often developed in an ad hoc way, rather than by overall advanced planning. Whether brought about by assignment by the president or the initiative of staff members, a consequence sometimes was overlaying and crisscrossing of individual tasks. Persons constantly worked in a variety of areas of activity. This made collaboration across loose boundary lines imperative. The collaboration was in the main improvised in response to immediate pressures. The flexibility may have reflected a normal attribute of staff work and a need in an operation where tasks are multiple and in constant flux. It certainly reflected the personal style of the president.

White House Communications

In the Johnson presidency the decision function was tightly held where the Constitution placed it—in the president himself. Formal delegation to the staff would have been illegal; virtual delegation was narrowly restricted by the president's personal grasp of total activity within the White House. Hence, the primary role of the staff was communication—upward and outward. And for the president's function of decision making, the key staff role was processing information that flowed to him.

The White House staff was the primary channel of information flow to the president. It was to a large extent assembler, gatekeeper, selector, organizer, creator—in sum, intermediate processor in the president's information system. Its performance in this process was affected by the allocations of function and the flexibilities within these. But perhaps even more it was influenced by the president's work habits within which the staff had to fit.

The central feature of staff aid was the flow of memorandums that went to the president for his night reading. The president's night reading was voluminous. Memorandums from departments and agencies and from executive office heads, accompanied more often than not by memorandums from White House staff, and a large stack independently generated by the staff accumulated at the end of the day. Staff rushed their memos to completion and then got them to the appointments secretary, the president's personal secretary, the chief usher, or to any other staff member strategically located to place them in the day's stack.

Typically, at the end of the staff memorandum were two blanks for the president's option opposite the words "Approve" or "Disapprove." The president often added comments, rejecting or amplifying the simple, dichotomous options provided him. He occasionally wrote, "See me." The system forced action-oriented memorandums and staff definition of options; it provided for the president also a ready means of prompt instruction of staff on next actions to be taken.

The president's checks on memorandums and the numerous comments inscribed in his writing witness to the historian the tremendous volume of issue-oriented material that the president read and the large number of quick responses that he was called upon to make. Yet each day started with an additional flow of materials to him. As he lay in his bed with his breakfast brought to its side, he received about 7 A.M. from an NSC staffer in the Situation Room edited reports of cables reporting on developments in Vietnam or elsewhere and a little later perhaps marked copies of the *Congressional Record*, both of which he avidly scrutinized. The early copy of the *Washington Post* would have been delivered to him the night before and now he would rapidly read the political and business sections of the *Post*, the *New York Times*, the *Baltimore Sun*, the *Wall*

Street Journal, and the *Christian Science Monitor*, all the while viewing the three television networks concurrently. An aide who witnessed him in these morning sessions said he "absorbed news and current events like a blotter."[66]

Usually two members from among the president's closest staff associates were assigned bedroom duty. Moyers, Valenti, Jacobsen, Christian, Temple, and Jones were among those who had the assignment over the years. They came at about 7:30 A.M. and remained with the president usually until he was dressed about two hours later. As he flipped through memorandum after memorandum, perhaps completing his night reading, he gave them instructions on action to be taken: set up appointments, make telephone calls, get further information. Temple said that they became "couriers of information."[67] These oral instructions supplemented the approvals, disapprovals, and comments on memorandums that would be returned to those who had authored them. Staff members found themselves with new tasks and new or amended instructions, and new persons were drawn frequently into the communications process.

Johnson had an insatiable thirst for information—more facts, new facts, instant facts. He went frequently to the ticker tape in his office, or turned on the pictures of the three TVs that were there. His telephone was in almost constant use. Direct lines connected him with staff members he needed to contact quickly. His closest staff members talked to him several times a day. One staff member reports that on one of the first days of his White House service, after he had gone out of the building for lunch, the president let him know that he shouldn't be where he couldn't be reached quickly.[68] And when the president gave assignments, he expected quick, if not instantaneous, follow-up.

The thirst for information was not merely for knowledge for public decision making. He craved public acclaim and was unusually sensitive to criticism. He watched for public opinion polls.[69] As the protest against the Vietnam War grew, his sensitivity mounted and his interest in favorable comment increased.[70]

Johnson wanted more than facts: he wanted ideas—ideas on items to be added to his legislative program, ideas on solutions. As we have noted, the president gave Cater no assignment of specific duties but asked him to generate ideas. Others were given the same commission, and feverishly speechwriters and program planners fed ideas into the campaign platform and legislative grist.

The president reached widely and persistently for fresh, action-oriented suggestions for a domestic program. This will be detailed in a later chapter, but special elements in the communication flow to the president through the White House staff should be summarily noted here: Moyers' and Califano's network of contacts within departments, outside task forces, visits to universities, and contacts with individual academicians—all for the purpose of gleaning ideas for legislation. And the staff added ideas. As noted earlier, Goodwin is credited with suggesting the term "The Great Society" for a presidential speech and thereby a standard for the legislative program. Aides exerted influence in various ways: Cater elevating education to top priority in preparation of speeches in the campaign of 1964;[71] Markham, Levinson, and W. Devier Pierson getting the president to go for a meat inspection bill;[72] McPherson trying to help develop alternate courses of action in Vietnam.[73]

Grist for the White House communication channel came also from the regular sources of information to the president. From the departments and agencies came regular reports which went to the White House aide assigned for contact; special reports requested by the president, such as those on progress on cost reduction;[74] memorandums suggesting policy or replying to requests from Califano or others for information or position; participation in conferences with White House aides or in-house task forces. Similar communication came from the executive offices, particularly from a daily flow of memorandums and numerous conferences from the Bureau of the Budget and the Council of Economic Advisers. The White House system was not merely an open one; staff reached for help.

Those who sorted correspondence channeled its flow in line with detailed instructions. Someone determined what would go to the president. Valenti has said that he "read everything that went over the President's desk. I *had* to. . . . you'd better be damned sure it's important enough for him to take the time to do it."[75] One staff function was to shield the president. This could be done by Jenkins with such understanding of the president's desires and such diplomacy, even humility, that his opposites on the telephone would accept his statements as though they were from the president.[76] Or it could be done in a manner to create a feeling occasionally that the staff was interposing itself between the president and other officials. But Valenti also stressed that as appointments secretary he tried to insure that the channels to the president were open to important people.[77] Temple, who worked closely with Watson, denies that Watson kept people from seeing the president and argues that it was easy to see the president.[78]

The President at the Top

The foregoing discussion of Johnson's staff system and communications within it would convey an incomplete, indeed incorrect, picture if it were not understood that it was only a part of Johnson's communication network. He was supported by but also floated above the staff system. From his office and wherever he moved he constantly reached for information or gave directions. He was habituated to grabbing the telephone for instant contact. His direct and feverishly pursued contact with Cabinet and other executives, congressmen, trusted advisers, and numerous other persons supplemented the staff system and often left even the top staff assistants uncertain about the sources of his information.

But the discussion of the staff system makes it possible to focus certain interrelated questions about its service to the president. Could a president have the capabilities required for using the kind of staff system that developed? Would he obtain the kind of help he needed?

Presidential Capabilities

Johnson's staff system, with its elements of looseness, undoubtedly increased the burdens of staff supervision and coordination. His work capabilities were great, but additional qualities would be needed if the president were to be capable of using the system in his processes of decision.

His staff identified other abilities. Some spoke superlatively. Goldstein thought he was a "genius";[79] McPherson that he was "smarter than anybody I ever saw."[80] Yet his capacity for retention seems to be what most impressed his staff. Cater said, "I often marveled at his capacity in meetings, cabinet meetings or other places, to range over the widest range of government activities and have quite precise recollections in each area."[81] Goldstein, elaborating on his judgment on genius, said, "I've never known anybody with a better grasp of information once it has been fed in, nor with an ability to dredge back in the memory bank and pull relevant stuff that hits or fits the problem. . . ."[82] Reedy, who has recorded sharp criticisms of President Johnson, said he was "capable of looking at a page of type, almost glancing at it, and then standing up and reciting it almost word for word."[83] Jacobsen said he had a "sponge mind."[84]

Knowledge gained from years of public experience was an ever-present base for his continuous grasp for more. Peter B. Benchley, who came to the White House without knowing the president, said,

"His knowledge is a sandbag, because you can be all too sure to say, 'Oh, he won't have any idea what this is,' and the next thing you know he'll come up and slap you with knowledge that you had no idea of, of profundity and breadth that you wouldn't have conceived."[85] Gaither remarked that at a meeting with Charles Zwick, Califano, Orville L. Freeman, and him on a food program, Johnson "baffled every one of us" with his questions.[86] And Mike N. Manatos found his knowledge was current: he could look over a list of sixty, seventy, or eighty bills and know them all and where they were.[87]

Roche thought that ". . . one of Johnson's problems was he knew too much. If he'd known about half of what he knew he probably would have been better off." He recounts a session of the president with Secretary John W. Gardner in the presence of Charles L. Schultze, Califano, and him. The topic was the budget, on which Gardner would testify the next day. The president embarrassed Gardner with questions beyond Gardner's knowledge and went on to coach him on how to deal with a senator who had had a bill on one of the subjects in 1956.[88]

Nevertheless, Johnson would sometimes delay decisions as he sought further certainty that he had gotten all the information or options he could. One of his staff has told about the president's deliberations on signing a farm bill. He carried the bill with him as he went for a birthday call on President Harry S. Truman. He kept pondering the bill and making more contacts for information on it, finally weighing it again and signing it after returning to the plane.[89] Moyers has reported that

> He is a very pliant man—a man who refuses to make up his mind until he knows clearly what the choices are.
>
> He insists on asking questions until he thinks he has pried from you all you know on the subject. Just at the point you think he has satisfied himself, he starts hurtling questions around the table like popcorn.
>
> Only the other day, in a two-hour session on NATO, I counted more than 100 questions he pointed at the advisers around the table. This is an effort to define the options.[90]

Yet Goldstein felt that he sometimes made "a decision on too little data" though perhaps "forced to by circumstance"; that there was "a lack of flexibility"—"It's awfully hard to budge him once he has really locked into something, even though it's not too late to unlock"; that he had "a tendency sometimes to deal with too small a group for advice, and then all of a sudden expand" and do some "bouncing around."[91] Unquestionably, Johnson's position was rigid and his circle of advisers narrowed after major policy decisions on Vietnam were made.

The various reports on Johnson's capabilities and work habits cumulatively confirm that he was able to maintain command of his staff. As we have read his comments on numerous memorandums, we have seen only occasional instances in which he was surprised by something that had been done or was being done by his staff.[92] McPherson, in commenting on the contingent authority of the president carried by a staff member as he negotiated with congressmen, concluded, "Working for Lyndon Johnson, an assistant did not easily forget that he carried his authority on sufferance."[93] Christian stated Johnson's dominance clearly: "He ruled."[94] In preparing another volume one of us examined all available memorandums sent by Califano and returned by the president on numerous reorganization proposals considered during the Johnson administration. This volume firmly supports certain conclusions: Johnson relied on Califano for initiation, recommendation, mediation of conflicts, accurate information, and analysis. Yet only in one instance did it appear that Califano went beyond the president's authorization. The instance related not to the substance of a proposal but to the prospect of congressional committee approval; the president asked for clearance two or three days in advance in future instances.[95]

The Aid the President Needed

While the president's knowledge and work habits were sufficient for him to maintain his dominance in the White House, questions have been raised as to whether he obtained the aid he needed. Reedy has charged that the "environment of deference" for an imperial presidency isolated the president from reality. No one would expect the White House staff alone to maintain the president's contact with reality. Certainly, President Johnson didn't. But an "environment of deference" could adversely affect White House operations. Reedy wrote: "The trouble with the White House—for anyone who is a part of it—is that when he picks up a telephone and tells people to do something, they usually do it"—"the heel click . . . will be prompt."[96]

"Usual" compliance by staff aides with directives from legitimate authority appears to be a necessary condition for preventing staff independence. Yet there were instances when seasoned members of Johnson's staff—such as Jenkins, Moyers, and Califano—knew that Johnson had issued directives that he would not expect to be carried out. They knew how to judge his moods. White said, "If you know the man with whom you are working, then I think you're able to find out when he absolutely means it; know when he sure as hell doesn't mean it; and kind of understand the hazy area in between and then develop techniques for handling it. . . ."[97] Califano has written: "Anyone who has worked on a presidential staff has been subject to commands inspired during instants of anger. Most who have served there recognized that, when such orders were issued, it was best to ignore or at least to sleep on them, and wait until the President raised the matter again in a cooler moment."[98]

The more serious question than compliance was, as Reedy recognized, whether deference foreclosed staff aid to the president's judgment. Certainly aides knew the hazards in presenting inadequate or sloppy staff work. Everyone knew he was being tested, conscious, as one staff member said, that Johnson was always "sizing you."[99] Certainly, they knew he expected them to reach to every source for ideas. Also, the very character of the staff system created opportunities for multiple sources of staff aid, an atmosphere of competitiveness, and opportunities for aides to expand their areas of activity. But were aides free to reason with him and to tell him when they thought he was wrong?

While the normal psychological gap between decider and staffer may have been accentuated by Johnson's forceful presence, evidence of confrontation between the president and his top assistants was abundant. Roche was emphatic: McPherson had "tremendous integrity," "a guy who used to lay into Johnson, too. I mean he used to really sock it to him." McPherson recalled a long, "very tough, candid" memorandum sent to the president soon after his appointment that apparently led the president, in McPherson's view, to proffer him, through Moyers, another position.[100] Yet McPherson was undeterred and did not hesitate to tell the president when he thought he was making a wrong decision. On one occasion McPherson sent a memorandum asking the president not to be intransigent about Paris as a site for peace talks. When the president called him at his home at 7:30 the next morning, McPherson recalls: "Well, we argued and argued and I, for the first time I think since I'd been working for him, I started shouting. I said, 'Goddamn it, I'm trying to help you! I'm trying to get you out of a fix! If you can't listen to me, go listen to somebody else! I'll take my advice somewhere else!'"[101]

Roche also reported that he, Christian, Watson, and Califano frequently disagreed with Johnson. "I've heard Califano stand with President Johnson and say to him, 'Mr. President, you are wrong.'"[102]

Califano recalled seeking permission to release portions of a complicated task force report: "We argued half a dozen times about that, and he wouldn't let me do it."[103] He said that he and the president would sometimes be estranged to the extent they would not speak to each other for two days, but that the flow of memorandums from Califano to the president would continue unabated.[104] Other assistants forcefully disagreed with the president. When Johnson was considering government organization proposals, Cater was a tenacious policy advocate. One memo from Cater to the president recorded Johnson's rejection of a proposal for the third time,[105] while another began, "This is to appeal your decision."[106] Reedy himself wrote of threatening to resign if the president persisted in a decision, refusing to do what the president commanded and talking Johnson out of a course of action.[107]

Despite their advocacy roles, Califano and other assistants recognized that there were limits to the number of times an aide could "go to the mat" in attempts to persuade the president. "There are only so many arguments that a White House aide can have with the president before he begins to be regarded either as a pest, a man unable to make the judgment essential to the performance of his duties, or someone who argues indiscriminately for every program he favors."[108]

Other limits on the free flow of advice developed. The course of events in Vietnam heightened Johnson's volatile nature and pervaded the advisory role of the top assistants. As public criticism of his foreign policy mounted, the president became progressively more defensive and intolerant of divergent views within the White House. McPherson came to have "colossal" doubts and held "essentially negative views about Viet Nam," but believed that if he openly voiced them he "would have no hope ever of taking part in either decisions or even of having such an effect as a speechwriter can have—that I would be aced out of the whole Viet Nam thing."[109] Consequently, he resorted to subterfuge. After preparing a lengthy memo to the president arguing against the bombing of North Vietnam, McPherson paused: "I started to send it in and realized that it would very likely mean the end of my participation in matters with Viet Nam, so I appended a paragraph saying, 'This is the way doves feel about the bombing,' . . . without saying whether I felt that way or not."

McPherson considered the procedure "hard to justify" and became so unhappy with his inability to approach the president forthrightly on the issue that he considered resignation. He refrained, however, because he had so frequently seen Johnson's "skill and sagacity and long-range capacity to anticipate" exceed those of his aides. Despite his growing unease, McPherson continued to hope that the president "would probably be found ultimately to be right."[110]

As the momentous tragedy of Lyndon Johnson's presidency unfolded (a legislative leader seeking the use of government for human welfare, but mired inextricably in a costly and unpopular foreign war), the capability of advisers to reach him was undoubtedly diminished. While aides seeking to influence him on Vietnam were stifled, those concerned primarily with advancing key parts of the Great Society became discouraged. Cater believed that his usefulness was diminished and that "this is particularly true when you're working on domestic things in a time of war abroad in which you know the war is gradually encroaching on the President's preoccupations more and more."[111] Although the president continued to launch new domestic initiatives, Cater recalled that Johnson's absorption in the war "affected my sense of my own utility."[112]

In Johnson's case, personal qualities could have inhibited some assistants. Johnson's mercurial nature, his moods, his explosiveness, and his castigation of assistants have often been the subject of comment. He was a "clean tube" man, "blowing everything out," said McPherson.[113] Yet Hardesty said characterization of his temper was exaggerated. "He never raised his voice to me," Hardesty said.[114] Rostow and Wilbur Cohen have each said that he only once shouted at them, in both cases over the telephone.[115] Califano said that he thought Johnson gave vent to his anger only toward those who were in a sense "his boys," those who had grown up in his service.[116] Christian said they learned to understand him,[117] and Gaither that once they knew him they didn't take him personally.[118]

Whether or not the president got the advice that he needed depended not only upon the quality and frankness of the staff's recommendations, but upon their ability to judge the president's moods and to pay attention to the timing of their advice. During 1966 Califano was ready to present a new higher education program to the president, but Valenti suggested delay because he knew that Johnson had been angered by a statement critical of the Vietnam War that a group of college professors issued. "If you want him to consider it dispassionately, you ought to wait a few days," Valenti warned. Califano held the program back, submitted it a few days later, and won the president's enthusiastic approval.[119]

Greater hazards than an "environment of deference" and personal reticence or fear were spotted by McPherson and White. McPherson wrote that the "real danger" in staff work was "that we would weigh it wrong." Reducing pages of staff papers to a three-page memorandum created dangers that "our judgments colored what we wrote."[120] At another time he said there was a tendency of a staff aide to see "it all" in terms of the president's interest.[121] McPherson noted that presidents were "not helpless" but that "the danger is always there, and it is unavoidable so long as Presidents make twenty decisions a day on the basis of information they can only receive through the filter of other men's convictions."[122]

McPherson saw the danger as inaccuracy in the communication that reached the president because of limitations on staff skill or from bias, either personal or for the president's interests. Johnson's protection from such distortion lay in his knowledge of his staff, his knowledge of public policy, the competitiveness in his staff system, and his own urge to constantly seek for more information.

Yet "twenty decisions a day"—with the volume spread and speed of decisions—increased the dangers for the president. The hazards were discussed by White:

> . . . it was too easy to get sucked into the day-to-day operations and . . . it seemed to me that what the administration and the President could stand was somebody who had, as I believe Cater does have, the good mind, good feel for history and experience and the way the political process functions, to be able to stand back and be somewhat reflective and didn't have to do something every day. If he were simply able to assimilate information and thoughts and begin to shape them, this would be a very valuable contribution.[123]

White may have summarized significantly the Johnson White House operation. The White House was action-centered. The president was continuously informed by information added incrementally to his own vast storehouse. The information included cream from the top of the intellectual community and was filtered through young men who had recently acquired senses of history and purpose in their own educations. They fed it to a president who could fit it to his views of national welfare. But the White House was not a study center, a think tank, or a debating circle. With Johnson's drive for accomplishment, and the constant pressure of events, the White House was a beehive of quick processing of data and ideas to supply options and guidance for one whose decision processes had been shaped for the world of action and who wanted action quickly.

Experience in the Johnson presidency suggests the roles of the White House staff in the advisory system and of the president's relation to it. The president will be heavily dependent on the ability, integrity, and adequacy of a staff that can, as McPherson saw, weigh things correctly and move on a fast-paced treadmill. Yet he will be dependent also on the base of knowledge, experience, and ideas in the various parts of the government and in the think centers of society, for which a small immediate staff will necessarily be retailers to him. Beyond all this, his successes—as Johnson's in domestic programming—and failures—as Johnson's in Vietnam—will rest on his own ability to manage the total advisory system, to judge the credibility of his advice, and ultimately to weigh things correctly himself.

5. Developing the Legislative Program

In chapter 3 we charted and summarized functions of White House management. The preceding chapters described the structure, personnel, and general operations of the White House during the Johnson presidency. The next four chapters will deal with the substantive (core) functions and the representational activities of White House personnel.[1] We begin with the development of the legislative program.

Executive leadership in legislation had evolved in a definite pattern under presidents Franklin D. Roosevelt, Harry S. Truman, and Dwight D. Eisenhower. Clearance of departmental legislative proposals by the Bureau of the Budget (BOB), established initially for proposals having appropriations effects, was expanded after 1939 to include the substance of legislation. The Bureau became a center for examination of proposals on the president's behalf. In contrast to the early years of Roosevelt's administration, in which legislative proposals developed in diverse ways, including congressional committee initiatives, a systematic process of presidential programming evolved.[2] Under Truman and Eisenhower departments were canvassed annually for legislative proposals, and the Bureau assisted White House staff in packaging an annual legislative program for presidential presentation to Congress in annual messages. The institutional service of the Bureau and the personal assistance of the White House staff served the president in development of his legislative agenda.[3]

President Kennedy initiated the outside task force as a supplementary source of ideas,[4] and Johnson with his momentous plans for legislative accomplishment in 1964 made it a central feature in development of his legislative agenda. Although he continued to use the processes developed by his predecessors, the leadership of White House staff in task force use enlarged the role of that staff and contributed to creativity and positive leadership by the president in legislation. Concentrated White House management was the striking feature of the process.[5] The exercise of the function is the subject of this chapter.

Emergence of White House Leadership

By the fall of 1964 major elements of the legislative program that originated in the Kennedy administration were law: the Revenue Act on 26 February and the Civil Rights Act of 1964 on 2 July. Yet before the specific obligations to the predecessor administration were fulfilled, Johnson seized the opportunity and responsibility to develop his own program.

The president outlined the philosophic base and unifying theme for a program at the graduation ceremony at the University of Michigan 22 May 1964: "For in your time we have the opportunity to move not only toward the rich society and the powerful society, but upward to the Great Society."[6] Amidst references to many specific goals for such a society, he spoke of the "three places where we begin to build the Great Society—in our cities, in our countryside [to prevent an ugly America], and in our classrooms." The president referred to the method he would use: "I intend to establish working groups to prepare a series of conferences and meetings. . . . From these studies, we will begin to set our course toward the Great Society."[7]

The task force approach was one that the president was familiar with and that was compatible with his management style. Johnson recalled that his first task force experience was with a group established by Roosevelt during the 1930s to study economic conditions in the South. Throughout his Senate career and as vice president Johnson relied "extensively on advice gathered by independent groups of experts."[8] The task force process reflected central elements of Johnson management: reliance on ad hoc, informal bodies, maintenance of personal control of process, and retention of flexibility through confidentiality.

Bill D. Moyers became the sponsor and coordinator of the working groups, called task forces. At least six White House staff members assisted him, including Francis M. Bator, S. Douglass Cater, Jr., Myer Feldman, Richard N. Goodwin, Donald F. Hornig, and Lee C. White. About equal number from the executive offices provided additional help; they included Gardner Ackley and Walter W. Heller from the Council of Economic Advisers (CEA), and Kermit Gordon, Charles L. Schultze, and Elmer Staats from BOB.[9] Although the White House contingent met separately on occasions, the collaboration between that group and other participants extended to all aspects of task force planning. By 30 May Gordon and Heller were able to send Moyers "a joint submission, based on several conversations and a lengthy evening discussion with our combined staffs."[10] It outlined suggestions for fourteen task forces and contained descriptions of nine that would be included in the final group. White House aides also made suggestions.

The first year task forces were called "outside" task forces because their membership was predominantly from outside the national government. One or more persons from BOB, CEA, and the White House served as liaison to each task force, and BOB and CEA also provided an executive secretary and other staff support. Selection of members for each task force was the responsibility of the liaison person. They cleared with BOB and CEA to ensure that there was no duplication in membership[11] and reported their lists to Moyers.

The president gave a full report on these plans at a Cabinet meeting on 2 July 1964. He said that "In 1965 the chances are very good that the Administration will have an *unparalleled opportunity* to make a further major impact on American society."[12] He explained the reason for the task forces:

> The time to begin planning the Administration's program for next year—and the years after—is *now*. But you and I are going to be exceedingly busy during the next few months. Therefore, as the first *step* in drawing up a 1965 program now, I am establishing a number of program *task forces made up of outstanding experts, from within and without the Government.*

He also wanted "to get the advice of the best brains in the country on the problems and challenges confronting America, and I want their help in devising the best approach to meeting them."

Despite the objectives of moving "now" and getting the "best brains in the country," the president sought to assure the Cabinet members of a role in developing the legislative program. The White House and executive office group

> will be in touch with you shortly about the task forces which relate to your areas of responsibility. In many cases people from your departments will be serving on these committees. I expect that they will be freed from their duties to the extent necessary to do this work.
>
> The task forces are *not* a new planning group in Government. Rather, their reports will provide the background for discussions among the Cabinet agencies and the White House in formulating the 1965 legislative program.

> You and I will still have the final task of accepting or rejecting, or making the judgments as to what is feasible and what is not.

The president made three significant points. The first was his purpose: "I believe you share my desire that this be an activist Administration, not a caretaker of past gains." The second was the role of task forces: "I am going to instruct each of the task forces to come up with *practical* program ideas." Third was the role of the established government: "You and I will have to exercise judgments later about what is feasible."

The president stated that the task forces would "operate *without publicity*." The existence of task forces could not always be kept secret. The week after the Cabinet meeting Cater reported to the president that Walter Lippmann, the prominent journalist, had queried him about the task forces. The president approved his request for authorization to brief Lippmann and "perhaps one or two other opinion leaders" on the general areas and key problems being worked on, without divulging the names of members of the task forces.[13] But eleven days later Moyers informed task force liaison officers that the president had instructed him "to re-emphasize his concern that all conversations pertaining to Task Force matters be treated as privileged."[14]

The strict demand for staff secrecy served the president's interests in two ways. It fostered complete candor, even boldness, in task force recommendations. It maintained his mastery of the process: public discussion and development of adverse reactions were avoided while he considered his policy options and the political feasibilities and consequences. If he did not like a task force report, he could suppress it; if he liked some parts and not others, he could suppress knowledge of the rejects; he could avoid unwelcome questions. Matthew Nimetz, an assistant involved with legislative program development, asserted that confidentiality gave the president "a great option of moving with it or moving with it at his own time limit."[15]

The president announced to the Cabinet fourteen task forces and later added a fifteenth. From what sources did the administration seek ideas? Table 4 lists the sources of task force membership. These figures are revealing. The representation of universities and of the U.S. government accounted for approximately 35 percent and 26 percent, respectively, of the membership. In contrast, state and local government and business and labor had relatively small representation. This is emphasized by the fact that seven of the eleven business representatives were on the Improvement of World-Wide Travel Task Force.

Table 4. *Membership of 1964 Outside Task Forces*

Employment Category	*Number of Persons*
Universities	54
Government, U.S.	39
Government, State	8
Government, local	3
Business	11
Labor	0
Research or management organization	14
Private association	2
Law firm	8
Publishing	2
Foundations	2
Other	10
Total	153

Because the chairmen exerted strong influence on these task forces' final reports, their institutional affiliations were especially significant. Of the fifteen 1964 outside task forces, seven chairmen were from eastern universities, three of these from Harvard and two each from Princeton and MIT. Three were from research organizations, three from the public sector (one current and one retired federal official and one state official), one from an international organization, and one from the private sector.

Extension of White House Structure

The responsibility for development of the legislative program was reassigned in mid 1965. On 9 July Moyers became press secretary and on 26 July Joseph A. Califano, Jr., moved officially from the Department of Defense to the White House. Johnson assigned Califano responsibility for development of the legislative program, a duty that he retained to the end of the Johnson presidency. He supervised, therefore, the preparation of presidential proposals for four sessions of Congress. During this time the White House processes were refined, systematized, and elaborated.

Califano's duties, as Moyers' had been, included more than the legislative program. He has summarized the breadth of his assignments:

> But in July 1965, nowhere in the White House were the legislative program and the coordination of domestic departments brought together and related to economic policy. The new domestic programs created the need for such an office and that was my assignment. The president gave me three tasks: to prepare legislative programs, to assist him in developing and coordinating domestic programs and related economic policy, and to guide the response of the federal government to domestic crises.[16]

Califano operated the first year with only one assistant, Lawrence E. Levinson, his deputy at the Department of Defense, whom he brought with him to the White House. Robert S. McNamara told Califano: "You take Levinson to the White House. You'll need him more than I will. That job over there is going to be infinitely more difficult for you than this one has been."[17] Fortunately Schultze, the new director of BOB, was familiar with the process and was a strong collaborator in the development of legislative programs.

Enlarged by stages, Califano's staff ultimately included four others: James C. Gaither, Nimetz, Frederick M. Bohen, and first John E. Robson and then later Stanford C. Ross. Gaither came to the White House on 7 July 1966, Nimetz and Bohen by July 1967. Robson and Ross devoted "virtually full time to the jawboning program of the president to hold down wages, prices and interest rates."[18] Thus, for legislative program development Califano's staff included for the first year Levinson (who helped Califano on other tasks as well), for the second year Levinson and Gaither, and for the third and fourth year Nimetz and Bohen also, with some help being given by Robson and Ross.

Prior to Gaither's selection Califano and Schultze informed the president that the person selected should be an "experienced career civil servant."[19] Gaither and Nimetz had staff experience in the national government, Gaither in the Department of Justice, Nimetz in Defense. While Bohen had been assistant dean at the Woodrow Wilson School at Princeton, the others had legal experience. Gaither and Nimetz had been clerks to Supreme Court justices and Robson and Ross in private law practice. Califano noted his heavy reliance on lawyers and the absence of an economist on his staff.[20] A staff of program generalists with broad assignments resulted. Indeed, a staff of generalists was necessary because Califano assigned them program and liaison task force responsibilities in diverse areas.

Although Califano recognized the advantages of a small, "tightly controlled" presidential staff that was in "daily contact with the president" and could "understand the president's objectives,"[21] his operation suggested the limitations of this model. The load on Califano was more than most persons could carry. After his belated recognition of the need for help, he had in Gaither a full-time systems manager for legislative programming who was engaged in scheduling, overseeing, and coordinating processes. Califano's staff was not able to contribute materially to the content of the program they helped put together until the recruitment of Nimetz and Bohen.[22] Califano also borrowed staff occasionally from executive offices.[23] More significantly, a small, overworked staff could suffice only because its functions were primarily collaborative of large and rich resources elsewhere in the White House. Califano obtained the aid of persons in the White House office who had functional assignments (congressional liaison, speechwriting) or policy assignments. He also had frequent contacts with the president. He relied on the assistance of BOB, which had a general function with relation to program development, and other executive office units (particularly CEA), which had specialized institutional responsibilities for assistance to the president. Finally, he enlisted the assistance of departments and agencies. The success of the Califano operation depended, in sum, on the effectiveness of a small, hard-working, and hard-driving group in unifying resources spread through the government.

Cater's role in legislative development illustrates the requirement for cooperation. On 11 July 1965 he asked the president whether Califano's newly assigned role would "not result in putting me off from a chance to work in the legislative program field—an area in which I have gotten more satisfaction and, I hope, served you better than in any other area." The president circled "putting me off" and returned the memo to Cater with the reply: "No thought of this. You do well & I would like to have you continue with it and add to it."[24] Califano could say later: "Just because you had a mandate you can't walk in and say, 'All right, Cater, from now on everything you send to the president on education that involves any programs you send through me' . . . So that process had to be done gradually."[25]

As the task force system was extended and became more refined, distinct, sequential parts of legislative programming evolved: the search for ideas, the study and staff review of ideas, the decision on programs, and the preparation of the program for Congress. We shall examine each.

The Search for Ideas

The president's public remarks and numerous staff memorandums reflect the push for "new," "bold," "imaginative" ideas that the activist president sought. The search produced the base for the legislative program and was the most distinctive feature in its development. Each year it was organized and extended to innovative sources.

The president desired the intensive search to reach widely and discover practical means of realizing his ideal of "The Great Society." The outside task force provided an immediate vehicle in 1964 for tapping the intellectual resources of the nation, particularly in academia. In successive years outside task forces had a significant but diminished role as other sources for ideas were sought or assiduously cultivated.

President Johnson's conviction that the historical process of departmental and agency transmission of proposals to BOB was inadequate partly accounts for the continued use of the outside task forces. He wrote retrospectively in *The Vantage Point*:

> I had watched this process for years, and I was convinced that it did not encourage enough fresh or creative ideas. The bureaucracy of the government is too preoccupied with day to day operations, and there is strong bureaucratic inertia dedicated to preserving the status quo. As a result, only the most powerful ideas can survive. Moreover, the cumbersome organization of government is simply not equipped to solve complex problems that cut across departmental jurisdictions.[26]

Califano thought the departments were intransigent and lacked breadth of vision,[27] but he and other White House staff members believed bright men within departments and agencies could be tapped individually for ideas. In addition, Schultze strongly believed that a public commission would not "get real solutions to problems."[28] The belief that reliance upon academicians would yield "practical" proposals the president desired was prevalent among his advisers.

The function of outside task forces was quickly clarified: they were to be bold and innovative; they were not to be concerned with political or budgetary considerations; they were to give confidential, off-the-record recommendations.

The impact of outside task forces on public policy was undoubtedly considerable. With respect to housing and education policy, two authors concluded:

> Specifically, the rent supplement program authorized by Congress in 1966 was the major recommendation of the 1964 Wood task force; and, the model cities program enacted in 1966 was the major recommendation of the 1965 Wood task force. The major

innovative programs authorized in the Elementary and Secondary Education Act of 1965, Titles III and IV, originated with the 1964 Gardner task force; and, virtually all the recommendations of the 1966 Early Childhood task force were adopted, although at lower funding levels than those the task force recommended, including the establishment of parent-child centers and of Headstart follow through.[29]

In 1965 the president considered other means for generating ideas. Cater referred to one in a memo to the president:

> After mulling the matter over, I think there is great merit in your idea to bring a small task force of thinkers into the Executive Office Building to come up with ideas for Project '66 and beyond. They should get to work fairly quickly before the regular program review gets too far underway in the departments. My only caution would be to make clear to them that they are merely being borrowed, and that this is a short term exercise. In case they start leaking their existence to the press, there should be a quiet and quick way of disbanding the operation.[30]

Also, the president apparently thought that the recently announced new budgeting system—Planning-Programming-Budgeting System (PPBS)—ultimately would set a framework for developing legislative goals. Yet Califano wrote to the White House staff in mid 1965 as follows:

> As the president stated on August 25, 1965, the new program-planning-budgeting system will not be ready in time to establish national goals for next year's Congressional session. Instead, the Task Forces listed above will constitute the ad hoc mechanism by which these goals will be met.[31]

There were, of course, additional sources for legislative ideas. In addition to departmental recommendations flowing to BOB, proposals issued from presidential commissions. In response to a variety of factors, twenty-eight presidential commissions were created—5.4 per year, more in total or per year than in any previous presidency. After a careful analysis of presidential advisory commissions from presidents Harry S. Truman to Richard M. Nixon, a competent scholar concluded that if such commissions had not existed, "the general course of policy would not have been altered in any major way but would have been altered in innumerable lesser ways"; his appendix, listing the follow-up actions on the twenty-eight Johnson commissions, demonstrated that Johnson's recommendations of legislation to Congress contained many ideas that were included in commission reports.[32]

While the president drew on these diverse sources, after 1965 the search for ideas centered in Califano's office. Califano has claimed that he "knew nothing about domestic programs" when he first came to the White House. He embarked on a "crash course" by reading the 1964 task force reports, studying BOB program materials, and attending "a host of meetings almost instantly with cabinet members."[33] He regarded the task force system as "chaotic and anarchic." "Aside from whatever the Bureau of the Budget was doing,"[34] effective oversight and management were lacking.

BOB officials also recognized this problem and worked with Califano to refine the task force system. On 6 July Director Schultze had sent Califano a memorandum and backup materials that summarized specific proposals for study, listed chairmen and members of both interagency and outside task forces, and proposed a schedule of task force meetings.[35] BOB assistance enabled Califano to report to the president on 11 August on the formation of a group of Cabinet and sub-Cabinet task forces.[36]

An important shift from reliance on outside to interagency task forces occurred during 1965. Four outside task forces and about a dozen interagency ones reported in 1965. From 1965 to 1968, inclusive, twenty-seven outside task groups (an average of six and one-half per year in comparison with fifteen in 1964) and ninety interagency task forces reported. In addition, Califano asked the White House staff and Johnson asked the department and agency heads to provide innovative suggestions.[37] The White House was clearly using the outside task force as only one element in a multifaceted search for ideas. Nevertheless, testimony of participants confirmed the greater productivity of task forces in generating new ideas.[38]

The greater use of interagency task forces occurred for at least two reasons. First, an in-house task force could refine proposals and consider means to implement task force recommendations.[39] Second, interdepartmental exchange and accord on issues that cut across the program boundaries of departments and agencies were often required.[40] The interagency task force was an ad hoc method that broadened and coordinated institutional deliberation and recommendation.

In 1965 a second significant change occurred: the president became much more involved in selection of task force members. Califano wrote:

> Johnson personally approved the memberships of each task force, which was usually composed of experts outside the government—academicians, economists, scientists, doctors, businessmen, labor leaders, lawyers. When I would submit a list of names, he would often call suggesting additional members. Pointedly he would say to others, "Joe thinks the Great Divide is everything between the Berkshires and the Rockies and that no one with any brains lives there."[41]

Gaither reported that the charter for each outside task force went to the president, and that while the president never to his knowledge rejected a charter, he "often rejected membership." Further, Johnson wanted regional diversity and to avoid over-reliance on academicians. An effort was made to get businessmen, labor leaders, lay leaders, and, in instances, local and state government professionals.[42]

Johnson continued to draw heavily upon academicians when appointing task force chairmen, but after 1964 he relied less on eastern universities. For example, all of the academicians who chaired the 1964 outside task forces were from eastern universities, while five of the twelve academicians who chaired those reporting after 1964 were from other regions. Two chairmen came from research organizations, three from the private sector, and six from the federal government.

Table 5 reveals that despite the president's asserted interest in task force diversity there was only slight change: the representation of the academic community (44 percent) was even greater than in 1964; there was, in comparison to 1964, a moderate increase in representation for business and labor.

In 1966 the experience in the White House in development of a legislative program largely repeated that of 1965. Although administrative coordination and economic policy absorbed much of Califano's time, he obtained no additional help for legislative program development until late in the year. Gaither had to start with BOB's preparatory work and with incomplete White House integration. The new assistant hurriedly assembled a group of aides from BOB, CEA, and the Office of Science and Technology (OST), held numerous meetings, and studied the many memorandums responding to Califano's request for ideas.

Visits to leading universities were another important innovation. Califano and other White House aides met with academicians in sessions to seek their ideas on federal legislation and broad policy alternatives. In 1967 the number of these increased. They consulted 115 academic figures at Harvard, Yale, and universities in North

Table 5. ***Membership of 1965–1968 Outside Task Forces***

Employment Category	Number of Persons
Universities	113
Government, U.S.	32
Government, state	9
Government, local	12
Business	29
Labor	7
Research or management organization	16
Private association	8
Law firm	9
Publishing	5
Foundations	8
Other	10
Total	258

Carolina, Texas, Chicago, and New York City. Califano headed the White House delegation on all the trips, with Gaither accompanying him most of the time. Also, McPherson, Cater, Levinson, Edward E. Hamilton, John P. Roche, Ervin Duggan, and Bohen each accompanied him on two or three trips.[43]

From these visits Califano acquired both new ideas and an appreciation of the regional aspects of national problems. For example, he learned that the primary environmental problem was smog in Cambridge, Massachusetts, but was preservation of open space in North Carolina; that the South and Southwest were unique in their concern for future energy needs; and that in many respects racial integration in the South posed fewer problems than in the North.[44]

By 1967 Califano's system was in place and operated on a timely schedule with carefully developed procedures. Intensive work began in May and the first stage was virtually finished before the end of August. The idea search extended to the following sources:

1. White House staff. In 1967 Califano asked thirty White House aides, Mrs. Johnson's press secretary, and White House fellows for "ideas."[45]
2. BOB and other executive office staff. The ideas came through the institutionalized processes of BOB, the supplementary suggestions of executive office heads and their top staffs, and from aides borrowed from these.

3. Departments and agencies directly.[46]
4. Individuals within departments and agencies that the executive office and White House staff regarded as "bright and imaginative." BOB was the primary source for these names.
5. University personnel in teaching and administrative positions.
6. Lists that BOB prepared of (1) expiring laws and bills pending for their extension; (2) annual program reauthorizations; (3) unenacted presidential program items; (4) unfulfilled commitments of the president to submit legislation; and (5) recommendations of statutory or presidentially mandated study commissions or committees.

By 1967 the process had reached a peak of systematization. The first step was to get ideas from internal government sources by 19 June. Second, a background paper for each proposal was sought. Third, by 20 July a program development book listed unfulfilled presidential commitments, pending legislation, and new proposals. This volume was arranged in categories such as health and education, but with each idea or problem on a separate sheet that recorded existing studies and proposals for outside and interagency task forces. Fourth, White House and executive office staff (Califano, Cater, McPherson, Levinson, Gaither, Schultze, and Ackley) reviewed the program development book. Fifth, meetings were held with the relevant department or agency heads "to collect their ideas and make decisions concerning ways to develop the ideas we have collected."[47]

After these steps the process of accumulating ideas would be extended to the task forces and by call later in the year to departments and agency heads for specific draft materials for the State of the Union message.[48] Concurrently, study and staff review of components of the legislative program began.

Study and Staff Review

The August reviews determined subjects for further study. Projects were frequently assigned to task forces but in other cases to individuals or agencies.[49] During the Califano period the task forces were established usually after the August review and hence became more important for study, elaboration, or implementation of ideas than for a search for an idea base.

Califano coordinated the establishment of both outside and interagency task forces, although in instances BOB or other agencies took initiatives. In the case of outside task forces, the usual sequence of events was illustrated by the establishment of an education task force. After the idea search generated both a broad overview of education problems and many proposals, Secretary John W. Gardner and Commissioner of Education Harold Howe were asked for suggestions on the charter and membership for the task force. Next, Gaither and the head of the Education and Science Division of BOB developed a chart of interests and professional groups appropriate for representation on the task force and a list of persons who might serve. Gardner, Howe, and others held another meeting to review the membership list to send to the president for his changes and approval.[50] Califano then obtained the chairman's consent while his staff secured an agreement to serve from the other members.

The outside task forces were asked to forgo considerations of political feasibility and to recommend the most desirable public policy. To ensure candid advice and preserve his own control, the president continued the rule of secrecy that he announced to the Cabinet in 1964. The existence of a task force, its membership, and its report were concealed from public notice. Only a small number of officials working on the legislative program were familiar with the recommendations. Gaither recalled only two leaks: one was through a presidential announcement complimenting Chairman Gardner on his service, the other resulted from a request of the education task force for a portion of its report to be released.[51] Johnson prohibited release of task force reports throughout his presidency.[52]

Two elements in staff collaboration in the study and review phase merit special notation. One was coordination between legislative programming and budgeting. Califano has referred to the relative unimportance of immediate budget considerations in 1965. The escalation of war cost was not yet inhibiting domestic planning, and domestic programs that ultimately became large items in the budget were relatively small the first year. In the late phases of planning the president's program in 1967, however, the inclusion of new program items in the budget already prepared posed difficulties. Gaither remembered a "wild six or eight hour meeting with Califano and Schultze and me to try to put some money into the budget for the key elements of the president's program in 1967."[53]

In April 1967 Schultze reported to Califano that "Too often the agency budgets are prepared with no presidentially oriented program strategy in mind. Turning them around in late November and December after they have submitted their budgets can be very difficult."[54] Gaither identified another unfortunate result. Many elements in the program developed for the president called for small expenditures that fell "through the cracks" because of the failure to take the steps necessary for inclusion in the budget.[55]

The establishment of procedures for coordination with budget planning completed a process that Gaither regarded as the "final change to institutionalize" the legislative development process.[56] After receiving task force reports BOB reported to Califano's staff on implicit problems of inclusion in the budget. Conversely, Califano's staff attended the budget review sessions of the director of BOB.

The other important element in staff collaboration was between Califano and Lawrence F. O'Brien. When Califano concluded that he had "a pretty good program," he consulted with O'Brien and his assistants to gauge congressional reaction to proposals and to avoid "overburdening committees." Califano completed this consultation prior to reviewing the program with the president.[57]

Groups similar to those that worked on the earlier aggregation of ideas reviewed the proposals emerging from the task forces and other sources. From October to December, and occasionally into January, the White House staff, executive office staff, and department and agency officials held work sessions. While interagency task forces usually reported expeditiously, outside task forces sometimes required extended periods, in some cases even a year, to report. At the final stage of review, Gaither recalled that work sessions sometimes resolved all problems in one four-hour meeting, but that Cabinet-level consultation with the White House staff frequently required twenty to thirty hours, especially on such involved issues as education, health, and civil rights. Their ability to reach agreement at this stage meant that relatively few conflicts had to be submitted to the president for resolution.[58] But one White House aide has reported that putting together the presentations for the president "was the cause of great strain for the various White House offices—each of whom have their own versions of what legislation should be charted as reflecting the President's priorities."[59]

Decision

While the president made decisions on particular parts of the legislative program as it evolved, his decisions on the program as a whole came at two stages. In August he was presented with the various ideas that had been developed for study and the means suggested for their study, and thereafter with the "charters" or guides to the task forces and proposals for their membership. At this stage the president seldom rejected an idea for study but frequently added some others.

In December, after staff and departmental review of proposals, the president held an all-day session. Typical of these meetings was one on 28 December 1967, when the president met with Califano, McPherson, Larry E. Temple, and the five members of Califano's staff for review of the legislative agenda. The meeting began at 9 A.M. and ran through lunch to 3 P.M. At these meetings the president either signified approval or disapproval or asked for more information. At this time Califano and Schultze went to the ranch for consultation with the president on the budget and the legislative program.

The president was a constant participant in the interim between August and December and in the development of specifics after December. The process of final presidential decision making involved an enormous amount of oral communication, in addition to the constant flow up and back of memorandums during work days extending from 8 A.M. to 11 P.M. The president constantly approved or disapproved, requested additional staff research, or made suggestions for securing congressional approval. His participation was especially prominent when Califano was unable to obtain agreement from departments or others who had been involved in the consultations. In sum, while Johnson assigned his staff the tasks of discovering, collecting, and studying ideas and mediating conflicts within the executive branch, he actively directed, constrained, and supported the process at all stages.

Preparation for Congress

Following the president's final decision, the subpresidency entered a period of concentrated activity that Califano called "an indescribable part of the year."[60] The task became preparation of the legislative program for presentation to Congress. The immediate necessity was the preparation of the State of the Union Message and the budget message for presentation to Congress, but the work of preparing bills and messages on the particular parts of the legislative program soon followed.

This collaborative process involved virtually all parts of the subpresidency. Within the White House intense collaboration between program and functional specialists broke down the normal lines of staff specializations. Except for nonlegislative decisions in foreign affairs, Califano became more nearly a chief of staff than at any other period.

Immediately upon his return from the ranch in December Califano would "fan out" the policy decisions to those who would be engaged in their implementation. He also developed a flexible schedule of dates for preparation and transmission of special messages and a listing of persons responsible for cooperation in the preparation of each message. For the 1968 legislative program twenty messages, other than the budget messages, were included on a schedule for transmission to Congress between 17 January and 29 February.[61] The president insisted that bills be ready for Congress the day after the delivery of messages. Before he sent messages and bills to Congress Johnson also wanted assurance that agreement existed within the executive branch and reliable soundings had been taken on the prospects for passage in Congress.

In making these preparations Califano turned to departments and agencies for base documents. He customarily asked them to prepare a draft of a special message and a draft of a bill. He engaged the departments and agencies in numerous discussions on the details of bills. He sought resolution of issues and mediation of conflicts between departments. He reported by frequent memorandums to the president on decisions, asked for the president's approval, and submitted to the president for decision or guidance issues on which conflicts remained.

The cooperation between the White House and BOB grew as the budget message was prepared and as budget consequences flowed from subsequent program decisions. And likewise, as BOB exercised its institutionalized responsibilities for legislative clearance, coordination of departmental legislative proposals, and consideration of organization and management consequences of legislation, it funneled ideas to Califano and participated in conferences on legislation. The process involved more than cross-clearance, or mutual exchange of information and opinion. It required joint decision making. For example, when it became apparent that the departmental official's proposal would not accomplish the desired objective, Califano and Schultze had literally to rewrite the formula for fund use in the Model Cities program the night before sending the message to Congress.[62] As in previous stages in program development, the collaboration of Schultze with Califano was close, constructive, and apparently harmonious.

Califano, however, lacked confidence in BOB's legal staff. He believed also that the best lawyers in the government were in the Department of Justice. Consequently, he arranged for drafts of bills to go from BOB to the Department of Justice before they came to him for final clearance.[63]

For judgments on political acceptability Califano relied heavily upon O'Brien or his successor, H. Barefoot Sanders, Jr. As the program was elaborated, Califano had the responsibility for developing concurrence on substantive details within the executive branch and O'Brien the responsibility for gauging acceptance in Congress. Continuous exchange between them was necessary. O'Brien arranged for authorship of bills in the two Houses, checked on the positions of strategically located members of Congress, and conducted head counts of committee members or of the members of the Houses. Undoubtedly, however, when program choices depended upon congressional acceptance, the separate reporting of these two White House chiefs enhanced the president's knowledge.

At this stage White House aides contacted outside sources knowledgeable about the effects of legislation or the attitudes of interest groups. For example, the staff sampled the opinion of college presidents when legislation affecting higher education was being finally considered for presentation to Congress. Business and labor leaders were consulted to get their reactions on the proposal for the creation of an executive department for transportation. Califano, his staff, or others assisting in a program area frequently held conferences with affected groups.

It is noteworthy, however, that specific attention to interest groups occurred at a late stage in the process. While there was some interest representation in the outside task forces and some reflection of interests in the organizational positions of members of interagency task forces, the search was for innovative ideas, expertise, and breadth of view in task force membership, rather than specific interest representation. The check with interest-related persons at the end was partly to ensure that nothing had been overlooked and partly to assess potential support or opposition.

At this last stage of program development the widest participation of White House staff was in the preparation of the message. And this often became, with the parallel preparation of the bill, the point of definitive commitment. The draft submitted by the department or agency would go to a person assigned to edit or rewrite the speech. This would usually be someone on the White House speechwriting staff but might be someone else—for example, Arthur M. Okun, member of CEA, on a consumer protection message. The speech normally moved through several hands and underwent considerable revision. During the process disagreements, often paralleling unresolved issues on provisions of a bill, resurfaced. Ultimately, a draft moved from the person assigned responsibility for the speech to Califano's office. He described the end of the task with respect to education bills:

> Gaither has now put the comments in. Read it with some care that night. But I know that a guy like Doug Cater has been over it, thinks it's okay, Gaither has been over it, thinks it's okay, John

> Gardner has read it, thinks it's okay. . . . I'm concerned about making sure in that message at that point in time there's nothing in there that I think the president won't like or that I think would create any problems for him with other messages or somebody on the Hill or something else that's going on that these guys don't know about. So maybe I spend an hour and a half or two hours that night going over it. . . . Panzer has got the education associations, O'Brien has given me the people that are going to introduce the bills. It's all in one package and that's typed up and all I have to do is initial that. It goes.[64]

The preparation stage was then over. As this final preparation stage drew to a close and as the legislative proposal began to take a definite shape, the president, with the collaboration of the White House congressional liaison staff, was engaged in a parallel process of informing appropriate congressional leaders and testing their reactions. "Throughout my Presidency," Johnson has reported, "I insisted that we brief the Congress fully before our messages were sent to the Hill. We made many mistakes, but failure to inform and brief the Congress was not one of them."[65] While he instructed the task forces to make the "best" policy recommendation, Johnson, former Senate majority leader and brilliant legislative tactician, monitored the process and read the proposals with an eye toward congressional acceptability. Moreover, as the legislative proposals germinated, the president took steps so that key congressional leaders would not be caught off guard. While the task force produced the "best" ideas, the processes also enabled the president to achieve his political purposes: "The trick was . . . to give the Congress a feeling of participation in creating my bills without exposing my plans at the same time to advance congressional opposition before they saw the light of day."[66] We shall examine this process of White House-Congress relations in greater detail in chapter 8.

Summation and Comments

By 1967 the process of legislative programming had been fully systematized. In the system that evolved the scope of White House involvement was broader and the period of White House gestation longer than in previous periods of legislative development. Despite serious Democratic losses in the congressional election of 1966 and waning presidential popularity, Johnson's legislative programming system served him well to the end of his presidency. The administration count of presidentially sponsored bills that became law for

1967 and 1968 numbered twenty-nine and fifty-six, respectively. These numbers compared favorably with the "major" bills passed in the landmark years of 1964 and 1965, thirty-one and forty-four, respectively.[67]

The process features of the system described above can be summarized as follows:

1. It added to the process of departmental and agency submittal and clearance through BOB used in preceding years a sweeping search for ideas through outside and interagency task forces and personal appeals.
2. It provided for an internal process of review, selection, and collation to convert ideas for legislation into practical proposals.
3. It assumed referral to the president of all ideas for legislation to obtain his guidance and his approval or disapproval.
4. It incorporated a complete integration of the total subpresidency—in departments and agencies, executive offices, and White House—in the development of the legislative programming.

In structural terms the system established a chief of staff for the legislative program. With a slender staff of his own, he integrated the diverse resources of the subpresidency.

The system developed in response to the desire of an activist president for extensive legislative accomplishment. The rule of secrecy that he prescribed probably enlarged the flow of ideas to him and protected his leadership from outside exploitation of internal policy uncertainties and divisions during the development stage. The system of collaboration gave the president the specific elements for a legislative platform to present to the Congress and the people.

Numerous articles and books have explained and commented on the process of program development in the Johnson administration. Usually these have emphasized outside task forces and their initiation of ideas. This chapter demonstrates the trend, after an initial period, toward the interagency task force and the integration of the resources of the government and outside contributions. It also shows that the process was centralized through delegation to a White House aide and collaboration of other aides and executive offices, yet it was open to and used the cooperation of departments and officials within them. Its strength was the mobilization of intellectual resources in prompt response to a president's purposes; its hazards lay in the immense concentration and burden on a small White House staff. The delay in full staffing of Califano's office until 1967 accentuated the burden. The consequences of volume of work and limited staff could include a lack of adequate professional and political input into decision making, a lack of deliberation, and a failure of coordination of contributing processes—as occurred in short-run budgeting. Speed and high volume of work were necessary—as in 1933 and 1981—to provide support for a president's purposes; but centralization accompanied by lean staffing brought action at the risk of loss of deliberation, which, as we noted at the end of the last chapter, was White's criticism of White House operations.

The blue ribbon Heineman Task Force on Government Organization, created by President Johnson late in his administration, recognized a need for strengthening institutional support for the president in domestic policy development. It recommended a new Office of Program Development within BOB "to provide year-round professional support to the president's personal staff in the vital work of constructing a domestic legislative program."[68] Almost concurrently a recommendation for further development of BOB's role in the legislative programming was contained in a self-study report by BOB.[69] As in previous instances in the past (establishment of BOB, CEA, etc.), the need for help to the president would be met by increasing executive office support.

President Johnson took no action on the Heineman Task Force proposal, and his successors have sought solutions different from this proposal and legislative programming practices of Johnson's administration. The Ash Council, President Nixon's advisory group on organization, recommended that development of domestic policy be assigned to a Cabinet committee called the Domestic Council and served by a professional staff. Although Nixon established the council and provided a staff, the effort toward larger Cabinet participation failed because the function of the Domestic Council moved to a large White House staff under the tight direction of presidential assistant John Ehrlichman. Presidents Gerald R. Ford and Jimmy Carter similarly sought to increase the Cabinet role, but at the end of the Carter administration domestic policy development remained highly centralized under about twenty-five White House professionals. President Ronald Reagan has made a more determined and continuous effort toward decentralization and Cabinet participation through the use of Cabinet councils, each chaired by a Cabinet member, integrated with a White House–centered professional staff (the Office of Program Development), and reporting to a White House assistant. President Reagan's emphasis on budget reduction, however, has meant that the Office of Management and Budget has retained an important role.[70]

Thus Johnson's successors have sought a method for institutionalizing departmental participation, but the pivotal role of the White House staff and the assistance of OMB (BOB earlier), initiated by presidents Roosevelt and Truman, have persisted. White House staffing for its role has been larger in numbers under all of Johnson's successors. The problems of successfully combining personal and professional assistance and balancing centralized and decentralized participation in domestic policy programming remain crucial for effective presidential management.[71]

6. Developing Executive Policy

In our description of functions on which the president would need assistance from White House staff (Figure 3 and chapter 3), we listed the large function of development of executive policy: "assistance on executive policy making and application in foreign and domestic affairs, whether through general policy decisions or engaging in case work on particular policy or administrative matters officially within the president's responsibility or assumed by him for his attention."

The means of providing assistance to President Johnson for his diverse executive functions varied among and within policy areas. In some areas of policy where special executive offices had not been created, continuous institutional assistance was provided primarily by departments, agencies, and interdepartmental committees. This was true of such policy areas as civil rights, education, microeconomic policy, and natural resource preservation and regulation. In such areas the assistance to the president was dual in that it came from executive departments and White House assistants, except as supplemented by ad hoc arrangements. In other policy areas—national security, economic, science and technology, budget, foreign trade, space, marine resources, and emergency planning—President Johnson had the help of executive offices. This chapter demonstrates the roles and linkages of White House staff in three policy areas—national security, economic, and science and technology—where a triadic subpresidency consisting of departments and agencies, executive offices, and White House staff existed. And finally, the chapter presents a case illustration of the adaptations in White House role in crisis situations.

National Security Policy

Except for the president, no one in the White House has been the subject of more study—and controversy—than the assistant for national security affairs.[1] This assistant has been closely scrutinized because who the president chooses and how he uses him reveal much about how a particular president manages national security policy. His choice will suggest the relation of the White House to the secretary of state and the secretary of defense. The roles assigned the national security assistant will reflect how deeply the president wishes to be involved in the policy process and whether the president wishes to rely primarily on formal, established structures or on personalized, informal patterns of decision making. How the president uses his White House assistant will also suggest how far into the bureaucracy the president wishes to reach and how wide a range of policy options he is willing to entertain.

Upon becoming president LBJ stepped into an on-going policy-making process that President John F. Kennedy had established. Since Johnson chose to maintain many of the Kennedy innovations, practices, and staff throughout his presidency, we must first briefly examine the far-reaching changes in the role of the national security assistant under Kennedy. This will enable us to examine and identify important modifications and changes traceable to Johnson's own operating style.

Impatient with routine channels, skeptical of the bureaucracy, and determined to play an active role in all aspects of U.S. foreign policy, Kennedy centered the management of policy in his national security assistant, McGeorge Bundy, and transformed the National Security Council (NSC) staff from a separate unit in the executive office of the president into a more personalized staff responsive to the president.[2] Following the Bay of Pigs invasion Bundy moved the NSC staff from the Old Executive Office Building to the West Wing basement of the White House. Bromley K. Smith, executive secretary of the NSC staff from 1961 to 1969, recalled that

> One of the reasons he [Bundy] acquired greater authority was that he had quite a few people behind him to whom he could delegate assignments and get back papers and memoranda, drafts of speeches . . . which went to the President in Bundy's name. . . . The Council staff members were in effect White House staff members, although they were paid by the NSC and their line to the President was usually through McGeorge Bundy.[3]

The nature of these changes was clear to both Bundy and members of the NSC staff. Bundy realized that Kennedy wanted "a small personal staff whose members worked 'outside the system' and who were sensitive to the president's own information needs."[4] He arranged for a prodigious flow of information from the State and Defense departments and the Central Intelligence Agency (CIA) to converge on the White House and to be available to the president. Smith vividly described the changes that Bundy instituted:

> When we first set up the shop over there [at the White House] we did two things: we moved in to gain control of communications, and we opened up the channel for the first time fully between the State Department and the White House. We rode piggyback on the military's command and control communications system. Very quickly, State was giving us automatic relay of practically all State cables. Then gradually we pushed into the Defense Department. We centralized CIA inputs.[5]

As a result of these innovations, Johnson entered the White House with enhanced capacities for exercising initiative and control of the foreign policy process, an ability to delve into the day-to-day operations of policy, and a flexible, open advisory system that revolved around personal (rather than formal and institutional) relations with the president. He inherited a system that was weighted heavily toward reliance on the national security assistant, working with the NSC staff, for policy integration and coherence rather than the formal processes of NSC deliberation or the lodging of coordinating responsibility with the secretary of state. The crucial role of the national security adviser was strongly process-oriented: managing the president's decision process and providing the president with linkage with other foreign policy principals.

The fundamental role and purposes of the White House/NSC staff forged under Kennedy remained unchanged during Johnson's presidency, and its organization and numbers were remarkably stable. The president's foreign policy staff consisted of four parts. At the head of the structure was the special assistant for national security affairs, his staff, and secretarial support. Bundy's immediate staff consisted of three aides. One, detailed from the CIA, assisted Bundy with intelligence matters and served as the secretary of a classified interdepartmental intelligence committee. A second, detailed from the Defense Department, served as a liaison with the Joint Chiefs of Staff. The third was a part-time staff officer detailed from the Office of Science and Technology (OST) who specialized in military technology and disarmament issues.

One step lower in the White House than the special assistant during most of the Johnson presidency was a deputy special assistant. Robert W. Komer, a Bundy staff assistant since 1961, was promoted to that post in November 1965. A specialist in Middle East and African affairs, Komer was assigned two junior staff officers and three secretaries. Komer remained with the White House until January 1967, after Bundy's departure, when Johnson sent Komer to Vietnam as "deputy for pacification."[6] The other deputy special assistant was Francis M. Bator, who served from October 1965 to September 1967. Bator had responsibility for U.S.-European relations and for foreign economic policy. He was aided by one junior staff officer and three secretaries. Johnson relied upon him on a wide range of subjects having both technical and political aspects: international monetary reform, tariff negotiations, relations with NATO, and the nuclear proliferation treaty.[7] Johnson named no deputy special assistant after these departures. Komer's responsibilities were scattered throughout the NSC staff, while Bator's fell largely to Edward R. Fried, who moved to the White House after having worked under Walt W. Rostow at the State Department.[8]

The third part of the foreign policy staff was Smith, executive secretary of the NSC. Smith was a career Foreign Service officer with the State Department and a senior staff member of NSC during the Eisenhower administration. Under Kennedy he played a key role in building the NSC's substantive staff. When Bundy moved from his office on the third floor of the Executive Office Building and established a "temporary" office in the White House basement, Smith helped the special assistant develop the space into the map-lined, top secret center of communication that became known as the Situation Room. His service as executive secretary from 1961 to 1969 imparted continuity to staff operation.[9] Smith frequently aided the special assistant directly. He routinely filled in for the special assistant in his absence, assisted in handling communication to and from departments, and conferred with him on the selection of items for the agenda of NSC meetings. His most important day-to-day activity, however, involved responsibility for the Situation Room. He had two secretaries and two administrative assistants who helped him with the NSC files, mail, and presidential correspondence. Additionally, a Situation Room supervisor with a secretary was directly responsible to him. Routine communications duties in the Situation Room were conducted by three duty officers and five junior intelligence officers, all detailed from the CIA.[10]

In addition to the special assistant, the deputy special assistant, and the executive secretary, a group of four senior NSC staff members did much of the substantive work of the White House/NSC foreign policy staff. Although they shared some overlapping responsibilities, the senior staff officers had specific assignments that roughly corresponded to the geographical divisions of the State Department. Additionally, the work of the senior staff reflected presidential interests and priorities. One of the group served as liaison with the Atomic Energy Commission (AEC) and the National Aeronautics and Space Administration, while another was responsible for internal security coordination and NSC personnel security matters.[11]

One of the most important tasks that Bundy confronted during the transition was developing a feel for the type and quantity of memos Johnson wished to see. For example, an exchange between Bundy and the president indicated that Johnson wanted Bundy to furnish information that enabled him to follow diplomatic developments with the Soviet Union and Vietnam in considerable detail. On 1 March 1964, Bundy sent the president a cable that reported conversations between Foy D. Kohler, the U.S. ambassador to the Soviet Union, and Soviet foreign minister Andrei Gromyko, and another reporting an exchange between Henry Cabot Lodge, U.S. ambassador to Vietnam, and General Nguyen Khanh. "I pass them on to you," Bundy wrote, "partly for their own sake and partly as an illustration of some of the cables which I have not been showing to you regularly and which you may wish to see." At the bottom of the memo Johnson checked the entry "I want to see this sort of cable," and scribbled "Many Thanks—LBJ."[12] Through this trial-and-error process Bundy developed a clear recognition of the type of memos that the president wished to see.

The national security adviser's ability to anticipate problems and bring them to the president's attention at the proper time was also of crucial importance. For example, on 6 March 1964 Bundy sent the president a memo informing him of intelligence reports indicating that

> [Fidel] Castro may have an itchy finger on the trigger of the surface-to-air missiles in Cuba. It seems to me very important that we take every possible step to warn both the Cubans and their Soviet friends of the risks involved in any interference with our high level surveillance.[13]

To help prevent a crisis, Johnson followed Bundy's recommendation to order the State Department to prepare a plan to warn "the Cubans and their Soviet friends" against any interference with U.S. surveillance of Cuba.[14]

Bundy's work was not completed when Johnson issued his order, since the national security assistant was also responsible for assuring that presidential orders were executed. For several days Bundy closely followed the deliberations of State Department officials who prepared a response. He fully briefed the president concerning past U.S. policy on the issue and provided the full context for any decision Johnson might make. Bundy made sure that the president received texts of various statements President Kennedy and Secretary of State Dean Rusk had made indicating that interference with the flights would "invite a dangerous situation."[15]

On 24 March Bundy notified the president that the State Department had prepared a plan calling for "a diplomatic warning" to the Cubans by way of the Czechs and for "covert statements which will reach Cuban ears and show that we are entirely serious."[16] The department plan, however, avoided speaking directly to the Soviets, as the president's original instructions suggested. Ambassador-at-Large Lewellyn E. Thompson cautioned that approaching the Soviets directly might force them into a strong statement supporting Cuba's right "to defend their sovereignty over their air space." Should the Cubans shoot down a U-2, it would be more difficult for the United States "to treat our retaliatory action as a purely United States/Cuban affair." Bundy informed the president that "I now find his [Thompson's] argument persuasive." He also recommended that the president make "an appropriate public warning . . . at some appropriate time—perhaps an answer to a question at an early press conference," and added that "I will see to it that such a question comes up." Johnson approved the plan.

In the process of developing a policy toward Cuban surface-to-air missiles, Bundy had performed several tasks expected of the national security adviser. He anticipated a potential problem and brought it to the president's attention. He coordinated the flow of information and decision papers to the president. He monitored departmental activity to see that the president's orders were followed. He had served as the point of liaison with the secretary and State Department officials on matters such as drafting the exact wording of the communication that did not require the president's attention. He called to the president's special attention a recommendation that originated in the department that called for a modification of the president's original instructions. He served as a policy adviser. Finally, he assisted the president in implementing the policy by arranging a public forum for its enunciation.

During the transition, and especially during the election year of 1964, Johnson spent little time on new foreign policy initiatives. He made clear to his staff his disinclination to become involved and took measures to monitor the bureaucracy closely to prevent them from drawing him into a crisis unnecessarily. Michael V. Forrestal, a Far Eastern expert on the NSC staff, recalled that Johnson "did everything to convey to his associates that their principal job in foreign affairs was to keep things on the back burner."[17] While the president reposed great confidence in Secretary Rusk, he was apparently somewhat skeptical of State Department officials and sent Forrestal to the State Department to assure that they "didn't do something stupid while he was out in the hustings trying to get elected."[18] Forrestal believed that "the only thing he hoped [for] from us [the NSC staff] is that we would somehow hold things together until the election. And that's what we did."[19]

Johnson's aversion to action, however, did not preclude policy planning activity by the staff. In a 22 May 1964 memo to the president titled "Planning Actions on Southeast Asia," Bundy detailed his role as an initiator and coordinator of Vietnam policy.[20] "A small, tightly knit group meeting at my call has now had two long sessions in working forward the two basic plans which you asked. . . ." Bundy indicated that the planning sessions had included both Secretary of Defense Robert S. McNamara and Under Secretary of State George W. Ball. Under Bundy's direction, William H. Sullivan, special assistant to Secretary Rusk, headed a group preparing a three- to six-month program "for major stiffening of our effort in South Vietnam." Sullivan prepared this program in close cooperation with General Andrew J. Goodpaster, special assistant to General Maxwell D. Taylor, and various members of the Joint Chiefs of Staff. John T. McNaughton, assistant director of defense for international security affairs, worked on "an integrated political-military plan for graduated action against North Vietnam." Bundy directed Chester L. Cooper, senior member of the NSC staff, to prepare "on a crash basis" predictions of enemy reactions to both the Sullivan and McNaughton plans. Bundy arranged for a small group under Ball's direction to draft alternative forms of a resolution providing "Congressional validation of wider action." Finally, Bundy briefed S. Douglass Cater of the White House staff on these developments and asked him to begin drafting a statement that would precede any action based upon the plans that were evolving. On 25 May Bundy presented the president with a five-page memo that reported a policy recommendation from these various ad hoc committees.[21]

While Johnson eschewed new policy initiatives during the transition, he spent considerable time acquainting himself with the national security machinery and conferring with foreign heads of state. Consequently, much of the staff's time was devoted to routine in-house matters. A schedule of brief meetings with foreign dignitaries was among the first requests Johnson made of Bundy. During the first half of 1964 Bundy developed a program for allocating Johnson's time with foreign officials. The special assistant checked with the appointments secretary and compiled a list of all Johnson's foreign visitors and the amount of time spent with each and developed a strategy for classes of visitors that Johnson would receive.[22]

In an effort to master the national security process Johnson held an unusually large number of NSC meetings during the transition. Between December 1963 and October 1964 the president held twenty-five NSC meetings, but the number rapidly declined thereafter. During the next four years the NSC held a total of fifty-one meetings, or an average of about twelve each year. According to Smith these meetings were major occasions for staff work. "The government was not organized to produce papers that the staff could suggest that the President spend thirty or forty minutes discussing."[23] He indicated that the staff spent much time preparing briefing papers for Johnson to study prior to NSC meetings.

Despite the president's emphasis on his domestic program, numerous crises demanded his attention and drew him into the details of foreign policy management. Bundy's management of communications contributed to readiness for presidential intervention as needed. The Cyprus crisis, the outbreak of anti-American demonstrations in Panama, the shut-off of water at the Guantanamo Naval Base, and the Gulf of Tonkin attack drew the president and the White House/NSC staff deeply into both the policy-making and operational aspects of national security during the transition.

In sum, while the president was preoccupied with the campaign of 1964 and busy formulating his Great Society program, Bundy and his staff were involved with policy planning that the president closely supervised. Despite Johnson's heavy domestic policy emphasis during 1964, the necessity of acquainting himself with the national security decision-making process, meeting heads of state, presiding over NSC meetings, and responding to numerous international crises placed heavy demands on the president's time. The effect was to maintain the White House as the focal point of national security policy and to preserve the roles of the national security adviser, the White House/NSC staff, and the president himself.

The foregoing discussion illustrates the wide-ranging nature of the national security assistant's activities. He coordinated and, when necessary, supplemented the flow of information and intelligence to the president from the departments and agencies. He had to be keenly aware of the president's interests and priorities and prepared to provide more information upon the president's request. In addition to these strictly managerial roles, however, Bundy was also at the center of national security policy making, not only because of his own enterprising nature and solid grasp of policy, but primarily because of his proximity to the president. His contacts with Johnson were far more frequent than those of any Cabinet officer. Because of his daily interaction with the president, he frequently was the first to bring an issue to the president's attention and the last to see the president before a final policy decision was made. Thus, Bundy's initiatives in increasing and coordinating the flow of information to the president were extended to enlargement of options for decision. As Richard Neustadt has noted, Bundy did more than administer a process of "honest brokerage" of departmental suggestions, but it was "not the same as advocacy." He rendered, rather, a service beyond one and short of the other: to lean "against consensus (or the president's own impulse) for the sake of enlarging his choice."[24]

These enhanced expectations of the national security assistant that Kennedy introduced and that Johnson maintained blurred the distinction between policy facilitator and coordinator on the one hand and substantive policy adviser and advocate on the other. Students of the presidency have largely concluded that it has been extremely difficult, if not impossible, for the national security assistant to be fully engaged in the processes of policy development and implementation and remain neutral and aloof from spirited debates among the foreign policy principals.[25]

A presidential assistant uniquely positioned to facilitate decision making will have the power and flexibility to assume a greater role. Bromley Smith succinctly stated the dilemma:

> The theory was that the special assistant's greatest usefulness to the president is to be absolutely neutral so that the principals have full confidence that their views will be presented to the President, and that the assistant is not taking advantage of his position by introducing his own views. Once that uncertainty develops, then it's a very difficult situation.[26]

While Bundy did exhibit a strong process orientation, he also played a key role as an adviser and, at critical intervals, an advocate of increased U.S. military involvement in Vietnam. We have already noted his role in advancing military contingency plans during May 1964, all of which Johnson eventually adopted as policy. Bundy routinely offered his assessment of alternatives as they were evolving. His comments on a memo reviewing "a number of contingency plans for limited escalation," sent to the president on 31 August 1964, are typical:

> A still more drastic possibility which no one is discussing is the use of substantial U.S. armed forces in operations against the Viet Cong. I myself believe that before we let this country go we should have a hard look at this grim alternative, and I do not at all think that it is a repetition of Korea. It seems to me at least possible that a couple of brigade-size units put in to do specific jobs about six weeks from now might be good medicine everywhere.[27]

In January 1965, Bundy joined Defense Secretary Robert S. McNamara to urge a major change in policy toward the use of more military action "to force a change of Communist [North Vietnamese] policy." Bundy reasoned as follows:

> We are pinned into a policy of first aid to squabbling politicos and passive reaction to events we do not try to control. Or so it seems. Bob [Secretary of Defense McNamara] and I believe that the worst course of action is to continue in this essentially passive role which can only lead to eventual defeat and an invitation to get out in humiliating circumstances. We see two alternatives. The first is to use our military power in the Far East and to force a change of Communist policy. The second is to deploy all our resources along a track of negotiation, aimed at salvaging what little can be preserved with no major addition to our present military risk. Bob and I tend to favor the first course, but we believe that both should be carefully studied and that alternative programs should be argued out before you. Both of us understand the very grave questions presented by any decision of this sort. We both recognize that the ultimate responsibility is not ours. Both of us fully supported your unwillingness in earlier months, to move out of the middle course. We both agree that every effort should still be made to improve our operations on the ground and to prop up the authorities in South Vietnam as best we can. But we are both convinced that none of this is enough and that the time has come for harder choices.[28]

Significantly, in January 1965, Bundy and McNamara were more eager to push ahead in Vietnam than Secretary of State Dean Rusk, who believed that "the consequences of both escalation and withdrawal are so bad that we simply must find a way of making the present policy work."[29] Maxwell Taylor, ambassador to South Vietnam, regarded the prospect for a stable government in the south as so dismal that the U.S. commitment should be re-examined. Taylor cabled the president that if a faction under the leadership of General Khanh seized power the United States would confront in the south "a hostile government which will ask us to leave while it seeks accommodations with the national liberation front and Hanoi." The consequence, he concluded, "might entail ultimate withdrawal."[30] With Bundy joining McNamara, two of the president's top four civilian advisers on Vietnam clearly recommended further escalation. In addition to this policy advocacy role, Johnson had Bundy assume operational responsibilities when he sent the national security assistant to Vietnam to further assess and evaluate conditions prior to a final decision concerning deployment of troops.[31]

As the momentum of escalation accelerated during the spring of 1965, Bundy—and other Johnson policy advisers—raised incisive questions concerning the premises, assumptions, and long-term viability of policy.[32] By June, Bundy regarded McNamara's push for expanded military moves involving up to 200,000 troops as "rash to the point of folly." Bundy asked:

> If we need 200 thousand men now for these quite limited missions, may we not need 400 thousand later? Is this a rational course of action? Is there any real prospect that US regular forces can conduct the anti-guerrilla operations which would probably remain the central problem in South Vietnam? . . .
>
> It is not at all clear that we should make these kinds of decisions early in July with the very fragmentary evidence available to us now on a number of critical points: the tactics of the VC, the prospects of the Ky government, and the effectiveness of US forces in these new roles. *Any expanded program needs to have a clear sense of its own internal momentum.* The paper does not face this problem. If US casualties go up sharply, what further actions do we propose to take or not to take? More broadly still, what is the real object of the exercise? If it is to get to the conference table, what results do we seek there? *Still more brutally, do we want to invest 200,000 men to cover an eventual retreat? Can we not do that just as well where we are?*[33]

Doubts concerning the soundness of the Vietnam policy that Bundy expressed in this memo were widely shared throughout the advisory structure of the Johnson administration and eventually played a part in the resignation of not only Bundy but of Secretary McNamara and others. Bundy announced his departure in December 1965, and on 31 March 1966 the president designated Walt W. Rostow as the new national security assistant.

The Rostow appointment was significant for a number of reasons. First, it reflected the president's growing absorption and preoccupation with Vietnam. Moreover, the appointment indicated the president's very strong desire for a strong advocate in the White House for the established policy and signaled the president's resolve to doubters in the foreign policy bureaucracy. Rostow was an early exponent of bombing against the north and, more than any other civilian policy adviser in the government, had consistently sided with military options advanced by the Joint Chiefs of Staff. Rostow was noted for his publications on Third World development and, along with General Taylor, had headed an important fact-finding mission to Vietnam in 1962 that recommended a large expansion in the U.S. advisory contingent. Additionally, the appointment of a former Ivy League professor meant that Bundy would be replaced by another intellectual. Johnson regarded Rostow "as a catalyst for ideas" to whom he would look "for the development of long-range plans."[34] By interest, experience, and policy orientation, Johnson considered him uniquely qualified to deal with the administration's most important foreign policy problem.[35]

While Rostow, like Bundy, continued to enjoy the unique advantages of proximity to the president, another source of influence was through his role as organizer of and participant in informal discussions with department and agency heads. These evolved into a regular weekly meeting called the Tuesday Lunch.[36] By the time of Rostow's appointment, the meetings "became a kind of regular National Security Council (NSC) meeting, with an agenda reaching far beyond Vietnam."[37]

Rostow's responsibility for setting the meetings agenda provided a regular and systematic means for him and his staff to keep in close contact with the foreign policy principals. Rostow has described the procedure for organizing the Tuesday Lunch:

> I would check on Monday with Rusk and McNamara (later Clark Clifford) to see what issues they wished to raise. If I had suggestions for the agenda, I would discuss them with one or the other, or both, depending on the issue. I would also arrange that any necessary documents be assembled; e.g., a draft cable, a negotiating proposal, a factual background paper. I usually sent the agenda and attached annexes to the President on Monday night, although occasionally an annex—or the agenda itself—might not be ready until early Tuesday morning. The agenda always contained an item "Other" to permit anyone around the table to

raise a matter newly arisen on Tuesday morning. I recorded the decisions taken by the President.[38]

Rostow pointed out that the Tuesday luncheons were "only one of many ways Johnson received advice before making decisions in military and foreign policy."[39] In addition to the regularly scheduled and impromptu NSC meetings "a great many other sessions were organized to consider specific problems at particular moments."[40] Bundy and Rostow frequently arranged ad hoc meetings for the president of foreign policy advisers other than those at the Tuesday Lunch when a foreign crisis developed or when a major decision point approached. Johnson periodically held lengthy sessions in the Cabinet room with a "Vietnam group" which ranged in size from eight to seventeen advisers. While the Tuesday Lunch was the "most important regular, high-level meeting in the national security process," it was part of a much more extensive and complex pattern of advisory meetings.[41]

The establishment of a special assistant for national security affairs in the White House with backup staff opened a new era in the organization of foreign policy advising. While Rostow and Bundy may have considered their role as policy adviser secondary, they both often held strong policy positions and as right-hand men to the president were in an unrivaled position to shape and define presidential perception of policy options. Partly because of Johnson's high confidence in Rusk's and McNamara's abilities and his insistence on policy consensus, neither national security adviser worked at cross purposes with the departments heads, and there was no confusion over policy because of conflicting White House and department statements. The expanded role of the White House assistant gave rise, nevertheless, to the difficult problem of relationship of the assistant to departmental secretaries in the president's total advisory system in national security policy. This and other problems growing out of the role of the White House national security adviser have plagued subsequent administrations and presented intractable institutional problems not readily apparent under Kennedy or Johnson.

Macroeconomic Policy

While White House responsibility for national security policy was clearly lodged in the special assistant for national security affairs, at the beginning of the Johnson administration there was no comparable point of integration in the White House for economic policy. During the Kennedy administration Theodore A. Sorensen assumed some coordinating responsibility. When Johnson first took office, Bill D. Moyers shouldered some duties but was largely involved with legislative program development, speechwriting, and management of the campaign. Memos to the president from departments and agencies that participated in economic policy making were variously routed through Moyers, Jack J. Valenti, or Walter W. Jenkins; none of them had an adequate view of government-wide economic activity. Not until the appointment of Joseph A. Califano, Jr., in July 1965 did Johnson clearly fix White House responsibility for economic policy. Also, until then no White House aide coordinated the legislative program with economic policy. Additionally, Califano believed that only a few Bureau of the Budget (BOB) officials "had a sense of how critical it would be to relate domestic programs to economic policy."[42]

As the costs of the Vietnam War posed fiscal problems and the administration became increasingly concerned with the economy, Califano became the key figure in pulling together the various parts of the economic subpresidency,[43] trying to develop and coordinate government-wide policy. Moreover, Johnson involved Califano in operational aspects of economic policy that the president considered critically important to the success of his administration.

Although Johnson eventually placed responsibility for economic policy in a single aide, no role of directing an institutional staff, similar to that of Bundy or Rostow, emerged. Part of the explanation is that Califano personally was less specialized than Bundy and Rostow. As noted above, he divided his time, developing the president's legislative program, coordinating departmental programs, as well as coordinating economic policy. Of greater significance, however, was the more independent status, compared with the NSC, of the three-member Council of Economic Advisers (CEA), from which the president obtained expert advice. Califano never had more than five assistants to help in all areas of his responsibility. Moreover, Califano and his two assistants most involved in economic matters, John E. Robson and Stanford G. Ross, had legal backgrounds and were not trained economists. Robson joined Califano's staff in 1966 after serving as a consultant to the director of BOB. Ross assumed Robson's position at BOB and was detailed to the White House when the latter returned to private law practice in 1967. They mainly assisted Califano in operational aspects of economic administration.[44]

Although Califano had no specialized economic staff at his disposal, he rendered valuable aid as a coordinator and facilitator of the economic policy process. The need for this service was as great in the economic policy domain as in national security affairs. In contrast to the highly focused departmental representation in the making of foreign and national security policy, the structure of the executive branch for participation in making economic policy was widely dispersed. In addition, the executive structure in the former fostered a national perspective, while that in the second often represented and accentuated fragmentary economic interests. Thus, Califano's economic responsibilities centered on stimulating, coordinating, and seeking agreement among the president's major advisers in the departments and agencies. He spent much time arranging meetings, participating in them, and informing the president concerning policy deliberations. He did not, however, have similar importance in origination and analysis of economic policy, this being shared not only with departments but with CEA and BOB.

Califano has described his role in terms that are strikingly similar to the description Rostow provided for the national security adviser:

> The most important thing is to get the alternatives clearly laid out, and in such a way that the President can understand the differences between them. Next, I try to get the alternatives narrowed down to two or three real choices. The alternatives that are sent over here by the Council are usually too many and too complicated. Third, I organize a number of meetings and consultations to get agreement on one or two of the alternatives. This is sometimes a fairly time-consuming process. Finally, after the President has made a decision, I write or coordinate the writing of the President's message announcing his policy decision.[45]

When disagreements arose among the president's advisers on the appropriate economic policies, Califano tried to get the parties to the dispute to compromise their differences. For example, in 1966 Califano facilitated compromise during a dispute within the administration over the suspension of the investment tax credit. By late in the summer of 1966, most of the president's advisers had settled on the suspension of the investment tax credit as the most effective tool available for slowing down investment in capital goods. Action on this measure was stalled, however, by Secretary of the Treasury Henry H. Fowler, who argued that the investment credit had been instrumental in increasing productivity and the competitiveness of U.S. products in world markets. To remove the credit would make businessmen lose confidence in the government's commitment to increasing productivity. The dispute was passed to the White House when Califano met with representatives of BOB, CEA, Treasury, and

Commerce. Califano convinced Fowler that it was the suspension of the investment credit or nothing and, thus, persuaded him to go along with the proposal.[46]

While Califano was responsible for resolving conflicts, he played a crucial role in stimulating a range of alternatives for presidential consideration. When the administration became concerned with the seriousness of the balance of payments, Califano let CEA members know that Johnson was reviewing a proposal for restriction of outbound tourism, one of the major causes for the outflow of dollars. "That excited us terribly," Arthur M. Okun, a member of the council, recalled.[47] CEA chairman H. Gardner Ackley ordered the CEA staff to prepare an elaborate memo arguing against restrictions. Only later did CEA realize that Johnson was not taking the proposal seriously but had used Califano "as a little bit of a goad to get better alternatives."[48]

Difficulty in securing agreement among the various actors in the economic subpresidency did not mean that Califano received no cooperation or support from others in his general staff responsibilities. The top members of Johnson's economic policy team included the secretary of the treasury, the chairman of CEA, and the director of BOB, who met regularly. Each realized that such a format required a consensus that satisfied their conflicting goals. Secretary Fowler noted that

> A set of policy prescriptions are no good if they can't be implemented, and in deciding on the mix of tax policies, debt management policies, and expenditures in the budget . . . I want to be sure that they can be influential and they can work. A second concern of mine has been that fiscal policy be fully coordinated with monetary policy.[49]

Califano received support from CEA in another one of his primary tasks: shielding the president from the barrage of biased and irrelevant economic information that flowed to the White House. In this role, the council and its staff cooperated with the White House staff to filter out the irrelevant, resolve conflicting reports, and condense incoming economic reports to manageable proportions.[50]

As for substantive economic advice the CEA, located in the executive office, was by far the dominant part of the economic subpresidency. Under highly capable and activist leadership the council was at the peak of its power during the 1960s. According to Califano, Johnson "relied heavily" on the council and was well served by three chairmen: Walter W. Heller for a brief period after the Kennedy assassination; then Ackley from the University of Michigan; and finally Okun, who came from Yale.[51]

Early in the Johnson presidency Heller took steps to assure that the council and the new president would work closely together. Heller had been with other Cabinet members on their way to the Far East when the assassination occurred. Upon his return to Washington he immediately met with the other members of the council, Ackley and John P. Lewis, in an all-night session and produced a memo presenting to Johnson the major economic issues that he confronted.[52] The following week he sent "a bird's eye view of CEA's major operations and work in progress."[53] The purpose of the memo, Heller explained, was "to aid you in deciding how best we at CEA can serve your Administration."[54] Moreover, Heller explained his role vis-à-vis the Kennedy White House and, by implication, the type of relationship he wished to build with the president.

> As you know, President Kennedy asked me to serve both as his White House economic adviser and as Chairman of the Council of Economic Advisers. It was not always clear which hat I was wearing. But it didn't matter, since the two jobs are really one—supplying the President with economic advice and staff services.[55]

The role that Heller outlined was one that went well beyond serving as a disinterested expert on economic issues. Heller and his successors served very much as personal aides to the president and played an active role publicly advocating policy and advancing the president's larger political purposes. Heller advised Johnson of their support of the tax cut that was part of the unfinished business of the previous administration.[56] A few months after Congress passed the tax cut, it became clear that the economy would be invigorated. As a result, according to Okun, the CEA was "riding about as high a crest of esteem and respect for the success of the tax cut as has ever been achieved."[57] CEA played a highly visible role in building support for the policies. "The largest emphasis of the council's activity was on the salesmanship of a product rather than on the development of a superior product, because that was what the real need was."[58]

By the second week of Johnson's presidency Heller was helping with representational activities. For example, Heller sent the president several memos concerning "Notes for the Business Council Meeting," "Notes for the AFL-CIO Meeting," and "Labor's Gains in the Democratic Administration."[59] Moreover, Heller served as a presidential liaison with the business and economic press. On

17 January 1964 he sent Johnson a memo informing him of the displeasure of the editor of *Business Week* because the president seemed to be paying more attention to the conservative Business Council than to the Committee for Economic Development, "the progressive wing of business."[60] Heller also represented the president's policies before wide public forums such as "Face the Nation."[61]

Another reason that Johnson relied heavily on executive office support was the ability of CEA to communicate effectively with the president. In fact, this ease of communication was one of the first characteristics of Johnson's relation with CEA to catch the president's attention. On 23 December 1963 Johnson replied to a Heller memo, "I like the way you write memoranda—crisp, to the point, and concise. Work–Think–Think Hard on the State of the Union," he continued. "I depend on you."[62] Ackley regarded the ability to write memos that Johnson could absorb as the "secret weapon" of CEA. "We really worked very, very hard in developing a style which was clear, said everything that needed to be said—but not another thing more. No other agency learned this."[63] The president frequently received lengthy, single-spaced memos from the Treasury Department that he sent to either CEA or Califano with a handwritten request at the top demanding, "Tell me what this says."[64] Ackley recognized that Johnson "just loved information, just ate it up, but he wanted information that he didn't have to work too hard to get."[65] He believed that "a lot of the possibly undeserved influence that the council had on economic policy . . . resulted from the fact that we could write."[66]

The real key to the maintenance of CEA influence, however, was the fact that the White House had no economists on its staff. While Califano claimed he never considered developing an economic staff, the CEA remained wary that the White House would develop an expert staff capacity. Early in the Kennedy administration Heller had requested that no economist be included on the White House staff, and he and his successors sought to prevent it by performing numerous "chores" for the White House. "One of the things we were interested in was making it unnecessary for Califano to want to have his own economists," Okun recalled.

> We would do anything that he needed to be done. He didn't need an economics staff of his own. We managed to convince him several times when that issue came up. "You really don't need to recruit a young economist . . . you know, Joe, we've got all the young economists you need around."[67]

CEA succeeded in protecting its access to Johnson.

Califano's task of coordinating economic policy was greatly simplified because of two informal bodies that the key members of the economic subpresidency evolved. One was the so-called Troika, composed of the chairman of CEA, the director of BOB, and the secretary of the treasury. Troika largely set the administration's fiscal policy that was the focus of economic concern during the Johnson years. The staffs of the two executive offices and the Treasury continuously communicated with each other regarding the formulation of fiscal policy and the generation of the quarterly reports on the economy. Johnson met with the Troika each quarter for a formal review of economic conditions and to consider the need for adjustments in government policy. Califano was responsible for assembling the papers for the president's briefing prior to Troika meetings.

A second coordinating body consisted of the Troika and the chairman of the Federal Reserve Board (FRB). Meeting with the president from time to time, this was called the Quadriad and provided an opportunity to discuss the relations of monetary policy to other economic policies. Established in the early days of the Kennedy administration, the number of meetings of the Quadriad declined in the Johnson presidency. On the other hand, informal contacts between the principals in the Troika and the FRB and among the professionals on the staffs of the several agencies facilitated continuous interchange of information and opinion and some cooperation in various policy developments.[68]

Califano's relation to these bodies differed markedly from the roles of Bundy and Rostow with respect to the Tuesday Lunch. One of Bundy's and Rostow's primary duties was planning and preparing the agenda for the Tuesday Lunch. By contrast, Califano was primarily a monitor of Troika and Quadriad deliberations and a reporter of the president's views rather than an agenda formulator. Generally, Troika's reports constituted the agenda for Troika meetings, while the agenda for Quadriad meetings was prepared by the chairman of CEA.

While Califano did not play as active a role in substantive policy development as his counterparts in national security affairs, he did become deeply involved in the operational aspects of economic policy. His role in operations is exemplified in an important aspect of the Johnson economic policy—the use of wage-price guidelines. In the absence of a statutory delegation of authority to a particular agency or department for this activity, the policy was made and administered at the presidential level. The web of interactions brought together CEA, BOB, Califano with his aides (Robson and Ross), and the relevant departments.

The point of continuity in guidepost activity was the CEA. It "played the central, integrating role in guidepost activity through the Johnson administration."[69] The council had the central role in policy initiation and in continuous reconsideration. The president's explicit declaration of support for guidelines in 1964 was based on policy set forth by the council as early as 1962. The 3.2 percentage standard for allowable wage and price increases around which so much of the administration's activity centered came from CEA. CEA sent to the president a stream of information and policy reports and special weekly price reports. The council served on numerous ad hoc groups of departmental executives along with Califano or his representative and, occasionally, the BOB staff. It provided leadership for interagency committees that considered price policy and the implementation of the guidelines. It kept close track of major price movements in key industries and participated in development of ad hoc responses to these. Although an "operational role was not consonant with its regular staff and advisory responsibilities, it fell to the CEA by default."[70]

The secretaries of the treasury, commerce, labor, and defense were the departmental officials most frequently involved in price guideline deliberations. They communicated directly with the president on guideposts. Secretary of Commerce John T. Connor frequently voiced dissatisfaction with the guideposts, while Secretary of Labor Willard W. Wirtz often reflected the dissatisfaction of labor groups. Fowler made numerous suggestions and reported on the work of a task group that he chaired. Secretary of Defense McNamara reported on the relation of stockpiling to price restraint. There was, however, some sentiment in CEA and the White House that the departments did not consistently support the guidepost policies.[71]

Despite CEA's positive and persistent role, Califano carried a heavy load of work on the guidelines. His contacts with the president, CEA, and departments were numerous. The president occasionally directed him to get public statements or action from the departments. He held regular Friday morning roundup sessions with the chairman of CEA. He or his aides were on all the ad hoc price committees that CEA arranged. After he acquired Robson's help, he regularly shared operating responsibilities with CEA.

> The early warning reports on prices now went to Robson, who, with the assistance of Duesenberry [a member of CEA], reviewed them to see what might be done to fend-off or reduce proposed

> increases. Robson's time was spent seeking information, identifying "levers," proposing actions, attending the weekly price meetings, working on stockpile releases and the like. He was assisted in his endeavors by an ad hoc "Price Policy" committee which included representatives from Commerce, Labor, Treasury, Defense and BOB.

Later, Ross gave most of his time to similar activities in guidepost administration.

Nevertheless, case-to-case activity in implementing the guidelines was, like policy deliberation and advice to the president, dispersed. Since industry and labor compliance was voluntary, department executives, CEA members, Califano, and his aides engaged in persuasion and jawboning with industry leaders. CEA reported that it had been involved in "perhaps 50 product lines" to avoid price increases during 1966. Shortly after joining the staff, Robson informed Califano that he had been involved in seventeen "principal price actions." These activities were often conducted with CEA leadership but at other times were "orchestrated" by Califano. During an effort to hold down aluminum prices, Califano talked with the president by telephone more than twenty-five times and met eight times with Cabinet officers at the White House.[72] In one instance CEA sent a report to the president on price increases that was, according to a handwritten note on CEA's file copy, "Written at Joe Califano's orders."[73]

The president participated both in general policy formulation and in particular applications. Ackley reported that Johnson "got very much involved and was intimately interested in every price increase." He considered a major price rise "a personal blow to him as well as to the economy. He wanted to know what was being done, and he often gave instructions about what ought to be done."[74]

The president explicitly approved the 3.2 percentage guideline and rejected a meeting to discuss voluntary notification of major price and wage changes. Yet he alone seems to have favored serious consideration of mandatory controls. He intervened in details of implementation. Thus, he asked the attorney general to investigate food prices in selected cities and the Bureau of Mines to give generous estimates of oil production needs. In January 1966 he sent telegrams to executives in the steel industry to appeal for recision of an announcement of a price increase and on another occasion brought 150 business executives to dinner at the White House to urge cooperation.

The White House staff played an increasingly important role in the coordination of economic policy advice during the Johnson presidency. When Johnson recruited Califano, the White House acquired a central point of contact with the economic subpresidency. Increasing inflation, changes in tax policy, and a worsening balance of payments deficit magnified Califano's importance. The existence of CEA made his role less comprehensive than that of the national security adviser. Yet he performed a crucial role in coordinating the key substantive advisers, fostering policy alternatives, and resolving policy differences. He became involved also in the detailed administration of economic policy and this was the reason for the addition of two members to the White House staff.

The president relied primarily upon the chairman of CEA, the director of BOB, and, to a lesser extent, the secretary of the treasury for substantive economic advice. Johnson's dependence on the executive offices was especially strong because, as already noted, the White House developed no economic staff capacity and because the chairman of CEA, as Heller noted, made no clear distinction between personal service that was normally expected of presidential assistants and institutional service that included offering expert advice and directing a specialized staff.

Science and Technology Policy

An advisory structure to the president on science and technology had evolved in the White House and the executive office by the time Johnson became president.[75] A special assistant for science and technology was a position created by President Dwight D. Eisenhower in 1957 and continued by presidents Kennedy and Johnson. The special assistant presided over an interagency Federal Council for Science and Technology (FCST) composed of the main units that spent federal funds on research and development. In addition, an Office of Science and Technology (OST) was created by executive order in 1962 that took over the staff of the special assistant. During the Johnson presidency the OST staff grew from about twelve to twenty-five professionals who were assisted by about two hundred consultants representing every field of science. The President's Science Advisory Committee (PSAC) worked closely with OST. PSAC was composed of eighteen presidential appointees and operated through study panels of consultants. During Johnson's presidency Donald F. Hornig was simultaneously special assistant, director of OST, chairman of PSAC, and chairman of FCST. As a White House assistant he drew upon the analytical capability of OST and PSAC, both executive office structures, and relied upon FCST as an instrument of coordination.

The general function of the four-part structure was to advise and assist the president in matters affected by or relating to science and technology. Since the staffing pattern was one of a White House adviser with an executive office staff, it was similar in form to the arrangement in national security affairs. The staff was comparable in size to those of NSC and CEA but much smaller than that of BOB.

President Kennedy announced Hornig's appointment as special assistant nine days before the assassination. After a conference with Hornig, Johnson confirmed the appointment and sent Hornig's nomination to the Senate for director of OST. Johnson thereby continued the combination of the White House and executive office appointments that Kennedy initiated in 1962.

The science and technology adviser assisted the president through a full range of matters from military, space, and atomic energy to health and housing. His responsibility was peculiar because the president's policy decisions were dependent upon technical information in highly specialized segments of knowledge. Hornig said that he was a "liaison between the president and the scientific and technical community."[76] Through the membership of PSAC and the use of consultants, Hornig was able to obtain studies and advice from universities and private industry. Yet he and the staff of OST also maintained contacts with the government agencies sponsoring or using science and technology. Hornig had lunch every two weeks with Secretary of Defense McNamara and more frequently with other officials in the Defense Department.[77] He linked his staff to all the centers of technology use within the government. One member of his staff, Spurgeon M. Keeny, Jr., served concurrently on staffs of OST and NSC and coordinated these offices' studies of nuclear nonproliferation issues and strategic arms limitation.[78]

Through his various positions Hornig could direct and coordinate the technical base and advice to the president in what W. Henry Lambright has called the "science and technology subpresidency."[79] The president had confidence in the analytical support of the White House/executive office in science and technology. He asked Hornig for studies on such subjects as world food supplies and pollution problems and in 1967 made Hornig responsible for an energy study, responsibility that clearly involved more than purely scientific and technological considerations.[80]

Hornig's dual position as a White House aide and as a director of a structure for analysis gave him some ability to influence decisions outside the White House. For example, Cyrus R. Vance, deputy secretary of defense, was within hours of signing an agreement with COMSAT which Hornig rather late decided would be a dangerous grant of the frequency spectrum into the commercial domain and the hands of other countries.

> . . . I called Katzenbach and said, "Look, we've got to do something about this." Well, he's not a technical man, but he said, "Well now look, Don, we've been having formal sessions for six months. The committee has signed off on it. It's just too late." . . . Finally I called Cy and just told him flatly, "You can't do it." I was mightily surprised myself when his reaction to that was, "Okay, I won't do it. But let's convene a group right away to start looking at the questions you raise." By three-thirty that afternoon, we did have a group convened to start looking at the details. And eventually the original agreement was discarded.[81]

For the personal aid the president needed, Hornig claimed: "It's not any different, maybe less so, than if Joe Califano or Walt Rostow made a similar call."[82] Yet he did not have the day-to-day contact with the president that was an essential feature of the national security adviser's job, and his staff dealt with much more long-range problems than the NSC staff did.[83] He believed that Johnson was not entirely comfortable with science and technology specialists and that this discomfort affected his relationship with the president. "He listens to me very seriously; he's responded on what I thought were major issues . . . but there has never been any easiness about it."[84]

While the president relied upon Hornig as a personal aide, Johnson regarded him primarily as a technical specialist. Hornig recalled an incident that indicated Johnson was aware of Hornig's lack of political experience:

> While flying from Washington to the Ranch, I was trying to persuade him [Johnson] to say something about population and birth control in the State of the Union Message. He said, "Don—have you ever been elected to anything?" to which I replied "The Harvard Board of Overseers."[85]

There was some incongruity in Hornig's dual position. As executive office head he testified on numerous occasions to congressional committees, but he had to avoid testimony as a White House aide. On another aspect of the problem, Hornig has said:

> The biggest problem—the central issue—is to define the right boundary line between a small, nimble top group which is very responsive to the president, and a more formalized structure

> which can in fact do something in greater depth to study the complete range of things from time to time he gets into.[86]

The issue, differently stated, is whether the requirements of institutional aid and personal aid can be combined in the same person without limitation of one kind of service. In Hornig's case, any sacrifice was on the personal and political side, with influence yielded to other White House aides.

Whatever effect these structural or personal factors may have had, it seems that decisions on science and technological matters are affected by a wider distribution of functions in the government and greater necessity for collaboration of different sets of actors than in either national security or economic affairs. This is because science and technology is less a subject area than a diverse set of capabilities to be used in public programs. Where the issue was federal participation with the state of New York in a nuclear reactor–desalting project, the agency actors were Glenn T. Seaborg, chairman of the Atomic Energy Commission, and Stewart L. Udall, secretary of interior, and the president appointed a committee composed of these two and Hornig and Ackley to report on the potentialities and possibilities of desalting in the Northeast.[87] In the White House Lee C. White became political adviser to the president on the issue. New York governor Nelson A. Rockefeller and New York congressmen were pushing for a decision contrary to agency positions, the questions were political as well as technical, and on this White had competence and the trust of the president.[88] When a desalting proposal for the Middle Eastern nations was broached, actors in the international arena were involved, and Hornig reported to the president on discussions but forwarded a detailed report to the national security assistant.[89] Johnson communicated with Rostow on action aspects of the proposal.[90]

In another area—the development of space technology—Horace Busby, Jr., acquired a liaison position with James E. Webb, the administrator of NASA, and Edward C. Welsh, the executive officer of the Space Council.[91] When Hornig became concerned that budget ceilings would adversely affect university research, he appealed to James C. Gaither, thus revealing Hornig's need for the stronger access of Califano in budget decisions.[92]

Consideration of the supersonic transport (SST) project clearly demonstrated the attention from diverse centers within and outside the White House. Decisions on the project would involve considerations of project design, cost, economic feasibility, apportionment of cost between the government and companies, and sound effects. Presumably, the benefits would be both for national security and domestic welfare. President Kennedy initiated the first phase of the project, and President Johnson acquired knowledge about it as chairman of a special committee appointed by Kennedy. Early in his administration Johnson appointed a President's Advisory Committee (PAC) on Supersonic Transport representing Defense, Treasury, Commerce, the Federal Aviation Agency (FAA), NASA, CIA, and two persons outside the government, with McNamara as chairman. The administrator of FAA had administrative responsibility for the project. The PAC assigned problems for study and developed recommendations. Communications flowed to the president individually from Hornig, FAA administrators Najeeb E. Halaby and General W. F. McGee, McNamara, Secretary of the Treasury C. Douglas Dillon, and Welsh. Beyond these advisers within the substantive area, the president received the usual summaries and recommendations on financing and organization from the director of BOB. Charles L. Schultze of BOB met several times with McNamara and McGee on the financial aspects.[93]

What role on this matter accrued to persons within the White House other than Hornig and those who served the president only in representational functions? In the early period some communications from the substantive actors went to Jenkins, Valenti, and Busby, but there is no indication from the memorandums that this was more than keeping them informed, particularly as they tried to get a grasp on carry-over activities to the Johnson administration. The president did, however, assign Moyers some responsibility for interagency reconciliation.[94] Since the SST project was primarily a domestic matter, Califano, who had worked on it while in the Defense Department, submitted to the president summaries of information, positions of the actors, and his own recommendations.[95] At least two other White House aides were active on the problem. Myer Feldman held meetings in his office on the issue of designating the Department of Defense as the executive agent in project development and advised the president on various aspects of the project, including contracting, financing, and notifying Congress.[96] Another legal aide, Milton P. Semer, advised the president that there was "no objection" to his signing a declaration of "highest national priority" under the Defense Production Act to the project, but, like Feldman, he extended his advice to the nonlegal aspects.[97]

When the problem of selection of a corridor for a sonic boom test for the SST arose, Hornig organized an interdepartmental Coordinating Committee for Sonic Boom Studies.[98] Califano, however, sent the president his own summary of events and recommendations on the project and attached memos on it from the relevant parts of the government.[99] When W. Marvin Watson asked the president if he approved of a step in procedure by Hornig, the president replied, "Leave this decision to the scientist."[100]

In sum, the president received advice from multiple sources on the SST issue. The basic information and recommendations came from the relevant technology agencies, BOB, and Hornig. While the interventions of Jenkins, Valenti, Busby, and Watson were routine, Moyers, Califano, Feldman, and Semer offered substantive advice on diverse aspects of the project. The subpresidency for science and technology included the four-part structure that Hornig unified and directed, the heads of the cooperating agencies, and White House aides who were responsible for various areas of public policy that the project affected.

Executive Policy Making during a Crisis: The Detroit Riot

The three areas of policy formation we have examined featured a White House assistant who partially coordinated an on-going policy process with various degrees of reliance on executive office staff and substantive input from top department and agency heads. The uniqueness, urgency, and unpreparedness that accompany a crisis situation modify the roles and the linkages among these participants. Activity is fused and integrated at the presidential level and roles of participants are less differentiated. A crisis magnifies the importance of immediate access in determining who has the most influence on the president. It heightens the necessity for the tightest possible cooperation among president, department, and executive officer. In addition to assistance for presidential decision making, an array of support services must be provided promptly and with utmost fidelity to the presidential directives. In consequence, the activity in the White House increases to a feverish pace.

The Detroit riot clearly illustrated these aspects of presidential decision making in a crisis situation. The riot produced White House activity at two stages: the first related to the president's decision to send troops; the second to the aftermath of the riot: political defense of the president's decisions on and administration of federal relief and the development of a long-range policy to prevent future disasters of that sort.

At 3 A.M. on 24 July 1967 the president's phone rang. Attorney General Ramsay Clark was on the line.

> Mr. President, Governor George W. Romney has just called me at home. The situation in Detroit looks bad. There are almost eighty fires unattended. There is extensive looting. The Governor thinks he might need federal assistance. I suggest we put the Army on alert just in case the troops are needed.[101]

Johnson agreed and authorized Clark to tell Secretary of the Army Stanley R. Resor to notify his men at Fort Bragg, North Carolina.

Clark's call marked the beginning of the federal response to the Detroit riot that began on 23 July. By the time order was restored five days later over forty people were dead, two thousand injured, and five thousand homeless. Estimates of property damage ranged from $250 to $500 million. The events of 24 to 28 July, Johnson wrote in his memoirs, "will remain forever etched in my memory."[102]

Immediately, the president needed assistance on two important decisions. The first was to determine whether legal requirements governing the deployment of federal troops domestically had been met. Once these conditions were established a second decision arose: did actual conditions warrant the dispatch of federal troops?

The White House staff was primarily absorbed with meeting the president's overriding need for quick, reliable information upon which to base these decisions. In fact, on Sunday, 23 July 1967, Califano had already established regular contact with the Federal Bureau of Investigation (FBI) Command Post and informed the president of the increasing level of violence, but he noted that Governor Romney made no request for federal assistance. At the president's request, Califano monitored events for the rest of the day. That evening he made Lawrence E. Levinson, his chief aide, responsible for liaison with the FBI and ordered him to keep the president fully informed. At 9:30 P.M. Levinson received a report that the rioting had intensified and that Governor Romney had ordered eight thousand guardsmen on duty with the backup of four thousand state and local police.[103] The staff had already provided the president with numerous reports on Detroit by the time Attorney General Clark telephoned him.

To keep abreast the president fully activated all White House communication facilities. He ordered the White House message center to be on alert for any communication from Governor Romney[104] and the Situation Room was used to monitor developments. A direct line was established from the Pentagon to Califano's office.[105] The top White House aides gathered frequently in the president's office to receive wire service reports. Before the crisis ended a large map of Detroit that dominated Califano's office revealed every contingent of troops, exchange of gunfire, and major fire in the city.[106]

Before making the decision to send troops into Detroit, the president utilized his authority as commander in chief to move troops from one military base to another. At 12:45 P.M., the president ordered an airlift of troops from Fort Bragg, North Carolina, and Fort Campbell, Kentucky, to Selfridge Air Force Base in Michigan so that forces would be positioned if their use became necessary. These military maneuvers were coordinated from the Division of Civil Disturbances at the Pentagon, which in turn relayed all information to the White House Situation Room.[107]

Getting a clear signal from Governor Romney regarding the need for federal troops was as difficult as obtaining reliable and up-to-date information. Presidential politics were involved to some extent. Romney, a northern Republican and counted as a liberal in his party, was an aspirant to its presidential nomination. In responding to the riot he faced a delicate and difficult dilemma in preserving his own reputation for leadership as well as the safety of Michigan citizens. At 8:55 A.M. Romney called Clark to read a statement "recommending" the use of federal troops. When the attorney general explained that a "request" and two other conditions were required, the governor said that he would draft a full statement. When his telegram reached the White House two hours later, it included a request for troops but failed to certify that a state of insurrection existed beyond the resources of state and local authorities.[108]

"The whole issue for hours was whether the governor and the mayor would request troops" in accordance with all necessary conditions, Harry C. McPherson, Jr., recalled. "We were determined not to send them until they did."[109] Throughout the morning of 24 July the White House staff received communications from local officials concerning the need for U.S. troops that they considered ambiguous. Beyond the legal requirements, a whole range of political and practical considerations was involved. Johnson was averse to sending in U.S. troops unless absolutely necessary. "The thought of blood being spilled in the streets of Detroit was like a nightmare," the president later recalled. "I could imagine the inflammatory photographs appearing within hours on television and on the front pages of newspapers around the world."[110]

White House officials also worried that an early commitment of troops would set an unfortunate precedent. They shuddered at the thought of governors across the country turning riot control over to the White House, not only to save lives, but also to save trouble, money, and political reputations. Attorney General Clark stated the dilemma:

> It's a very sensitive thing, because you don't want the federal government in the position of everytime there's a shooting of having the Attorney General and the President . . . doing something about it. On the other hand, you don't want to be called in at the last minute and not have any sort of feel for what's really going on.[111]

By mid-morning Johnson determined that he needed an independent assessment of conditions and summoned to the White House his key departmental officials for a meeting in the Cabinet Room that began at 10:43 A.M. Secretary of Defense McNamara, Attorney General Clark, Deputy Attorney General Warren M. Christopher, Assistant Attorney General for Civil Rights John Doar, and Director of the Community Relations Service Roger W. Wilkins joined the president to consider the federal response. Top White House aides also participated. Watson, who was busy rearranging the president's appointments, and Califano, who monitored incoming communications, did not attend but sent their chief deputies, W. Thomas Johnson, Jr., and Levinson, respectively. These two aides took detailed notes of the group's deliberations. George E. Christian attended and prepared to report publicly any decision that the officials reached and that the president might wish to disclose.

The president decided to send ex-Deputy Secretary of Defense Vance to Detroit as his personal representative to assess the situation. The president selected Vance, who had resigned only three weeks earlier, because he was thoroughly familiar with the procedures of the White House and the Pentagon and had worked on racial disturbances in the South. The president also had Christopher, Doar, and Wilkins accompany Vance to Detroit.[112] The hurriedly assembled Vance team arrived in Detroit shortly after 3 P.M. and spent several hours meeting with local officials and touring the riot-torn areas of the city. At 10:08 P.M. Vance reported directly to the president over a White House speaker-phone that "there is no doubt in the Governor's mind or anyone else's" of the need for federal troops.[113]

Upon receipt of Vance's report, Johnson went to his office to meet with McNamara, General Harold K. Johnson, FBI director J. Edgar Hoover, Secretary of the Army Resor, and Attorney General Clark. At 10:31 P.M. Johnson signed a proclamation calling on "all persons engaged in such acts of violence to cease and desist . . . and to disperse . . ." At 11:25 P.M. he issued an executive order authorizing

Defense Secretary McNamara to "take all appropriate steps to disperse all persons engaged in acts of violence" and to "restore law and order." Additionally, he authorized McNamara to call "any or all units" of the Michigan National Guard into federal service.

After signing the proclamation ordering the rioters to disperse, the president gathered his advisers to prepare TV remarks announcing the deployment of U.S. troops. McPherson was called to the president's office to write a statement for the president. When he arrived he found Supreme Court Justice Fortas reading over a statement concerning the president's decision to send troops to Detroit

> . . . with the greatest regret, and only because of the clear, the unmistakable and the undisputed evidence that Gov. Romney . . . and the local officials . . . have been unable to bring the situation under control. Law enforcement is a local matter. It is the responsibility of local officials and the governors of the respective states. The federal government should not intervene, except in the most extraordinary circumstances. The fact of the matter, however, is that law and order have broken down in Detroit . . . and the federal government in the circumstances . . . had no alternative but to respond, since it was called upon by the governor of the state, and since it was presented with proof of his inability to restore order in Michigan.[114]

"What do you think?" the president asked the aide after he finished reading.

"All right," McPherson replied.

"Really, are you really going to approve that?" Fortas inquired.

"Yes," affirmed the legal counsel.[115]

Actually, McPherson was uneasy with the statement because of the frequent references to Governor Romney's inability to contain the riot. McPherson believed the statement reiterated this point to make it clear that the statutory requirements were met and that the president was not usurping power or sending in troops where they were not wanted. He thought that the president had legal requirements in mind but that Johnson was also interested in "gigging Romney," who was an aspirant to the Republican presidential nomination.[116] McPherson considered the remarks "excessive" and believed that they "would come back to haunt us." Califano had a similar reaction. The presence of the Supreme Court justice, McPherson later claimed, prevented him from offering the president the type of frank political advice that would normally have been forthcoming.

> I was intimidated by the stature and the brains and the judgment and the reputation and my own relationship with Justice Fortas. I was very much the junior man and although I would have argued with the President alone about it, I didn't argue with Justice Fortas.[117]

The restricted participation of a strongly assertive White House aide is less astonishing than the mere presence of a Supreme Court justice in White House policy deliberations with implications that could have led to an issue requiring judicial decisions.

Following McPherson's clearance the news office and appointments office began to type and reproduce the statement. Deputy Press Secretary Robert H. Fleming notified the networks that the president was preparing a TV statement and summoned the teleprompter personnel. While the staff prepared for the TV appearance President Johnson conferred with Watson in the aide's office. When he returned he began reading the proposed statement as it was being typed and edited and then prepared for speech cards and the teleprompter. As the first card was typed the president began to read aloud and to rehearse his delivery with Christian standing beside him and making occasional suggestions. At 11:55 P.M. he began his ten-minute address to the nation announcing the troop deployment with Hoover, Clark, and McNamara at his side.[118]

The president went directly from the White House studio room to his bedroom with Christian, Fleming, Thomas Johnson, Califano, and McPherson to watch the analysis of his statement and to listen for the latest reports on conditions in Detroit. He returned to his office at 12:11 A.M. and read over the latest ticker reports.

In addition to keeping abreast of developments, liaison with departments, and legal advice, White House aides performed the miscellaneous services of a central staff. The proclamation and executive order were prepared under McPherson's direction. Watson busily assembled documents for the president's attention or signature.[119] H. Barefoot Sanders continuously kept Johnson appraised of congressional reaction to the riot and arranged for a White House meeting with congressional leaders Monday afternoon. The president ordered Sanders to call all of the Wayne County, Michigan, congressmen and to keep them informed concerning the federal response. Johnson directed Sanders to make definitely sure that prior to the official public announcement congressmen were aware of any decision to send in federal troops.[120] Levinson and Thomas Johnson prepared an elaborate chronology of presidential activities during the riot that McPherson, Califano, and Christian used to brief reporters concerning the White House role in the crisis and to defend publicly the president's action from various critics who charged that the president's response was either precipitous or tardy.[121]

On 27 July, Califano gave the president a telegram from Governor Romney and the mayor of Detroit, Jerome P. Cavanaugh, requesting that Detroit be declared a disaster area.[122] The president did not immediately accede to this request but did order a regional officer of the Office of Emergency Planning (OEP) to meet with Romney. Califano recommended that a top aide of Schultze's from BOB, William B. Cannon, go to Detroit so that someone familiar with the wide range of available programs would be on hand. Vance and Christopher kept in constant touch with Califano concerning the relief efforts going on in Detroit.[123]

When Vance returned on 29 July the president had him announce that Johnson was ordering the Small Business Administration to declare parts of the city disaster areas and therefore eligible for appropriate assistance to homeowners and businessmen under the Small Business Act. He did not, however, act on Romney's request that the city be declared a disaster area.[124]

Califano played a central role in coordinating the relief effort. He maintained contact with OEP head Farris Bryant. Since the president did not declare Detroit a major disaster area, however, OEP was not fully mobilized. Instead, all requests for assistance and proposed responses were channeled through the office of the deputy attorney general with whom Califano worked closely in coordinating relief.[125] He reported to the president not only on the details of administration of relief but the political reaction. Califano monitored the congressional reaction to the federal efforts and was in constant contact with John Conyers, Jr., and Charles C. Diggs, Jr., two Detroit congressmen, both black.[126]

As the disturbances subsided and federal relief efforts got under way the staff began work on a long-range policy for responding to future disturbances. The president wanted a thorough inquiry into the cause of civil disorders and established the national Advisory Commission on Civil Disorders. To McPherson, Califano, Clark, Schultze, and Levinson he set forth the commission's agenda: to find out "What happened, why did it happen, and what can be done to prevent it from happening again and again?" These aides immediately went to work to plan the commission's activities. They assisted the president in the selection of commission members, prepared the executive order creating the commission, and assembled information on civil disturbances for the commission to begin preliminary work. Watson was responsible for contacting the various members of the commission and making sure of their attendance at the first meeting. On the morning of 29 July, Clark, McPherson, and Califano met with the commission heads, Governor Otto Kerner of Illinois, and Mayor Johnson V. Lindsay of New York. Califano appointed one of his staff members, Frederick M. Bohen, as White House liaison with the commission and had him follow the commission's work on a day-to-day basis.[127] Schultze prepared funding and administrative arrangements.[128] Califano worked with his staff to develop "talking points" that the president used in his first addresses to the commission.[129]

The major decisions of the Detroit crisis clearly involved presidential rather than departmental choices and automatically required numerous forms of White House staff service—largely facilitative rather than substantive. Under the pressure of a crisis the assistants' work of transmitting information, preparing documents, writing speeches, providing legal advice, and arranging press coverage became merged and intimately coordinated with the action of the department and agency heads.

In the Detroit crisis the striking attribute of White House assistance was the readiness for prompt response to the president's needs. He placed heavy reliance on the departments for bringing in key advisers and implementing presidential decisions. The White House role in policy advice is illustrated by McPherson's approval of the draft of the president's public statement on his decision to send troops and by Califano's recommendations on disaster assistance, but more important for the president was the reliance he could place on proximate aides for coordination and supplementation of information and for support services that became vital in an emergency.

Conclusion

In the three areas of executive policy development discussed above the role of White House assistants was primarily one of coordinating, facilitating, and managing a policy process, including giving advice and sometimes participating in administrative operations. Without examining the adequacy of information and the quality of substantive advice given to the president or whether different institutional and personal arrangements would have modified his decisions, this chapter has presented the mix of personal and institutional help for a president.

The small size of the White House staff designated as such and who interacted with the president directly in the broad scope of executive matters is noteworthy: in foreign affairs, the White House assistant, his deputy, and a few aides; in economic affairs, a senior White House aide and an assistant; and in science and technology, a single White House aide. In all these cases, the service of the White House aide or aides was made possible by the existence of an executive office. Two of these offices—foreign affairs and science and technology—were subject to the direction of the White House aide. The services of the primary White House aides were also supplemented on substantive matters by that of other aides, particularly for legal and political advice, and were regularly supplemented by the assistance of persons performing the representational functions.[130]

In two of these areas—foreign policy and science and technology—President Johnson inherited the structural system from his predecessor, under whom the distinctive features of each had developed. The union of personal and institutional service to the president was the salient feature of both. Bundy, Rostow, and Hornig were White House aides and also directed an institutional staff, Bundy and Rostow *de facto* and through the instrumentality of an executive assistant, Hornig legally and directly.

The system established by President Johnson in 1965 for his White House assistance on economic policy formally separated personal and institutional aid, the latter provided substantially by CEA. Nevertheless, the distinction broke down in practice because the mutual confidence and shared purpose between the president and CEA enabled it to give assistance to the president that reached beyond institutional service.

The experience in these three instances (and in budgeting, discussed in the next chapter) confirms that the combination of institutional and personal service is not only a viable option for presidents but probably an essential characteristic of presidential staff support. One function may be dominant in comparison with the other. Delegation of institutional operations enabled Bundy and Rostow to concentrate on personal service to the president; because institutional responsibilities engrossed Hornig's attention, other White House assistants provided the personal aid envisaged in his post. The circumstances of Hornig's appointment and his experience in professional rather than personal service accounted for these divergences.

The small size of the White House staff limited its capabilities and enhanced presidential dependence upon institutional help. This dependence and Johnson's habit of reaching personally for all sources of information justify another characterization of the system of decision on executive matters. While there were elements of stratification, not by any means the same in all situations and for all types of assistance,we find that sources of presidential aid were generally triadic. There was no concentration of responsibility such as existed in legislative programming, and only incidental superimposing of White House staff over departments and executive offices.

Yet there were differences in the requirements for linkage between the White House on the one hand and the executive offices and departments and agencies on the other in the several areas of policy. In foreign affairs there was a strong integration of functions in the departments of State and Defense. Johnson placed high trust in the secretaries of both. His decision-making system included direct communication with these and other advisers, a council (Tuesday Lunch) chaired by him and assisted by a White House secretary, and staff aid for information and definition of options. It centralized responsibility for staff aid in a special assistant for security affairs but was decentralized in the opportunities provided to department heads and by the president's dependence upon them.

For economic affairs, the dispersion of functions through departments and agencies amplified the need for coordinative arrangements. The system included consultative mechanisms (Troika, Quadriad, ad hoc committees), continuous executive office assistance, and loose and selective coordination by a White House assistant defining alternatives and striving for consensus. The degree of openness to departmental participation, variation in participants, and flexibility were high. The adoption of a presidential price and wage control policy without machinery for executing the policy drew the White House into distinctive administrative operations.

In science and technology the functions of government were even more widely dispersed than in the economic area. Yet the issues of policy are more separable and bring different agencies into the policy arena. During the Johnson presidency the elaborate structure of White House/executive office assistance facilitated technical and professional aid from the special assistant. Regularly, however, the agencies were participants in presidential policy, and White House aides other than the special assistant often contributed. Though formally integrated, policy assistance for the president was more ad hoc and more decentralized than either foreign or economic policy.

Executive policy making in a crisis required a somewhat different role for the staff than in a noncrisis situation. The most striking feature was White House centralization. Notable in this instance was the absence of any executive office assistance, except in the relief stage. In the earlier stage the important factor was the ad hoc mobilization of departmental and White House participation. Under pressure of a crisis the White House assistants were able promptly as needed to prepare documents, conduct policy research, write speeches, provide legal advice, and arrange press coverage. These activities were merged and intimately coordinated with the action of the department and agency heads.

7. Directing the Executive Branch

We have reserved for separate discussion those executive policy and administrative matters that related primarily to direction of executive departments and agencies. While the Constitution and statutes delegate extensive powers to the president, the practice of Congress has been to vest responsibility for implementation of most laws in departments, agencies, and bureaus. Yet presidents will be concerned, in general terms and in numerous particulars, with the development and execution of policy throughout the executive branch, even including agencies with much organizational independence or autonomy.

There are many reasons for presidential concern. The Constitution mandates that "he shall take care that the laws be faithfully executed." The manner of administration in departments and agencies can affect discharge of his responsibilities in national defense and diplomacy as well as other powers vested in him. The public will look to the president for leadership on the tone and trend of administration and particularly for some coordination of activities that crosscut departments. Finally, the president's achievement of his own policy objectives and the maintenance of his political capital will be affected by actions in diverse parts of the executive branch. In consequence, the president must be concerned or appear to be concerned with probity, economy and efficiency, effectiveness, fairness, and political effects of executive activities.

We approach the subject of White House operations with respect to presidential direction of departments and agencies in their responsibilities by describing the president's functions and posture and in each case showing the participation of the White House staff and the expectations of the president with respect to their service. We organize the discussion around two aspects of presidential leadership that are more or less distinct from each other: the basic resources available to the president for executive management and the uses of influence during the Johnson presidency.

Presidential Resources

Appointments

The president's power of appointment, even though mortgaged in part to political influence, is his basic and most important means of influencing the conduct of the executive branch. The power of removal, when it exists, adds further potency to the resource. President Johnson, his aides have repeatedly reported, did not like to remove anyone, and the records of his administration have revealed to us no instances of outright firing. Yet the constraint of the power of removal is in the threat of its use and the consciousness that its existence implies some obligation of continuing cooperation.

A continuing relationship is created by the act of appointment. Membership in the president's official family and partnership in his administration are implied. Nicholas De B. Katzenbach, who held a Cabinet post as well as the second-level position in two departments, has confirmed the importance of the appointment resource: "If you want the Department of State and the foreign policy to be responsive to the President, then the appointments that you make, not only in the Secretary's job but in the other key jobs—eight—ten of them here within the department—are the way in which you get a handle on it.[1]

Although Johnson initially retained President Kennedy's executives, the sense of membership and partnership continued in most instances to be strong. In making new appointments Johnson was extremely cautious in selecting people to meet his qualifications for executive performance and especially careful to assure their loyalty to his objectives and to him personally. Even when responding to political influence in appointments, he normally sought assurance of loyalty.

The appointments process during the first year of the Johnson presidency centered in Walter W. Jenkins. Jenkins checked with members of Congress and other sources for suggestions for appointments, prepared lists of possibilities for the president, and arranged for FBI checks and for political clearances. He has said, "That took more time than anything else I did."[2] He was assisted in a formal and routine way by Ralph A. Dungan, who had been Kennedy's chief aide in the appointments process but who became conscious of less dependence on his assistance early in the Johnson presidency and left with an ambassadorial appointment in November 1964.[3] In this activity there was a two-tier relationship between the new and the old White House aides, as Jenkins, assisted in the activity by Jack J. Valenti, Bill D. Moyers, and Horace Busby, Jr., took over.

With the departure of Dungan and Jenkins in November 1964, Johnson made new arrangements for help on appointments. In a companion volume to this one, Richard L. Schott and Dagmar Hamilton have described the new arrangement as being two-tiered in a different sense. There was a formal process and an additional, more informal, fluid, and ad hoc process that was in part parallel but largely subsequent to the other.[4]

The formal process was directed by John W. Macy, Jr. Within a week after the election of 1964 Johnson asked Macy, who had a full-time position as chairman of the Civil Service Commission, to take on a second responsibility. He was to be the "talent scout" for executive personnel. Thereafter until the end of the Johnson presidency Macy ran two distinct operations in two locations with two staffs, with a daily tour of duty in one followed by the other. Although Johnson gave him no White House appointment and he operated as appointments aide from the Executive Office Building, he was, in fact, and we have described him as an integral part of White House operations. In this instance the same person served in an institutional position outside the White House and gave personal service to the president within it, but his two roles were operationally separate.

The Macy operation as talent scout was one of the most distinctive elements in White House operations. Johnson asked Macy to act "in the same professional way" he did in the Civil Service and to leave political judgments to others.[5] When a vacancy was in prospect Macy developed a position profile, including conditions affecting the appointment and the qualifications to be sought. With a list ultimately of over sixteen thousand names of possibilities and with supplementary contacts over a wide net, Macy would send the president names for consideration. Johnson customarily sent back a note with follow-up instructions, one of which would be study of FBI files on a person tentatively chosen by the president.[6]

The second part of the process exemplified Johnson's conviction of the importance of appointments, the need for political input, and the caution that led him to search for more information and opinions before making important decisions. W. Marvin Watson, Jr., taking over much of the task from Valenti, became the center of the second operation. Johnson asked him in 1965 to make a second review of FBI folders, and he checked also through various political channels for reactions. These activities somewhat limited the scope and influence of the Macy operation. But the second system, which Schott and Hamilton call the surrogate system, included numerous persons. Suggestions and advice on particular appointments came unsolicited or on request from Cabinet officers, trusted friends of the president outside the administration, and various persons within the White House. Among the last were particularly Valenti, Busby, Moyers, Joseph A. Califano, Jr. (aides who had information about numerous persons in the executive branch), Myer Feldman and Lee C. White (particularly on appointments to regulatory commissions), and Lawrence F. O'Brien (with his responsibility for favorable congressional reaction).

Executive Structure

Another resource for presidential influence on executive branch policy and operations is decision on its organization. The president may exert influence in four ways: proposal of legislation for new departments or agencies, a reorganization plan for combination or transfer of organization units or functions, executive order, and influence on department or agency heads on reorganizations within their authority.

President Johnson sponsored and gave leadership for numerous reorganization changes that reflected his purposes or objectives to be achieved in the executive branch: creation of a new agency to unify direction of the anti-poverty program and new departments to gain greater attention to urban problems and new planning and policy choices for transportation; delegation of authority for coordination of interdepartmental activities overseas and of various domestic programs; and transfer of functions to attain greater effectiveness in particular programs. He failed in some reorganization efforts, notably the stillborn proposal to create a merged department to unify promotion of commerce and labor and a valiant but unsuccessful move to give home rule to the people of the District of Columbia. He took an active interest in some reorganizations effected or sought within departments. He devoted much time to consideration of changes in executive organization.[7]

For this function the president had the advantage of knowledge and professional help from an established executive office—the Bureau of the Budget (BOB) and particularly its Division of Management and Organization. BOB and its division supplied a consistent perspective for viewing organization change, a watchful and protective attitude on presidential authority, and a positive stance on changes that conformed with its perspective. Only occasionally did it fail to have a significant role in organization change. In addition to its readiness with information and organizational perspective, it was usually able to give direction because it was involved in the process of consideration at the beginning, participative throughout, and carried the burden—through organization of interagency task forces or other means—of working out specific details to implement basic decisions. Occasionally, however, BOB and its division were not an important agent of decision, as when Johnson on his own initiative rescued the decision on organization for the antipoverty program from BOB indecisiveness and delay,[8] or when BOB views were not accepted, or in the case of its division on management and organization when there seemed to be purposeful avoidance of its participation.[9]

When Califano joined the White House, issues of organization change were assigned to him. He was the chief channel of communication and advice to the president because most of the organization changes related to domestic policy. And he became the mediator among those with conflicting views, the liaison with Congress on questions of substance, aggressive promoter of organization changes approved by the president, and even advocate of changes to the president himself. Yet on organization change, as on development of the legislative policy program, Califano often had support from other White House aides or occasionally was supportive of them. This was the result of the area specializations that had developed. For example, S. Douglass Cater, Jr., was a participant on reorganization of the Public Health Service, White on reorganization plans related to civil rights and water pollution, Macy on the proposed creation of a department for economic affairs, Charles A. Horsky initiator and participant on District of Columbia reorganization, and General Maxwell D. Taylor the mover with respect to unifying field activities within the Department of State.[10]

Two comprehensive studies of government organization were made during the Johnson presidency. Don K. Price chaired a 1964 Task Force on Government Reorganization. Its report apparently received little attention by the president, but many of its proposals became part of the stream of ideas considered by BOB and Califano. With Califano serving as instrument for creation and BOB assisting, a Task Force on Government Organization, functioning from 1966 to 1967, brought in a series of reports that raised basic issues on executive structure. While the task force had strong support from the president and included some of the top executives of the government, the reports came too late and reached a president too engulfed in other matters to push, or even consider, a program of administrative reform.[11]

Budgeting

Structural rearrangements are made to influence the general directions of executive performance. In contrast, the budget process provides the president with opportunity for specific entry into executive affairs, both as to scope and direction. For assistance in this process President Johnson inherited in BOB an institutionalized and professionalized component of presidential assistance. Within the White House there was no personal, political, or intimate adviser assigned to assist on all budget matters. Communication of the three successive BOB directors with the president was direct and offered with full trust. We have seen that there was an effort, belatedly, to combine budget planning with Califano's legislative planning; and although Califano had constant access to the president, the central elements in the budget process were the president and the director of BOB. In the overall budget conferences prior to the annual January messages on the State of the Union and the budget, often held at the ranch, the top domestic and foreign affairs/national defense advisers in departments and agencies and policy and press aides in the White House were present, along with the director of BOB. There were also numerous presidential conferences with particular departmental and agency heads. For example, when Senator Harry F. Byrd demanded a cut in funds as the price for support for the tax increase bill, the president conferred with James E. Webb of the National Aeronautics and Spacc Administration (NASA), whose agency was to get a $500 million cut. In other instances, budget policies were integrated with macroeconomic or foreign affairs policies, where different advisers were involved.

Dependence on the director of BOB was, therefore, somewhat different from that in other areas: from appointments, where there was a professional layer and an informal and broader area, both centralized in the White House; from economic policy advice, where there was an institutional component in the executive office and delegation to Califano, a White House component; from national security and science and technology, where McGeorge Bundy, then Walt W. Rostow, and Donald F. Hornig served dual roles as White House aides and directors of executive office staffs. In budgeting, therefore, it could be anticipated that the aid expected by the president from the director of BOB would, particularly with Johnson's high requirements for personal loyalty, fuse the functions of professional and institutional help with those of personal service. A thorough analysis of Director Charles L. Schultze's participation in another aspect of his service—advice on executive organization—led to the conclusion that Schultze served the president in both capacities.[12]

Miscellaneous

In addition to these resources, the president had a variety of others, including veto or support of departmental and agency legislation, the executive order or other means of direction based on constitutional and numerous statutory grants to him, and the influences accruing from his position in government, with the public, and in international relations. White House staff assisting him on legal issues, substantive policy, and representational functions could be involved from these bases, as well as on appointments, organization, and budgeting.

Uses of Presidential Influence

It would be absurd to view the responsibility and actions of a president, either personally or through the White House or by any other means, as a systematic effort to govern the executive branch.[13] Since most of the legal delegations Congress has made run to departments and agencies and since the presidency is loaded with responsibilities, the direction a president gives the executive branch is to a large extent reactive, selectively interventionist, and episodic. President Johnson displayed instances of activism, but more generally he was cautious and sometimes a reluctant participant. His relationships with department or agency executives were mostly direct, with the White House staff in a more limited role than when direct presidential power was exercised. The main services of the White House staff were, first, to be alert to activities or inactivities within departments and the possibilities for action within them that would be of concern to the president and, second, to be available for the various kinds of assistance required in multiple types of presidential intervention. The general role of White House aides, with some specific illustration, is presented here.

Monitoring Executive Activity

The Johnson presidency made a systematic effort to obtain cues for presidential attention, both from agencies and executive offices. In part, these came from formal reporting requirements. Departments and agencies submitted regular reports on developments and problems and sometimes on separate subjects. Special reports were submitted as presidential interests demanded. For example, Califano has reported, "In 1967 and 1968, he [Johnson] established a weekly reporting system on the number of federally assisted new housing starts."[14] At certain stages in implementation of Title VI of the Civil Rights Act of 1964 and of the Voting Rights Act of 1965, daily reports were sent to the White House. "He monitored its [Voting Rights Act] implementation with the meticulous care of an obstetrician during a difficult labor and delivery. He prodded the Justice Department to make sure monitors were present at each voting place in the affected Southern states."[15] As the president pushed his cost reduction program, he could state that for the sixth time in the previous year and a half agency heads had reported on efforts to reduce costs and improve operations.[16] So numerous were reporting requirements that at least on one occasion Califano asked the help of White House staff members in a comprehensive review of the procedures.[17]

A steady flow of these reports went to the president himself. For example, in a pouch sent to the president at the ranch on 6 December 1966 there were nine reports from departments and agencies marked weekly or monthly or on some special subject. Another pouch at about the same time included weekly price reports and balance of payment reports from CEA.[18] Secretary of Interior Stewart L. Udall says that he himself prepared the weekly reports for his department—"terse," "tight," "set forth major issues"—and that "Because of the playback, it was always clear to me that President Johnson saw most of them because he reacted occasionally."[19]

Reports were referred to White House staff members who had competence, interest, or functions related to the reporting agency. Thus, a memorandum of 21 October 1965 set forth the allocation of eleven departments and forty-five agencies to ten aides who had responsibility for day-to-day contacts.[20] Yet Secretary Udall says he never had a counterpart in the White House, as Cater was for Health, Education and Welfare (HEW).[21]

Irregular and informal communications usually tended to move in the same channels as formal reports. Within the White House, awareness of the tasks of others led to transfer of the information as needed—to Califano, Rostow, or others who had broad responsibilities to which the agency information related.

For the day-to-day business of government, reports are forbiddingly numerous and inclusive and undoubtedly many if not most of them received scant attention. More meaningful channels of communication were usually the memorandum, personal visit, and telephone call. Staff members developed numerous points of contact within departments from which they extracted information. Involuntarily, they gained information from departments seeking attention or support from the president, from the media, and from Congress or private interests with complaints or importunities.[22] The president himself learned directly from these sources about departmental problems, but he was heavily dependent upon White House staff for alertness, selectivity, summarization, and supplementation of executive branch information useful to him.

Managerial Direction

President Johnson was exceptionally active in the broad area of managerial direction of the executive branch as a whole. Yet this was an area in which White House aid was minimal because of the service provided to him in executive offices. For example, in 1965 he inaugurated an expansive and comprehensive effort to centralize budgetary planning called Planning-Programming-Budgeting System (PPBS).[23] Although Califano (who had come from the Defense Department, where it was used) was undoubtedly influential in its adoption and viewed it as the future instrument for coordination of program planning, BOB was the instrument for the largely unsuccessful effort to direct and coordinate departmental and agency implementation.

Johnson's activism is exemplified also in his cost reduction program, which may have had largely symbolic and public relations values but which he persistently pursued in line with his genuine interest in government economy. It was launched during the first month of his administration after numerous meetings with executive staff, and BOB was the natural organ for its administration, with temporary assistance from a task force and council. White House staff received primarily quarterly and special reports. These came to Busby, Robert E. Kintner, and Charles M. Maguire—the Cabinet secretaries—for use in preparing for Cabinet meetings, to George E. Reedy and Moyers successively for use in their work as press secretaries, to Califano, and later to E. Ernest Goldstein, with some prodding from all of these on a skeptical BOB.[24]

Parallel to this effort and his overall budget management were the president's distinctively more personal and more particularized pursuits of economy: freezing purchases of filing cabinets, curbing purchases of typewriters and office furniture, restricting June buying, directing reduction of questionnaires and reports, consolidating purchases of coffee, cutting off White House lights, and examining (through Watson) expenditures of the First Lady's press secretary. Watson, as we have noted, was persistent, meticulous, and even obnoxious to other persons in his pursuit of Johnson's desire for economy in the White House.[25]

The president's managerial direction extended to human services.

Johnson was an activist in this field also. As in finance, statute had provided him with institutional assistance. The chairman of the CSC for the duration of the Kennedy/Johnson administrations had the special confidence of President Johnson, making representation within the White House on general public service matters unnecessary. The president's directives to departments and agencies, enforced by the Commission, extended to such diverse aspects of administration as personnel ceilings, increased compensation, classification, labor-management relations, opportunities for the handicapped, employment of women, standards of ethical conduct for public officials, and retirement.[26]

Undoubtedly, however, the largest effort of the president in personnel policy was to eliminate racial discrimination in the public service. While vice president, he had been given this responsibility by President Kennedy, and his zeal was heightened by his campaigns for civil rights legislation in 1964 and 1965. He issued executive orders, gave the CSC the responsibility for enforcement, importuned his Cabinet,[27] studied the reports from departments and agencies, appointed interagency committees, and directed particular departments to give attention to minority employment.[28] In this matter, the White House staff seems to have sensed that the president wanted any bit of meaningful information, for memos flowed to him from Cater, White, Harry C. McPherson, Jr., and others.

Policy Development and Application: Presidential Abstentions

In the broader arena of substantive policy development and application, an important element in the president's stance of which his immediate staff was conscious was his desire for protection from unwarranted, unnecessary, or politically dangerous interventions by him or his staff. On numerous occasions he instructed a staff member to work toward a solution for a problem without involving the president, at least publicly. For example, when McPherson reported to the president that the Department of Agriculture's anticipated action on milk price support was being contested by congressmen Wilbur D. Mills (D.-Ark., chairman of Ways and Means Committee) and Carl B. Albert (D.-Okla., majority floor leader), the president responded, "Get Mills and Albert with [Secretary of Agriculture Orville L.] Freeman and get president out of this."[29]

Many considerations could contribute to a president's avoidance of involvement: among others, consciousness of personal vulnerability, deference to other governmental authorities, desire to remain out of issues where his political capital could be diminished, and the objective of holding the ultimate political power in reserve. Johnson was, in addition, "inordinately sensitive to his characterization in the press as a 'wheeler-dealer.'"[30] He was acutely aware of personal vulnerability in two areas of public policy: oil and gas, and communications; the first, an area in which he might be accused of concern for the interests of persons in his state and region, the other, one in which his family's financial interest was strong. He let his staff know that he would be reluctant to take positions on administration in the two fields. With respect to oil and gas, he is reported to have remarked, "I'm very vulnerable in the resource picture."[31] In his first meeting with Udall, he instructed him: "I want you to make all the oil decisions, you run the oil program; I want oil out of the White House."[32] On communications, a study of Johnson's seven appointments to the Federal Communications Commission concluded that "President Johnson was determined to avoid even the appearance of impropriety in his dealings with FCC."[33] Goldstein, to whom Johnson assigned "care of the regulatory commissions," said he got a "very distinct impression" he was expected to make judgments on matters that dealt with the commission so that Johnson "would be completely insulated and divorced from it."[34]

The inclination to avoid involvement, however, was not always realized. Udall has said that oil issues entangled him with several other departments and agencies, but that the White House intervened only once: on legal grounds the White House overruled him.[35] But Udall was apparently not thinking of the course of decision on oil import quotas, a matter on which the president himself is delegated statutory authority and on which the interests of sections and groups were sharply divided. The White House was kept informed and often consulted on key decisions and in a few instances decision was actually made in the White House by the president independently or based on staff recommendations.[36] Appointments to the Federal Power Commission involved the president in consideration of the effects on the oil and gas industries. Similarly, in making his seven appointments to the FCC, Johnson dampened the regulatory activism prevalent under Kennedy.[37]

One reason for restraint on presidential involvement is administrative rectitude. This may have been an important consideration in a communication to Secretary of Defense Robert S. McNamara during Johnson's first week as president. "I shall make no recommendations or suggestions with respect to contract awards or negotiations, and I shall not permit any person on the staff of the White House to do so."[38] Jenkins has said: "LBJ didn't allow the staff to contact the Justice, IRS and FCC."[39] Jenkins was obviously referring to particular cases and with some overstatement, yet Califano says "that he [LBJ] repeatedly prohibited his staff from involvement in any antitrust or regulatory commission cases."[40] The president at a later date prescribed a strict rule that, at the penalty of firing, no staff member should make any contact with a department or agency in behalf of a private citizen.[41] Watson at one time elaborated the president's instructions to all staff members and sent them suggested form letters for response to private requests.[42]

The delicacy of the position of White House staff on private importunities was particularly apparent in relations with the regulatory commissions. The general stance of the president was stated by White: "The president has a firm policy against White House staff involving themselves in any proceedings before regulatory bodies. . . ."[43] Johnson remonstrated with McPherson, who had advised noninvolvement of the president but had himself met with a private party aggrieved by a regulatory decision: "I don't even think we should have meetings like this in the White House."[44]

Some members of the White House staff, especially those in the legal profession (such as McPherson, Califano, and White), were highly sensitive to the need for protecting the president from the appearance of involvement on issues before regulatory commissions. Watson and Valenti, as appointments secretaries to the president, were pressed on occasions to grant audiences with the president which legal staffers desired to avoid. Such avoidances were difficult when the persons seeking presidential attention on regulatory actions adverse to their interests were active in representing the president on other matters or exerted pressure through persons close to the president. Fortunately, instances in which parties were able to run through the gauntlet of White House obstacles were rare.[45]

A comparable delicacy could exist with respect to presidential interventions on prosecution of individuals or companies on such a matter as antitrust violations. The president's desire to avoid involvement was known to the staff. Thus, Watson wrote to a complainant "that the president does not become involved in matters of this kind."[46] Yet the president's interest was often known to the Department of Justice: by request to Justice to consider whether illegal actions contributed to food price rises, direction to staff for conversation with Justice on the relation of the structure of industry to prices and antitrust, communication of concern with maintenance of transportation service when governors or the Department of Transportation did not want Justice to pursue action in merger cases, reference through the White House staff of complaints of Justice's prosecution, and—it is alleged—Johnson's approval of two cases.

The president's legal counsel and Califano engaged in various liaison activities with the Department of Justice on antitrust matters. Yet Temple referred to the president's relationship to Attorney General Ramsay Clark on "anti-trust if any" as "personal between him and Ramsay."[47] The president was reluctant, at least in instances, to push a position on Justice. Typical of his stance was a note to Califano on an issue between the departments of Transportation and Justice on whether the government should try to prevent merger of northern railway lines (Great Northern, Northern Pacific, and Chicago, Burlington and Quincy): "I think he [Ramsay Clark] is out of step; Call Ramsay at *once* & tell him I strongly agree with [Secretary of Transportation Alan] Boyd but I will not force him to act against his conscience as I told him."[48]

Policy Development and Application: Presidential Participation

Multiple interventions in the affairs of departments and agencies would have neither served the president's interests nor accorded with the responsibility of executive officials. Yet Johnson selectively participated in departmental administration on matters of high presidential priority.

The president made numerous statements expressing his interest in the administration of particular policies. These could be largely hortatory and sometimes were undoubtedly issued on the plea of departments seeking support from the president. These involved the White House staff very lightly, perhaps mainly to prepare the statements.

Support of the president or absence of it can be the most meaningful element in departmental execution of public policy. This is illustrated in the experience of F. Peter Libassi, who became director of the Office of Civil Rights in HEW and special assistant to the secretary in January 1966. His office made thousands of investigations on compliance, chiefly of schools and hospitals, with Section VI of the Civil Rights Act of 1964, and Libassi signed several hundred notices for administrative hearings on compliance. The White House staff, he says, could not have avoided attention to his activities because of numerous calls from senators and congressmen, many of which required more than a mere reference to HEW. He was in constant communication with staff, usually White first, or Cater, and sometimes Califano. He says he never discussed the merits of a case with the White House nor was he asked to modify anything because of political pressure. But Johnson was anxious to gain understanding and political support for enforcement. Thus, when Congressman Jamie L.

Whitten (D.-Miss.) was holding up an agriculture appropriation because of Title VI action in his district, Johnson asked Secretary John W. Gardner of HEW and Libassi to see Whitten. Also, when a famous newscaster was airing complaints about withholding funds for a hospital in Mississippi, Johnson through Cater asked that an effort be made to get the government's side on television. When new school desegregation guidelines were being framed, Johnson sent word that he wanted contact to be made with leaders and numerous other members of Congress to obtain their views. And Johnson, with Wilbur J. Cohen present, met with governors at the ranch and told them in strong language that the law was going to be enforced. Libassi says he never thereafter had a protest from a governor. Summarizing enforcement of Section VI, Libassi said, "It couldn't have been done without Johnson."[49]

The president was often alert to steps necessary to inaugurate new programs. For example, at a reception marking the signing of the Elementary and Secondary Education Act of 1965, which enormously increased the activities of the Office of Education within HEW, he said,

> So I am asking Secretary [Anthony J.] Celebreeze and Commissioner [Francis] Keppel to immediately prepare the Office of Education for the big job it has to do, just as soon as the funds are appropriated. Upon their recommendation, I am notifying the Secretary now that later I am going to appoint a task force to carry out his recommendations to assist him in the next 60 days on organizational and personnel problems in this area to administer this bill.[50]

The president designated for full-time work a task force composed of a representative each from BOB and CSC, with Dwight A. Ink of the Atomic Energy Commission as chairman. With the assistance of staff from BOB and CSC, the cooperation of HEW, and the oversight of Cater from the White House Office, a new structure for the Office of Education and accompanying personnel requirements were worked out in detail and reported to the president, the Cabinet, and the press.

On the other hand, the president could act to interdict departmental actions. A notable incident was his intervention to prevent the consummation of plans for reorganization of administration of manpower functions in the Department of Labor near the end of his administration. After prolonged consideration in the department and BOB and an indication of sympathy from the president, the president was importuned by Califano to approve a reorganization. The president rejected the order and Secretary of Labor Willard W. Wirtz was notified of the rejection. The secretary nevertheless on 23 October 1968 issued a reorganization order and it belatedly came to the attention of White House staff. The president, in direct confrontation with the secretary, demanded the rescission of the order. When Wirtz refused, the president asked for his resignation. After a letter of resignation was submitted, the president pushed further for rescission of the order, which Wirtz announced would be held in abeyance. He was then allowed to withdraw his resignation and face was saved for each party. But the confrontation demonstrated, as in President Andrew Jackson's removal of Secretary of the Treasury W. J. Duane,[51] the strains that can exist between a departmental chief with statutory authority and a president with objectives of his own. In this instance, the White House staff supplied the president with what Temple called the "daily men" who manned the telephones and made appointments as needed by the president in a hectic period of presidential contacts to get outside interveners to exert pressure on Secretary Wirtz.[52]

Sometimes presidential intervention was activated by a political complaint. When HEW moved to withdraw funds from the Chicago school system because of alleged violations of antidiscrimination prohibitions, Mayor Richard J. Daley of Chicago protested to the White House. The president, contrary to the general policy described by Libassi, called for a conference in his office, attended by the secretary of the department, other executive officials, and a few persons from the White House. Wilbur Cohen, who had answered the summons along with others, was instructed by the president, without any policy guidance, to go to Chicago and "settle it." Cohen hurriedly gathered data on the case and left for Chicago, where some kind of arrangement was made with the head of the school system and cleared by a telephone call from Cohen to departmental officials. The president's action was the minimum intervention required for divesting himself of a troublesome problem.[53]

Multiplication of complaints could activate deep involvement by White House aides. For example, criticism from mayors, governors, and members of Congress led to White House involvement in the administrative operations of the Office of Economic Opportunity (OEO). A White House report detailed the attention the agency received: "Califano meets with [R. Sargent] Shriver more than 50 times during this 9 months period and has about 15 telephone conversations with Shriver each month (and as many as 26 in February)."[54] While much of this activity related to renewal and amendment of OEO's enabling legislation and engaged James A. Gaither, assistant to Califano on legislative matters,[55] involvement of the White House was generated by dissatisfaction with administration of the OEO program. Various means of improving administration were considered, such as transferring OEO functions to other agencies and appointing a strong deputy director.[56]

Manifestly, motivations for presidential participation could vary from case to case, including certainly the president's priorities in a policy or concern with political sensitivity. Also, the evidence is overwhelming that President Johnson's participation was generally directed toward policy objectives but extended sometimes to particular applications, as the Chicago event illustrated, and the absorption of the president in the detailed conduct of the Vietnam War.

A significant role, even a necessary one, for the president and White House aides often emerged in policy areas where responsibilities for execution crosscut departmental or agency lines. Here are three illustrations of staff responsibility. First, Cater reported to the president a conflict between Director Shriver of OEO and Secretary Celebreeze of HEW over OEO grant funds for birth control and family planning programs. The president responded, "Celebreeze makes sense to me" and checked "see me" on the memo.[57] Notice of and reconciliation of conflicts required staff help in administration as well as in development of legislation.

Second, when Title VI of the Civil Rights Act of 1964 required presidential approval of regulations and the largest role in administration was to be in HEW, conferences on the regulations went on among officials of HEW, the Department of Justice, and the White House. The White House staff was preparing for issuance of the regulations and alerting the agencies prior to the passage of legislation. Readiness to meet new responsibilities required an alert staff looking after presidential interests.[58]

Third, the president designated White House assistant Lee White to act as liaison among the several units of the government administering laws on narcotic and drug abuse, in effect making him responsible for policy execution. This delegation to someone within the White House appears unusual and preceded the later solution to the problems of coordination by consolidation of the functions in the Department of Justice. This was accomplished by a Reorganization Plan pushed by Califano.[59]

The main impact of presidential intervention on crosscutting responsibilities was to establish some structure outside the White House for coordination. Continuously, task forces or committees with interdepartmental representation were established. Delegations or directions were made to executive authorities; for example, the extension of the authority of the Department of State in coordination of interdepartmental activities overseas,[60] the request to Assistant Secretary of State for Inter-American Affairs Thomas C. Mann "to undertake the coordination and direction of all policies and programs . . . relating to Latin America,"[61] and the direction to Secretary of the Treasury C. Douglas Dillon to establish procedures to insure that agencies with regulatory authority over banks act in concert.[62] Executive orders were issued prescribing arrangements for interagency coordination: by the attorney general of enforcement of the Civil Rights Act of 1964; by the secretary of Housing and Urban Development (HUD) of federal urban programs; by the secretary of agriculture in rural development; or by the creation of an interdepartmental organization such as the Advisory Council on International Monetary and Financial Policies.[63] More immediate and activist intervention to facilitate interagency cooperation might exist where unusual circumstances arose. Thus, when riots occurred in the Watts district of Los Angeles in August 1965, on the president's instructions an interagency task force composed of representatives of departments and White House aides, with then Deputy Attorney General Clark as chairman, was set up in the White House.[64] When an electric power failure with threatening dimensions occurred in the northeastern portion of the country, Johnson even directed the Federal Power Commission (FPC), an independent regulatory commission, to coordinate government-wide efforts:

> You are directed to launch a thorough study of the cause for this failure. I am putting at your disposal full resources of the government and directing the Federal Bureau of Investigation, the Department of Defense and other agencies to support you in any way possible. You are to call upon the top experts in the nation in industry in conducting the investigation.[65]

To stress the urgency, the president told Califano, "For God's sake, get the FPC on it."[66] The lesson is clear: both for long-term and emergency action the intervention of the president often sets the basis for collaboration within the executive branch.

The various presidential actions were normally ad hoc, involved White House staff participation, or sought solutions by delegation to individual department or agency heads or task forces. The discussion of these, like the discussion in preceding chapters, indicates nonuse or limited use of the Cabinet collectively as an instrument of presidential direction. While the Cabinet was neither a customary center of policy decision nor administrative coordination, it met regularly and was a means for communicating presidential purpose, interchanging ideas, and occasionally receiving specific presidential instructions.[67]

A White House staff role was required to facilitate presidential use of the Cabinet. The primary role was to prepare an agenda. Charles M. Maguire, Cabinet secretary for several years, has described this process:

> I had regularized Cabinet meetings on a fortnightly basis, every second Wednesday. On the Friday preceding every second Wednesday, a group of the staff would meet in one of the larger offices—Cater's or McPherson's, Cater's because it was the nicest—and we would kick around a Cabinet agenda. . . . It meant that five or six principal White House staffers were setting the agenda for the Cabinet. . . . Out of these meetings and through simultaneous contact with the Cabinet departments I would prepare an agenda.[68]

Another role was to frame a list of people to be invited by the president to attend. Maguire explained this process also:

> The President would have on his desk the morning of the cabinet meetings the final attendance report, suggestions from me. Some he would strike out, and somctimcs hc'd just check the whole list. But interestingly enough he never checked the page, he checked name by name. If there were thirty names on it, with all participants and everything, there'd be a checkmark by every name.[69]

White House staff members themselves were included on the list. Rostow, Califano, Cater, and McPherson were invited regularly, as were legislative liaison aides Mike N. Manatos and H. Barefoot Sanders, Jr. Attendance of other aides, however, depended upon the topics included on the agenda. Cabinet meetings gave White House aides prestige and visibility to the secretaries, the opportunity to hear the president's and department heads' comments, and a chance to speak to a Cabinet member on a topic on which they were working.

Finally, when the president used the Cabinet meeting to give a directive, follow-up activity would accrue to a White House aide. For example, after secretaries John T. Connor, Wirtz, and Henry Fowler were requested to seek cooperation by business and labor in using payroll plans for the purchase of savings bonds, a White House assistant was requested to take action to see that these directives were acted upon.[70] Often the president's directions or requests at a Cabinet meeting created new reporting requirements to the White House.

Comments on White House Assistance

Personal Relationships

Thomas E. Cronin, student of the presidency and White House fellow during a portion of the Johnson presidency, has described "an executive office exchange system" in which White House staff and senior department officials communicate and negotiate with each other to satisfy their respective needs. "White House staff members can be viewed as performing important linkage in this exchange system, connecting a president with a vast network of administrative officials." He examined with much thoroughness the various causes for "tension and strain" between White House staffers and departmental executives.[71]

Cronin was analyzing conflict in all the relations between the White House and departments, but it could be expected that such conflict would be particularly present in White House activities related to matters conceived by departments to be within their own executive duties. Among other factors, it could be anticipated that government executives would sometimes feel that White House aides were too active and had excessive strength in White House/executive office relations.[72] But Johnson's activism and knowledge of events within the government and his dominance of his staff restricted it to its essential service functions to the president and the executive heads seeking presidential support.[73] The president's telephone and personal meetings with executives ordinarily gave him direct channels of communication.[74] Staff members were often uninformed on these presidential communications.

Yet staff members had proximity that facilitated their superior access to the president. Pierson of the White House staff explained that the president would say in Cabinet meetings that "no one is to stand between you and me" and added, "but that wasn't right. You had authority because you had access" not only to the president but to the facts: "Any memo from Freeman went to me."[75] HUD Secretary Robert C. Weaver was acutely aware of the staff's proximity to the president. Because the president did not always agree with the staff, however, Weaver was never certain whether the staff reflected the president's thinking.[76] Katzenbach said that somebody in the White House staff was going "to shape things up as far as the Department is concerned."[77] Temple attested to the importance of being part of the preliminary discussions: he would have "a considerable number of discussions with people of Justice before we got to the posture of recommending people."[78] And Johnson required staff recommendations. Access to the president, ability to "shape" things, discussion in preliminary steps, and expectation of recommendations gave opportunity for staff input to the decision process.

At least two executives would have preferred more decisive and prompt decisions through staff channels, as they had experienced in President Kennedy's administration. Secretary Freeman said "there was nobody in the White House who could speak for President Johnson. He made all the decisions."[79] During the Kennedy administration Cohen believed that "when you dealt with [Theodore C.] Sorensen you were . . . dealing with the president." With Califano, Cohen was a little unsure. "Well, don't do anything until we let you know," Califano would say. Cohen added that the president would reverse staff many times, or delay, or he would consult with someone else.[80]

The qualities of the president revealed in chapter 4—personal activism, knowledge of government, desire for more information—balanced against some avoidance of intervention infused Johnson's relationship with executives. Both the presidential qualities and the avoidances operated to confine the role of White House staff.

White House Inadequacy

More significant than personal relationships that inevitably differ substantially from presidency to presidency are the limitations on White House assistance to the president in general direction of executive matters. Its utility may be least in the large institutional obligation "to take care that the laws shall be faithfully executed." In this area of presidential performance the essentiality of institutional assistance is clearly apparent and is especially demonstrated by experience during the Johnson presidency. If indeed the president's resources other than appointment of personnel equip him mainly for reactive participation in executive matters, the White House staff is even more limited to that type of participation.

Even in areas where the president is delegated executive functions by the Constitution or statutes, arrangements are usually made for institutional assistance. For example, the Department of Justice gives most of the assistance to the president in grants of pardons and other forms of clemency and in appointment of judges, the Office of Management and Budget exercises much of the presidential discretion in preparing a budget, and the Office of Personnel Management assists the president in exercise of numerous grants of authority in personnel matters. The preceding chapter reviewed such aid for the president in the important areas of foreign affairs and national defense, economic policy, and science and technology. When responsibilities are delegated by statute to departments and agencies, the several kinds of White House activity detailed in this chapter can yield only piecemeal involvement by the White House staff.

In the case of the Johnson presidency, the limitations of reliance on White House assistants became obvious in the execution of the Great Society program. The crisscrossing of responsibilities among agencies administering the numerous programs created serious problems of coordination and leadership. The administration's own blue ribbon Task Force on Government Organization in a separate report on 15 June 1967 on "The Organization and Management of Great Society Programs" concluded that "*organization criticism is merited.*" It recommended a new executive office to monitor the administration of Great Society programs, provide a focal point for consultation with governors and mayors, and "settle" interdepartmental issues. Various other proposals for strengthening presidential oversight and direction were made within the administration. But none of these proposed expansion of White House staff for this purpose. There was implicit recognition that, while legislative programming could be successfully centralized in the White House and representation of the president to constituencies outside the executive branch would necessarily be centralized, the responsibility of the president to "take care that the laws shall be faithfully executed" depended primarily for even minimum effectiveness on strong institutional help.

8. Representing the President

The presidency is a political office, and the president is a political person and must have political help. Politics is, at least in a democracy, the art of gaining consent, and for the president the practical meaning of government by consent is that he can achieve and maintain capability to accomplish his purposes only if he and his programs are supported by domestic constituencies.

This fact is often overlooked in discussions of the president's needs for help. The Brownlow Committee, the Hoover Commission, the Heineman Task Force, and the Ash Council, which conducted renowned studies during the Roosevelt, Truman, Johnson, and Nixon administrations, respectively, all devoted attention to the core functions of policy and administration. A more recent report by a panel of the National Academy of Public Administration set forth a design of "Size and Functions of the White House Staff" to include assistants to the president for "core processes of policy coordination, policy advice, information flow, and management." The call for "a trim White House staff" included no design to meet the needs of the president in processes of government based on consent of Congress, organized interest groups, and the larger public.[1]

Presidents today will have been informed by the powerful arguments of Richard E. Neustadt's *Presidential Power* that presidential capability depends upon maintenance of presidential prestige and the gaining of consent for particular policies.[2] Yet they need no such literary presentation to realize the need for staff aid for representing the president. Immediately speeches and statements must be prepared, the press answered, and the importunities of congressmen and groups considered.

We distinguished in chapter 2 four parts of the process of representing the president. This chapter will discuss each of these separately: congressional liaison, speeches and messages, media presentations, and group contacts.

The purpose of these activities is to represent the president and his position so as to gain acceptance for his policies. In their performance the representational staff becomes involved with the policy staff and with the development of policy by the president himself. The processes for obtaining consent are part of the processes of policy deliberation and decision, as would be expected in government based on consent.

Representing the President in Congress

The activist president's legislative program created the largest presence of the executive in Congress since the early days of the New Deal and perhaps the most persistent and continuous presence in our history. A highly effective White House operation contributed to Johnson's impressive legislative record.[3] A major factor here was the commanding, intimate, and ceaseless participation of the president himself. With Johnson's insatiable urge for countable achievements, his unsurpassed knowledge of the arts of gaining consent from congressmen, and his own drive toward stretching himself personally into the movement of events, he was not merely a manager who refused to delegate responsibility for success but an operator who intervened whenever his position and persuasiveness would gain needed votes. Johnson realized that no matter how good a program he developed, without his continuous prodding the administration's bills would move through Congress "at the speed of a glacier."[4]

The president continued the weekly breakfast meetings in the White House of the congressional leaders of his own party that had been the practice of his predecessor. His appointments officers knew that the president had an open door policy for congressmen wishing to see him, and they customarily arranged for them to see him without public notice. He entertained congressmen in groups in the White House. He received weekly reports from his congressional liaison office on the status of legislation and a continuing stream of memorandums and telephone calls from those who were assisting in getting legislation enacted. In reverse, he continuously directed the staff through telephone calls, comments on returned memorandums, special assignments, and conferences in his office. His main contact with congressmen was through the ever-present telephone but was supplemented by personal conferences with congressmen strategically positioned for influence on passage of legislation. According to Lawrence F. O'Brien, the top congressional assistant, for Johnson "Congress was a twenty-four hour a day obsession."[5] It is probably not excessive to characterize the president as hyperactive in legislative leadership.

A basic guide for Johnson's operations with relation to legislative matters was stated in a memorandum to Joseph A. Califano, Jr., on one occasion: "I wouldn't start something I couldn't pass."[6] This usually meant extensive conferences with departmental executives, executive office units, and congressmen whose assessment of congressional reaction would be accurate and whose cooperation would be necessary for passage of legislation.

A second feature of White House operations for congressional consent was a system of congressional liaison that included two types of aides, policy and representational. Those on the White House staff who worked on the development of the legislative program worked closely with strategically located congressmen as they considered ideas for legislation, prepared bills, or considered amendments to meet congressional purposes. The top policy aides working with the task forces were instructed by Johnson to involve key congressmen behind the scenes during the programming process. Through congressional participation as the administration's bills evolved, the president and the staff obtained a clear indication of the chances for passage. Additionally, congressional participation enabled the White House to take early steps to assure passage by redrafting bills and doing preparatory work in committees to which they would be assigned. As was shown in chapter 4, the central responsibility for this function was focused during the last three and one-half years of the Johnson presidency in Califano's office, but the responsibility was shared with S. Douglass Cater and other policy aides.

In addition to the policy aides' deep involvement with program development, there was also in the White House a group whose responsibility was legislative acceptance of presidential policy. It was shown in chapter 3 that key members of this staff were carried over from the Kennedy administration and remained through much or all of the Johnson presidency. Lawrence F. O'Brien was the chief of this group until November 1965 when he became postmaster general, but he retained an office in the White House and continued to give help to the president in legislative relationships. He was succeeded in May 1967 by H. Barefoot Sanders, Jr., a Johnson recruit. O'Brien's assistant for the Senate was Mike N. Manatos, who served in that capacity through the Kennedy and Johnson administrations. Similar assistance was provided in the House of Representatives by Henry Hall Wilson until May 1967. A varying number of additional persons completed the liaison staff, and after its enlargement in 1967 it included ten people on a full- or part-time basis.[7]

One function of this group was to serve as a channel of information to the White House. Manatos said, "My job was to count heads and to make sure we had enough votes to pass legislation."[8] Manatos also has stated that O'Brien, undoubtedly reflecting the demands of the president for accurate information, wanted no soft counts but reports based on conversations with senators.[9] The counts were reported to Califano, Cater, or others who needed them and often to the president himself. For example, Sanders sent successive reports, sometimes only hours apart, to the president on vote counts and conversations with chairmen and other members of congressional committees when the tax increase bill was being considered.

Vote count was, however, only one aspect of the work of the liaison group. This office provided the president and policy aides with weekly reports on the status of legislation. Through this channel, as well as through the reports of policy aides, the president learned the objections to legislation and the difficulties to be overcome at specific points in the legislative structure and process. The liaison group, in reverse activity, could provide information, answer inquiries, and advance argument for the president's program. It assisted the policy aides in the White House and the legislative representatives of the departments in working out compromises.

Harry C. McPherson, Jr., has given his summary of the work of the liaison staff:

> The President needed a legislative staff to work the Hill. Theirs was largely a transmitting job—relaying the members' hopes, dilemmas, and complaints to the president, explaining to the members what the President wanted. Often they took part in our discussions about new programs, and provided a sense of the possible in tasks that by and large concentrated on the desirable. They put the pressure on when the votes looked tight, reported offers of compromise, and took soundings as best they could. Like many of our ambassadors abroad, they represented the needs and views of the principality to which they were accredited more often, if not more urgently, than they did ours to it. No doubt that was necessary for effective representation, and Larry O'Brien, Henry Wilson, and Mike Manatos were very effective. They were trusted on the Hill, and that was the main requirement.[10]

As in other areas of White House activity, access to the president was power and the congressional liaison staff had remarkable access to Johnson. The effectiveness of the congressional staff derived largely from the fact that aides were in such frequent contact with the president that they could be trusted to speak for him on Capitol Hill. The head of the staff, first O'Brien and then H. Barefoot Sanders, Jr., had a telephone directly connected to the president's desk. The White House switchboard was under instructions to put the head of the congressional staff's calls through to the president regardless of the hour. Manatos and Wilson regularly submitted memos that were part of the president's night reading. Manatos reported that he sent memorandums directly to the president when he desired and also that the president would read them, whatever length they reached. He could provide access through the appointments office for any senator who wished to see the president.[11] The several members of the group attended the weekly congressional breakfasts and various staff conferences on the legislative program.

A third feature of congressional liaison was that the dual structure for congressional contact was supplemented by participation in this activity by persons having other functions in the White House. Walter W. Jenkins, continuing service he had given when aide to then Senator and Majority Leader Johnson, assumed the liaison function with members of the Texas delegation and the "whales" in Congress with whom Johnson had maintained close relationships. Jack J. Valenti, along with his other duties, was very active in congressional liaison. When Sherwin J. Markham came into the White House from the Midwest, he was assigned responsibility for liaison with certain Midwest congressmen, a kind of assignment given to others on the staff.[12] Beyond this, the president expressed a desire that each assistant be assigned a list of senators and congressmen with whom he could become closely identified in order to provide backup for the congressional liaison operations as occasions arose.[13] These references illustrate the third feature of use of the talents and connections of the various members of the staff in gaining congressional consent.

A fourth feature was the collaboration with the legislative officers of the executive departments who participated in the preparation of legislation and in the coordination of legislative activities. Within each department there was some official, such as the assistant secretary for legislation in the Department of Health, Education and Welfare, who carried responsibility for legislative acceptance of presidential and departmentally sponsored legislation. Johnson asked each Cabinet officer to select a top official to serve as his legislative liaison and said, "Next to the Cabinet officer himself, I consider this the most important position in the department."[14] Ralph K. Huitt, who occupied the position in HEW during much of Johnson's presidency, has said that "A presidential program cannot be carried to Congress by the White House staff. That staff may direct, coordinate, solve problems, and give support, but like soldier ants pushing leaves, the agency legislative officers try to move their programs."[15]

Thus, White House liaison activity, which sought to maximize presidential influence in setting the legislative agenda, formulating the content of legislation, and facilitating enactment, was supplemented by departmental and agency capacities. The resources of the executive departments were particularly critical when dozens of bills were scattered in many different committees. At this point, the White House sought to harness the established departmental and outside clientele relations with the committees and to utilize these relations to advance the administration's program.

The collaboration of the White House and departmental groups was carefully planned and executed in the Johnson period. Each departmental legislative officer gave a detailed, bill-by-bill weekly report to the White House. Also, the White House liaison staff met each week with the departmental legislative officers, at first late on Friday afternoon, later on Monday morning. Departmental executives, usually Vice President Hubert H. Humphrey, and sometimes President Johnson would be present at these meetings.

Huitt reports that these meetings were helpful to departmental officials in providing access to the president and tactical advice from such knowledgeable White House aides as Wilson.[16] White House aides regarded the meetings as helpful in coordinating two levels of activity for congressional support of the administration's program. In the case of Wilbur J. Cohen—serving first as assistant secretary for legislation, then under secretary, then secretary of HEW—the two levels merged into one as Cohen's contacts with the president, as well as with Cater and Califano, made him virtually a member of the White House working group.

Obviously, close collaboration within and among the different staff groups was necessary in daily activities. O'Brien and Sanders held regular weekly conferences of their group and sometimes called staff meetings to which the policy aides were also invited. All members of the congressional liaison group attended regularly the weekly meetings with the departmental legislative representatives. Although compliance with procedures was not always perfect, regular reporting procedures from staff aides to O'Brien's office on all congressional contacts were prescribed and supplemented by the collaboration between the program aides and the legislative officers of the departments.[17] Apparently there was sufficient awareness among the different groups of their complementary roles to ensure the collaboration necessary for legislative achievement.

Writing for the President

Six hundred fifty items are listed in the *Public Papers* of the president for 1966, approximately two per working day. Included were a diverse set of addresses, statements, and remarks. There were communications to the Congress: the State of the Union Message, the Budget Message and supplemental messages, messages proposing legislation, veto messages, reports on studies or action, letters to presiding officers or to other congressmen replying to their inquiries or expressing the president's desires. There were announcements of appointments, statements at swearing-in ceremonies, directions to executive officials, messages to international committees, and remarks on an event of national significance. There were miscellaneous remarks such as a statement on the death of a foreign official, greetings to a noted writer on his birthday, remarks at the meeting of groups (e.g., the Boy Scouts) or at some ceremony. There were remarks prepared for introduction of press conferences.

Not included, of course, was the president's correspondence on public matters. The content of correspondence was largely routinized, but the attention of designated White House personnel was required, nevertheless. Assisted by the Correspondence Section and other sections in William J. Hopkins' staff, this activity was under the direction first of Paul M. Popple and later of W. Whitney Shoemaker, both of whom were authorized to sign mail under the title "Assistant to the President for Correspondence." Shoemaker's assistant was authorized to sign as "Administrative Secretary."

The preparation of released statements and of platform language could require as intimate an entrance into the president's mind as that of his correspondence, and was in addition one of the most extensive and diversified tasks to be performed in the White House for the president. It is also apparent that it was the most dispersed, loosely structured, and, for much of the Johnson presidency, poorly coordinated function of the White House staff.

The task was dispersed from the early days of the Johnson presidency. Except for Jenkins, who had no desire for this kind of participation, all the first Johnson recruits to the White House had interest and competence for the task. Horace Busby, Jr., Bill D. Moyers, Valenti, and Elizabeth Carpenter from Mrs. Johnson's staff all became engaged at once in speechwriting and George E. Reedy in the preparation of public statements. Theodore C. Sorensen remained for a time as coordinator of important policy statements.[18] Richard N. Goodwin, who had moved from the White House to the State Department in November 1961, returned to the White House early in 1964 to engage exclusively in speechwriting. Cater's first large task was preparation of a book to set forth the president's philosophy, and he too would participate in speechwriting, though he preferred to be engaged in policy development and was soon able to escape substantially from speechwriting.

Primary responsibility for the preparation of a speech rested at different points. Thus, Busby was the central figure in preparation of the president's Thanksgiving address to the American people the first week in office, Sorensen the person who put together the various drafts for the president's first message to Congress, Goodwin the next year for the Great Society speech, policy specialists sometimes for addresses to Congress related to their fields, and Moyers or Califano for other addresses related to the legislative program. Putting together a State of the Union Message and the annual Budget Message called for linkage of speechwriters with the legislative development office. In the campaign of 1964, speech material came from "every crevice and cranny of the government apparatus," then went to Secretary Willard W. Wirtz, who for this purpose occupied a desk in the White House, then to wordsmiths (Goodwin, Busby, and Cater among them) operating under Moyers' direction, then from Moyers to the president.[19]

For non-campaign and non-legislative addresses, the coordination tended to gravitate to Valenti, presumably in part because of his access to the president and in part because of his skill in speechwriting. He had a staff assistant who gave part of his time to letter-writing and speechwriting activity. Speeches were assigned by Valenti to writers, meetings of the writers' staff were held by him, and drafts were read, revised, and approved by him for transmission to the president. Yet in this period the chief speechwriting center was Goodwin and associates.

The authority to assign and provide a final draft seems not to have been fully integrated, for Charles M. Maguire reported that other channels existed and that when Valenti left some "commotion" and "stress" over who would control occurred.[20] But concurrently, Robert E. Kintner had come to the White House, and the president assigned to him the responsibility for managing the speechwriting operation and to Maguire the job of assisting him.[21] The records on Kintner's activities indicate that he gave more attention to the speechwriting operation than to any other responsibility. He did no speechwriting or speech clearance himself, but he sought to increase the size of the overburdened staff and to concentrate the management of the process in Maguire.

After some confusion when Kintner resigned ("chaos," Peter Benchley says),[22] the operation settled into a definite pattern.

Through collaboration with W. Marvin Watson and Jones, Maguire sought on Thursday of each week to coordinate the speechwriting assignments with the president's calendar. He then gave out assignments prior to the late Friday afternoon meeting of speechwriters to discuss assignments. Speeches were returned to Maguire for his reading, but they now went to McPherson or to John P. Roche for final revision. McPherson, Roche, and Maguire were assisted by six to eight speechwriters.[23] Among the latter were Robert L. Hardesty, who had been speechwriter for the postmaster general, and Harry J. Middleton, who came from the Department of Defense and worked closely with Califano's staff on legislative matters.

Speechwriting might follow a pattern of a single writer drawing from the bureaucracy and other sources the needed material and putting it together for the president. Two examples will illustrate what McPherson called the "rational" process of speechwriting.

Benchley, who had become a kind of specialist in consumer addresses, was assigned in October 1967 the preparation of a speech to the Consumer Assembly. The president wanted to set forth his consumer goals and to spike pressures for protectionism. Benchley asked every department that had a consumer function to give him an inventory of every consumer function the department had ever had. He then reviewed all the president's statements on consumer protection. From this base it was a simple process of lifting out the goals, adding some light touches, and taking a thrust at protectionism. Since there was ample time to prepare the speech, the content was not altered during clearance from Maguire, then McPherson, and finally the president.[24]

McPherson expounded the process in an instance where more varied inputs were present:

> Writing the cities draft was part of a rational process. I worked with the task force throughout the fall of 1965, as it debated technical amendments to the housing laws and sweeping changes in policy; used an excellent memorandum, prepared by Wood and staff, as the basis for the President's message; circulated the draft to Budget, the economic advisors, and Califano (though not to the new Housing Department, which was thought to be wedded to past programs and more responsive to congressional than Presidential goals); and then discussed it at length with the president. He made many changes in language, crossing out and writing in the margins, and many more in substance—"I don't want to say that on page 8; I want to tell 'em to give me a supplemental appropriation right now." He had designed the task force, and

> had given it its charter. He was aware of what it was doing throughout. His staff was deeply involved, as were his counselors on the budget. There were no last-minute surprises. Altogether the process was a model for the writing of Presidential messages. It was also atypical.[25]

There were, however, many variances in the writing of speeches for the president. Johnson might or might not have given leads on the content. Benchley says the president would say that they should call him if they needed clues, but that this was ridiculous because speechwriters could not call him every time they needed guidance.[26] Different writers might be assigned parts of a speech and the president often wanted more than one draft. Sometimes when a speech was a major pronouncement, it was almost a total staff enterprise. The famous speech of 31 March 1968, without the final withdrawal statement of the president, was McPherson's responsibility, but numerous persons assisted over a six-week period in its preparation and the president finally had Maguire cut its length on the day it was delivered. At other times, as on the trip to the western Pacific in 1966, a few speechwriters—in this case, Moyers, McPherson, and Roche—turned out speech after speech, and, referring to one as illustrative, McPherson said it demonstrates "that Presidents are called upon to speak too often, manufacturing words of no lasting significance for gatherings of little consequence to them."[27] Moyers is reported to have called many speeches "Rose Garden rubbish."[28]

Beyond all the things alluded to above (volume; unavoidable necessities for consent, favorable image, and serving the combined role of chief of government and chief of state; White House management and process), there is a lingering question of whether speechwriting means more in government than representation of the president. Does it impact upon the policy content of a presidency?

The speechwriters are often, and aptly, referred to as wordsmiths. Given certain admonitions from President Johnson (e.g., use short words, add some humor, etc.), their role was to put in language what he wanted to communicate. Some of them deny that they tried to go beyond this role and exert influence on policy or that except by occasional chance they did influence policy. Yet the disclaimer may not be accurate for all the writers. Maguire says, "I don't know if there are any great differences in this sense between a presidential writer, a presidential adviser, and a member of the President's Cabinet." "Everything a president says is presidential policy."[29] Speechwriters often have access to the president. Moreover, the phrase shapes content; rhetoric tilts the significance. Occasionally, a phrase like "The

Great Society" does more than encapsulate; it provides a standard for policy.

McPherson avowed an interest in influencing policy, evidencing that there can be policy activists among speechwriters.[30] Yet the constant vigilance of the president guarded his specific policy questions. "Who wrote that," he said on one occasion, and he discarded the speech and ad-libbed from the platform. The speech makers were important because they reflected the bent of the president. Moyers, Valenti, McPherson, Maguire, and others shared the populist mood and the faith of the president in the benefits of legislative change. They also knew the methodology for expansive policy. McPherson describes it and philosophizes about it. The Johnson speechwriter had first to show "an indiscriminate sense of urgency." He had then to express the president's concern for "immediate action." Writers for conservative presidents might show concerns for management and efficiency in administration, but a president striving for change, working within the philosophy of the New Deal, "had to convey, not only a poignant sense of the misery to be relieved, but confidence that money and organization and skill could relieve it." McPherson almost apologized for his role in this: "At the end of our time in the White house, I winced at the striving rhetoric I had written at the beginning." "I thought we might have been more cautious in claiming what we did for our programs." Yet he did not make a full apology: "But I would not have traded Johnson's vast hopes and intentions for another man's bookkeeping prudence."[31]

The intricate relation between speechwriting and policy development meant that the line between a speechwriting assignment and policy assistance was extremely blurred, particularly in Johnson's White House staff of "generalists." Moreover, speechwriting was far more loosely structured and decentralized than most other staff activities. Nonetheless, the pivotal role in coordinating the process that McPherson assumed toward the end of the administration meant that this operation, like others, became more orderly, regularized, and systematically coordinated as Johnson's presidency progressed. This innovation, along with the maintenance of a small, personalized staff, enabled Johnson to direct and coordinate this crucial aspect of staff activity.

Representation to the Media

An imperative for a president is attentiveness to the media in its various forms. In a symbiotic relationship he must both respond to the media's need for news and court their favorable presentation of his leadership, proposals, and actions. A corollary imperative is that he have spokesmen to the media who continuously have accurate information concerning the core activities. Inevitably, top staff members with media responsibilities will be positioned in close proximity to the president and to the assistants with primary responsibilities in the substantive areas.[32]

Johnson's exaggerated concern for media attention to his programs and his desire for favorable reporting shaped almost all aspects of the White House staff's relations with the media. Moreover, his sensitivity to media reports, commentaries, and editorials grew as criticism of his expansion and conduct of the Vietnam War mounted. He was concerned, however, with more than media reaction: he longed for popular approval. While constant concern for media and popular plaudit is a natural instinct of the politician, in Johnson's case it was accentuated by his consuming desire for accomplishment and, ultimately, by his ungratified desire for media and popular support for his Vietnam policy. Likewise, his drive toward personal involvement was exhibited in his constant attention to the media. He held numerous interviews with influential publishers, editors, and writers with their own by-lines. He frequently responded to requests for individual interviews if he thought the writer's attitude toward his administration was favorable.[33] He had the staff plan the number and types of appearances in order to obtain "maximum benefit from each appearance" before the media.[34]

Some competent observers and aides believed that Johnson became too involved in staff-media relations. For example, Cater wrote the president that "[*New York Times* columnist James] Reston believes you spend entirely too much time on the details of press relations which should be delegated to others."[35] Reedy considered the president's involvement with "trivial" details of press relations a serious staff problem. Reedy recalled that Johnson was "practically tearing my staff to pieces . . . on a couple of occasions on little knit-picking [*sic*] pieces of nonsense that really didn't deserve any time or effort at all."[36]

For assistance on media relations Johnson had four press secretaries. He began with Pierre E. G. Salinger, President Kennedy's press secretary, who resigned in March 1964 to run for the Senate. Reedy succeeded Salinger and served until July 1965. Upon Reedy's departure the president appointed Moyers, who remained in the position until December 1966. When Moyers left the White House, Johnson turned to Christian, who had gained experience in the service of the president's trusted friend, Governor John B. Connally of Texas, and who remained with Johnson until the end of the administration.

This pattern of frequent turnover is significant. First, it was a clear departure from the relative stability that characterized other White House operations such as appointments, legislative program development, and congressional liaison. The press operation was the one part of the White House where the "ceaseless turnover" that journalists and reporters frequently noted was a serious staff problem.

Second, it was symptomatic of the anxieties that attended media relations that we have noted. Since the elements of personal service and loyalty are necessarily a strong characteristic of this post, the departure of the Kennedy-appointed Salinger at the earliest convenience was natural. Yet the inability of either Reedy, who had years of dedicated service to Johnson, or Moyers, who owed his sudden rise to prominence exclusively to performing to Johnson's complete satisfaction, to stay on as press secretary suggests that personal service and loyalty were not sufficient. Ironically, Christian managed to run the press operation more to Johnson's satisfaction, although he knew the president far less intimately than either Reedy or Moyers and had served in a second-level staff capacity only seven months prior to his appointment as press secretary.

One important source of difficulty was Johnson's failure to discuss adequately the role of the press secretary vis-à-vis the press prior to making the appointment. Reedy recalled that when Johnson asked him to be press secretary he "very definitely did not want the job" because he realized that Johnson "would want the press to do things that it would not do and could not do, and I didn't want to be the man caught in the middle of it."[37] Nonetheless, he accepted because he "knew the President quite well, [and] was strongly devoted to him. . . ."[38]

Only later did the wide divergences between Johnson's and Reedy's views of the press secretary's job become apparent. Reedy described their different conceptions:

> He was thinking of the press office as a place that produces stories for the press. I thought of the press office as a point of contact between the press and the White House. . . . And the two concepts just didn't jell. . . . He thought I was pampering the press. I wasn't. I was just trying to set up rational procedures so that the press could cover him.[39]

Frequent arguments over how to deal with the press and threats of resignation punctuated Reedy's "stormy" service as press secretary.[40] As trust between Johnson and his aide deteriorated, Reedy believed that "the president had begun to cut me off from sources of information. He was afraid that whatever I knew, I might give to the press."[41] Reedy resigned as press secretary in July 1965 when he entered the hospital for a foot operation.

To replace Reedy, Johnson turned to Moyers, who had served effectively as an innovative and creative aide for domestic policy. The president, however, lost confidence in Moyers not only because his tenure as press secretary coincided with a steady fall in the president's popularity, but also because Moyers did not make a completely successful transition from policy aide to press secretary. According to McPherson, Moyers became "less and less successful" as press secretary:

> Bill had adopted a method of operation that included an awful lot of background on what the President was really doing, and most of it was intended to push the President—to show the President as a liberal and a bit to push the President as well. It was a way of effecting policy by going through the press.[42]

Despite the appointment of two press secretaries who held quite different views of their responsibilities from those of the president, Johnson made no attempt to explore the subject with his third appointee to the post, Christian. "Did he [Johnson] then, or anytime about that time, discuss with you his philosophy of dealing with the press?" an interviewer asked Christian. "No, not really," he replied.[43] The president called Christian to his office, handed him a letter that Moyers had written recommending Christian as his replacement, and asked the aide, "Do you think you can handle it?" After Christian replied, "I think I probably can," the president told Moyers to make the announcement concerning his successor.[44]

Nevertheless, Christian had served in the White House long enough to acquaint himself with the working of the press office prior to his appointment and, no doubt, profited from the insights of other assistants who had observed the conflicts between the president and his former press secretaries. According to McPherson, Christian "had an altogether different concept of his responsibilities" as press secretary than Moyers had.[45] "He understood that his first duty was to convey, as accurately as possible, what the President thought, did, and intended to do. He was an instrument who played Johnson's music, not a composer."[46] During a period when Johnson had serious difficulties with the press, Christian won the respect of both the president and the press.

Effective performance of the press secretary and the White House press office required continuous and close access to the president, open communication with other parts of the government, and supplemental contact with other White House aides. Therefore, each morning the press secretary or his deputy conferred with Johnson during "bedroom duty"—presence with the president in his bedroom as he absorbed the latest information and gave out instructions for the day.[47] Additionally, the press secretary had one of the direct telephone lines to the president and was in the president's office frequently during the day. Further, the press secretary was on the receiving end of antennae from departments, agencies, and other members of the White House staff. On the basis of information from various sources, the press secretary could anticipate reporters' questions and "call the president shortly beforehand and say, 'This is what we think we are going to get asked and what is your reaction?'"[48] Thus, the intimate knowledge of late information was gained for his two daily press conferences, preparation for presidential replies at the irregular presidential conferences, and numerous telephone inquiries.

The press office remained small throughout Johnson's presidency. Only two or three other professionals in the office assisted the press secretary. As in congressional liaison the specialized service of a central White House unit was supplemented by the contacts of other aides. As new programs were sent to Congress, those participating in their development explained them to press representatives. Contrariwise, the press importuned staff for information. Several members of the White House staff, including Bundy, Cater, Califano, and McPherson, had frequent contacts with segments of the media.

In 1966 Johnson apparently contemplated improved media relations as a reason for the appointment of Kintner, who had been a Washington columnist and president of ABC and NBC. Kintner promptly reported to Moyers, then press secretary, his resolve that media representatives speak to him "as freely as they do now" and that he speak the truth to them even if it were unpleasant for the president.[49] He provided more information to weekly news journals,[50] broadened contacts to more newspapers,[51] and coordinated Cabinet officers' campaign speeches.[52] He had numerous talks with leaders in communications, held meetings with a small circle of aides engaged frequently with the press, and sent suggestions to the president on press contacts.[53]

As Johnson's relations with the press deteriorated he took several measures that increasingly drew him into detailed oversight of staff-media contacts. For example, he reported to Cater his dissatisfaction "with the amount of commentary on substance of his messages to Congress, particularly by the columnists, the newsmagazines, and the editorial writers" and asked that he hold a meeting of certain staff aides to develop "themes and talking points" to use with the editorial press and "to divide up the columnists, editorial writers and others to be contacted."[54] This amazing expectation of journalistic cooperation with presidential desire was to be accomplished by a plan to be reported immediately in his night reading. Similarly, the president directed the staff to get the departments to report weekly on newsworthy events and to become more active in the release of favorable news stories.

Although the president aggressively involved the staff in efforts to obtain favorable coverage, he remained distrustful of the press, nervous about leaks, and wary of staff interviews with reporters. *"Measure each word"* was his advice to an aide who consented to an interview with Hugh Sidey.[55] "No, I don't trust him or the Times," was the comment written to another aide who requested an interview with a Los Angeles *Times* correspondent.[56]

During 1965, the president began to issue directives to the staff to report press contacts. This lack of trust of staff performance and the desire to be omniscient culminated in the issuance of a memorandum to White House assistants on 20 June 1966. It stated in unusually dogmatic language:

> From now on, the president wants a daily list, submitted to him by about 5 PM of all press people whom you have seen or talked to during the course of the day. This list is to be submitted to Bill Moyers. If you have no contact with the press during the day, he wants a negative answer. In either case, unless he receives a response from each Special Assistant on a day-to-day basis, he refuses to accept the night reading.[57]

The next day a secretary in the president's office directed the special assistants' secretaries that these reports should be with the president "by 5:30 each evening, red tag" for the president's night reading.[58]

This extraordinary procedure illustrated not only the president's detailed involvement in staff-media relations, but also his desire to route all contact with the media through the press secretary. In no other area of the White House was there so determined an effort to tie other operations to a single staff center. Christian summarized the president's underlying purpose: "He did not like for a fellow who wasn't the press secretary to be saying much to the press—saying anything to the press for that matter—unless the press secretary asked him to do it or unless he asked him to do it."[59]

Evidence is abundant that staff members scrupulously tried to report all press contacts but that the restrictive efforts put strains on staff members who sought both to perform their specific tasks and to present the president's interests as they could. Cater reported to the president on 19 June 1965 on contacts during the past week with ten reporters, including James Reston, Charles Roberts, Eric Sevareid, Rowland Evans, and Philip Geyelin. The contacts ranged over many subjects and apparently most or all of them were initiated by the reporters.[60] But four months later another report to the president reveals the problem, if not irritation, created by the president's instructions:

> My policy in dealing with reporters has been as follows: When called upon by them, to treat them courteously but tell them nothing (pursuant to your instructions). Those known to be treacherous, I give a swift brush-off. Many of my former colleagues I avoid altogether. Those whom I consider reliable, I have provided a minimal amount of background on subjects I judged to be within your guidelines.[61]

He added that "if at any time you have reason to doubt either my credibility or my judgment, I would like to make my departure as swift and silent as possible."

McPherson, with his own activist temperament, would bring whatever ideas or warning he could to the press secretary but would be candid to the reporters when they came to him.[62] He informed the president that he had not talked to a member of the press for six months and that he had a number of unreturned calls on his desk. He added:

> I do not relish talking with the press. They are birds of prey and apt to make use of whatever casual scraps are dropped their way. I don't think I am particularly naive, but I have on several occasions in the last ten years let my guard down to my later regret, and it is likely to happen again.[63]

While both Cater and McPherson carefully followed Johnson's directive, they also communicated their belief that the attempt to restrict staff contact with the press was counterproductive. Cater predicted that such a policy will "contribute to making the press stories about you and your Administration a great deal more snide."[64] Similarly, McPherson reported to the president his belief that abstention from contact with the press only heightened reporters' frustration and hostility toward the administration and that a less restrictive policy would actually lead to more favorable coverage. "I have operated on the theory that it was better to carry on a fairly credible dialogue with them than to cut them out."[65]

Despite these warnings, Johnson maintained the practice until the end of his administration. The strains such tight staff supervision involved were revealed in an extraordinarily futile display of pique one month before Johnson left office. He wrote to Califano,

> Joe—may I *again—again* ask you and *all* your *associates* to please meet with press members during your association with my administration upon request of Press Secretary Christian only. This request has been made before and will not be made again.[66]

The press office was one of the more distinctive and highly organized White House operations. It was systematically linked to departments, agencies, and the core activities of the top presidential assistants. Johnson recognized the need for a press secretary who was tied to him personally and who had complete access to all aspects of presidential conduct. Yet conflicts between him and his press secretaries led to more turnover at the top than was typical of other White House operations and to some extent impaired relations with the media. Moreover, his close supervision of staff-media contacts involved the president in detail, created tension between him and his staff, and further aggravated White House–media relations.

Representation to Other Groups

This section surveys a category of miscellaneous components that did not reflect any White House structure or any particular group of White House advisers. Representation of presidential interests to groups not discussed above encompassed work done by all or most aides. While some of this representational activity was definitely assigned, much of it arose from the discharge of substantive responsibilities. In other instances, personal interests, associations, and special capabilities of staff members were involved in advancing presidential interests to groups outside of the White House.

Governors and Mayors

For political representation to the nation's governors and mayors President Johnson relied upon the vice president and executive officers as well as White House aides. In 1966 the president designated Farris Bryant, former governor of Florida and director of the Office of Emergency Planning (OEP), as his "personal ambassador to the governors." This assignment grew out of the director's extensive contacts with state and local officials in the administration of OEP's responsibilities. For example, in 1967 Bryant held conferences with governors and their staffs in forty states. Some 285 Washington officials who represented twenty-five departments and agencies, 300 other federal officials, and nearly 1,900 state officials were involved in these conferences. When Bryant resigned and was succeeded by Price Daniel, ex-governor of Texas, the president continued the practice of designating the director of OEP as his representative to state officials.

In March 1965 Johnson had designated Vice President Humphrey as his liaison with the cities. Two executive offices, the Office of Economic Opportunity (OEO) and the Bureau of the Budget (BOB), also gave particular attention to city relations. OEO officials worked closely with mayors who frequently protested the administration of its programs, while BOB was involved with difficulties in intergovernmental administration of numerous grant programs.

Within the White House, as problems arose for cities from administration of various programs and as riots occurred in urban centers, several White House aides were involved in liaison with the cities, both for policy and representational purposes. From his accession to November 1966 the president had the help of David L. Lawrence, who had been mayor of Pittsburgh and governor of Pennsylvania. He also instructed Clifford L. Alexander, Jr., a black who had extensive experience in the administration of community programs, to serve as White House liaison with city officials.

Party

When Johnson became president he relied on Jenkins as liaison with the Democratic party. While Jenkins was at the White House Johnson's presidential drive dominated not only party affairs but much of the staff's work. During the 1964 presidential campaign the staff was fully mobilized to write campaign speeches, make advance arrangements for presidential appearances, plot strategy, arrange for advertising, and perform all of the other activity usually associated with election year politics. Johnson and his staff, rather than the national party structure, were the center of activity. Valenti recalled that "There really was not any single manager of the campaign, unless it would be President Johnson himself. . . . The Democratic National Committee played practically no role at all in the campaign."[67]

After the election Watson assumed responsibility as White House liaison with the Democratic National Committee (DNC) and began participating in important top-level party decisions. He met regularly with John Bailey, the national party chair, Arthur Krim, the chair of the finance committee, and Clifton C. Carter, executive director and long-time friend of Johnson whom he sent to the DNC "to represent his interests over there."[68] With these and other top party officials Watson helped to plan the agenda for party meetings and membership, fund raising, and voter registration drives. He kept a steady flow of memos to Johnson on the details of party activities.[69] Weekly "Activity Reports" that he sent the president included information on party officials' speeches, reports of meetings between party leaders and administration officials, and efforts to strengthen the party with key voting blocks.[70]

Watson was the president's deputy with respect to party affairs and saw that his directives were enforced. For example, following the election of 1964, Johnson directed Bailey to "reduce to a realistic monthly average" the national committee's expenditures.[71] Later he wrote, "I want you to submit a plan that will completely eliminate the Democratic National Committee debt by September, 1965 and a plan to further raise adequate funds to finance the Committee for the balance of the calendar year."[72] Watson saw that such directives were implemented with the same spirit of ruthless efficiency that characterized his White House administrative responsibilities.

As the 1966 congressional campaign approached, White House officials' contacts with the committee quickened. Preparation for the campaign began in May, when Moyers organized a meeting of top party officials, Jake Jacobsen, Cater, Milton P. Semer, Kintner, and McPherson to discuss strategy. "I particularly stressed the need for coordinating the efforts of administration spokesmen. We are setting up procedures to do this," Moyers reported to the president.[73] The aide wrote the president that Semer and Kintner were working together toward "careful coordination of cabinet speakers." Moreover, the group had agreed on the "need to provide candidates with good material on Vietnam. In this connection, I have asked Farris Bryant to stimulate requests from Democratic Governors for State Department briefing teams that you offered them at their recent meeting here."[74] As the election drew near Watson asked the president for additional help. "Between now and the middle of November," he wrote Johnson in September, "I suggest that Larry O'Brien be requested to take the assignment of coordinating political activities of the Democratic National Committee."[75] The president gave his consent to Watson's request.

While the White House worked in harmony with the DNC, Johnson was careful not to have his presidential assistants assume official responsibilities. An unsigned memo to the president suggested that the DNC "should be headed by someone who has the complete confidence of the President . . . Accordingly, it is recommended that one of the top assistants—Marvin Watson, Jack Valenti, Jake Jacobsen or Joe Califano, to mention several possibilities—be named Chairman . . . on either a part time or full time basis."[76] Johnson did not accept the advice and retained Bailey. He was especially concerned that no assistant in the White House become involved in party fund raising. Watson wrote the president that he, Bailey, Krim, and Carter had met and decided that Carter should be named treasurer. The president replied emphatically, "I don't want Cliff or any Texan to be connected with treasurer."[77]

Other Groups

To maintain and garner support from groups for his administration and policies, Johnson used his own wide personal acquaintances. He was in personal contact frequently with Henry Ford II and other business friends, with George Meany and other labor leaders, with the outstanding leaders in the black community, with Washington lawyers such as Abe Fortas, Clark M. Clifford, James Rowe, and others who had wide connections, and with numerous other persons and groups. As in congressional relations, Johnson's personal activism led to his direct intervention when he thought it critical for the result he desired.

A few groups were represented directly in the White House structure. In September 1964 Congress created the National Council on the Arts, with a chairman to be appointed by the president with advice and consent of the Senate. President Johnson appointed Roger L. Stevens to the chairmanship and also made him a special assistant to the president. Stevens' contacts with the president normally went through Cater, and he served in this position only until Congress created the National Foundation for the Arts and Humanities in 1965.

In December 1964 Johnson appointed Esther Peterson as special assistant for consumer affairs, a position held by her or her successor, Betty Furness, until the end of the Johnson administration.

With the departure of historian Arthur M. Schlesinger, Jr., from the White House in the spring of 1964, Johnson brought into the White House Eric Goldman, professor of history at Princeton University, to serve as liaison with the academic community. When Goldman left, Roche, professor of political science at Brandeis University, was brought in, and while many considered him Goldman's successor, Roche became speechwriter and adviser to the president and did not regard building relationships with the academic community an important responsibility. The position of Donald F. Hornig, special assistant for science and technology, gave to the science community special access and representation to the president. Also, the appointment for the first time by a president of two women—Peterson and Furness—and the appointment of two blacks—Hobart Taylor, Jr., and Clifford Alexander, Jr.—to positions in the White House perhaps gave added assurance that the particular interests or views of these two groups would not be overlooked, at least in some deliberations. The same was true of other groups, including Jews and Italians, who were represented by chance in the White House.

An effort to win support from and consideration of the views of special groups by presence of their members in the White House could change the nature of some aspects of presidential policy making. Johnson's primary consideration in White House appointments was loyalty to him, which excluded representation of special groups. Personal biases, even of those choosing the anonymity of White House aides, are of course inevitable; but to make the White House representative of groups, and policy making within it a mediation of group interests represented there, would rob the president and the nation of concentration of advice in terms of the problem to be solved.

There may have been some compromise in the positions of some of these advisers in the Johnson presidency. Yet clearly at that time loyalty to the president was not materially impaired by representation of other interests.

Moreover, the various economic interests were not directly represented at the apex of our political structure. Indeed, in the White House staff there were few who had had any substantial experience in business, labor, or agriculture. The winning of support from these groups was a task of White House members who stood substantially independent of them, aided by departments and agencies which had affinity to them.

This political activity generally accompanied the exercise of the policy and administrative roles assigned to White House aides.

Largely it was ad hoc and often supplemented departmental activity. Yet it was an essential part of service to a president who wanted assurance that policies would prevail before he adopted them. Aides might help the president establish foundations for general understanding and support, as when Lee C. White arranged promptly on Johnson's accession for contacts with leaders in the black community. They might have a continuous relationship with particular groups, as Hornig did with scientists and Cater came to have with educational leaders. But generally the contacts were related to specific decisions to be made. We have noted the pressure on industry leaders from Califano's aides for compliance with wage-price guidelines. A good example of Califano's regular search for assurance of interest group support or acceptance or at least lack of antagonism for contemplated legislative proposals is illustrated by his contacts with the various components of the transportation industry before the administration's recommendation for a department of transportation was sent to Congress or unveiled to the press.[78]

Conclusion

This chapter has set forth the important role of White House aides in the politics of the presidency. Quantitatively, about one-third of the sixty to sixty-five aides for substantive functions that we have established were present at a given time were assigned specifically to the type of functions discussed in this chapter. Beyond this, other aides participated in the functions to an extent that it can be concluded that the largest role of the White House aides, extending probably to more than one-half of their working time, was representational.

Centralization in proximate aides of assistance to the president for his correspondence and speechwriting and for his media relations is apparently necessary for his effective representation to the public. The centralization of assistance to him in legislative liaison to the extent it existed was a natural accompaniment to Johnson's interest in legislative goals and his centralization of legislative planning. The lack of differentiation between official and partisan roles contributed to the overload on White House aides and raises issues on the scope of their political participation. On the other hand, the general avoidance of representation of groups in the White House restricted the size and complexity of White House operations and preserved qualities of loyalty to the president and independence from group viewpoint.

For assistance in representation of his policies to Congress and the public the president requires proximate aides, intimately knowledgeable of his purposes and loyal to him officially and personally. Though these properties of personal aid may be impaired if the staff becomes too large or representational of outside interests, an adequate representational staff is essential for the president and endemic to the process of democratic government.

9. Conclusion

This conclusion does two things. First, it summarizes selectively the historical record in the foregoing pages. Second, it addresses the issues about the scope and methods of White House operations because these are illuminated in the history of the Johnson presidency.

The Historical Record Reviewed

The historical record substantiates the following statements of fact or interpretation.

Transition

Johnson's decision on his accession to emphasize continuity with the previous presidency led to a dual White House staff composed of John F. Kennedy carryovers and Johnson appointees that operated during a little over two years. The dual White House was partially a two-tiered operation but was at least equally characterized by parallelism between the roles of the two groups.

Whether initiation of a Johnson White House immediately would have served President Johnson better is conjectural. The experience in the Johnson presidency demonstrates that some strains are likely, perhaps inevitable, in dual staffing occasioned by a new president's decision to retain his predecessor's staff, but that with continuity in party and purpose and with presidential direction to assure mutual respect, a dual staff can serve the interests of a new president.

Continuity in White House staff was interrupted in the middle of Johnson's presidency by the resignations of many Kennedy and Johnson assistants. Thereafter a Johnson White House staff, with some Kennedy carryovers, came into being. Continuity and stability in White House staffing and operations marked both earlier and later periods in the Johnson presidency. Despite the heavy work demands under President Johnson, many White House assistants served either him alone or President Kennedy and him successively for long periods of time.

Profile of the White House

By the time Lyndon Johnson became president, the functions for which the president required help were extensive and diverse. Our analysis of White House operations at that time distinguishes types of White House functions: service, managerial and legal, representational, and core presidential functions of legislative and executive policy and action extending into almost every facet of American government. Although a large service component had evolved, its elements were institutionalized and managed in ways that freed the president from its potential burden or uncertainties. Also, staff performance of management and legal services protected the president and enabled him to direct his attention to more substantive matters. Representing the president to various external constituencies probably absorbed more staff time and energy than other substantive tasks. These service, management, and representational activities supported the core presidential functions of legislative and executive policy and action.

White House assistants engaged in essential and highly distinctive activities. Although they frequently offered advice to the president, their most crucial function was to pull together information for the president's use, selecting memos that merited presidential attention, organizing and focusing their content, and defining possibilities and perhaps alternatives of decision. Other important staff activities included mediating differences and winning support for presidential policy. They also communicated the president's wishes to others and facilitated the implementation of his decisions. Alertness to presidential interests, readiness to move into action, and flexibility in responding to situations were distinctive features of staff service.

For the substantive functions that were performed, both representational and core, the Johnson White House was lean in size and heavily worked. For the presidential purposes inherited from his predecessor or initiated under Johnson's leadership, the staff was minimal and perhaps less than was desirable.

While no single White House type emerged in the Johnson presidency, the profile of the group as a whole reveals high academic credentials, dominance of legal and public relations/journalistic background, experience in government and particularly national government, little experience in private industry, youth, and strong Ivy League representation in educational background for both Kennedy carryovers and Johnson appointees. The carryovers included a heavy representation of the northeastern portion of the country; correspondingly, a higher proportion of the Johnson appointees came from Texas. Typically, White House staffers were generalists. Philosophical orientations ranged from populism to conservatism, but the dominant spirit was one of reform along the Kennedy-Johnson line. Some—and notably from different sections of the country and different educational backgrounds—were idea men, some were skilled in consensus building, and a few supplied the needed managerial talents.

On the whole, the presidential assistants represented no special constituencies. Recommendations for such representation were usually rejected. Nevertheless, direct representation was given to consumers through a White House assistant. Also, the affiliation of an arts assistant (for the period required by statute) and of the science and technology assistant with particular external groups was strong. Appointment of a few blacks and of women as consumer advisers was not assumed to be for the purpose of representing blacks or women's interests. A presidential effort to provide direct representation of groups in the White House could greatly increase the size of the White House, change the nature of White House decision making, and vitiate the dependence of the president on undivided loyalty of White House aides. But in the Johnson presidency the pressures for representation of interests inside the White House had not mounted to a point where presidential reliance on advice biased only toward his interpretation of the public interest was threatened.

Structure and Personalities

More order and structure characterized the Johnson White House than was apparent to outside observers. Although staff assistants were never able to chart White House structure and many crosscutting arrangements existed in White House operations, identifiable points of internal coordination and an awareness of individual roles contributed toward orderly operations. The organization and points of integration were more clearly defined when the transition to a Johnson-appointed staff occurred. In the later operations of the Johnson White House the points of coordination were an administrative chief of staff (W. Marvin Watson, Jr.), a national security assistant (Walt W. Rostow), a domestic affairs assistant (Joseph A. Califano, Jr.), a speechwriting coordinator (Harry C. McPherson, Jr.), a press aide (George E. Christian), a congressional liaison coordinator (H. Barefoot Sanders, Jr.), and an adviser on appointments to executive positions (John W. Macy, Jr.). Specializations in science and technology, health and welfare, and other policy areas paralleled these key integrative points. Personnel assignments responded in considerable measure to natural distinctions in functions or alternatively toward area specializations. These two elements of structural unity overlapped. They were, moreover, overlaid with individual role specializations developed by the initiative of staff members or assigned to them by the president. The result was a mixture of functional, area, and personal assignments that was compatible with the president's administrative style and decision methods.

White House operations were highly personalized. Johnson's drive for accomplishment, engrossment in virtually all policy and many operational matters, wide and continuous search for information, and work habits that constantly created new activations and crisscrossed normal boundaries among the staff produced a highly individualized staff operation. The personalization did not create chaotic or disorganized operations or seem to prevent Johnson from making his decisions as these were required. These consequences were averted by Johnson's knowledge of public policy and governmental operations, his full dedication of his time and energy to the presidency, his dominance of his staff, the small number and continuity of staff, the structural integrations, and the coherence of purpose within the policy staff and between it and the president.

Developing the Legislative Program

In Johnson's presidency responsibility for putting together the president's legislative program and obtaining consensus for it from relevant Cabinet officials was centralized in the White House. Nevertheless, Johnson depended upon the collaboration of executive offices and departmental executives, particularly upon the latter, as frontline troops in gaining congressional consent.

The sheer size of the legislative programming expanded the workload of the White House staff and to a large degree determined the atmosphere and conditions of work. The White House was a center of feverish activity in which ideas for legislation were assembled, numerous programs of immense scope and impact on the welfare of the nation were placed on the agenda, details were worked out and agreements sought or compromises made, and decisions made in rapid succession by the president. Deliberation and contemplation on the effects of proposals were limited by the pace of recommendations. The philosophy and directions of change were firm in the president's mind, as well as the desire to make the most progress possible in those directions within the time of his presidency. The White House ran a catchup affair to put on the statute books the ideas being generated in academic and other centers. The time was for decision; the thought behind decision lay largely outside the White House and had to be transformed into actionable measures within it. By centralizing program development in the White House Johnson gained initiative, momentum, and quick action, but with consequent limitations on deliberation and consultation. The White House with its small staff could not be a center for thorough analysis of alternatives and results or for unpressured deliberation. Long-run problems in administrative implementation sometimes received scant attention.

Coordinating the Subpresidency

For areas of presidential activity other than legislative programming the methods of coordinating the contributions of a triadic subpresidency composed of White House assistants, executive office units, and departments and agencies conformed to no consistent pattern, either structurally or behaviorally. This was apparent in the uses of White House and executive office units. For science and technology the White House assistant and the director of an executive office were the same person. Similarly, for national security, the White House assistant was de facto, but not formal, director of the executive office staff. By contrast, on economic policy and the budget, the organization and management of executive office units were structurally separate from the White House. On economic policy the executive office came to have a counterpart in the White House, but no such counterpart developed for budget policy and execution. In each of these areas the relationships of president and White House aides, executive office units, and agencies were responsive to circumstances peculiar to it: the powerful concentration in State and Defense in national security matters; the diffusion of science and technology jurisdictions through the executive branch and the organized participation of outside experts; the dispersion likewise of economic jurisdictions and the particular necessity of Treasury and Federal Reserve Board participation; and the centralization of budgeting in a single agency.

Yet in all cases the distinction between personal and institutional staff aid tended to disappear. Differences were there. In science and technology the special assistant was heavily involved in his institutional directorship and was not as fully involved in personal consultation with the president as the national security assistant. The

White House assistant coordinated economic policy advice and to some extent science and technology advice for the president in a way that no one in the White House did for budgetary policy. Yet the chairman of the Council of Economic Advisers and the director of the Bureau of the Budget shared the purposes of the president and had his trust to an extent that enabled them to perform service similar to that of a White House assistant. They were among the president's intimate advisers.

The use of departments and agencies in developing presidential policy was determined more by situational and personal factors than by plan. Closer working relations developed with departments whose activities related to devising and implementing Great Society adventures than with some other departments. In general the president had an open door policy and favored multiple channels of communication to him personally. In national security matters he used a council of executive chiefs (the Tuesday Lunch) and numerous ad hoc committees, but also relied upon staff and close personal contact with individual executives and personal advisers. In some areas where the dispersion of functions in the executive structure was great, as in economic affairs and science and technology, no conciliar structure similar to the Tuesday Lunch developed, but the president relied on White House staff, executive offices, and interagency consultative arrangements. In economic affairs he relied heavily both on executive offices and a White House aide operating selectively. In science and technology, though the structure provided for unification of advice through a single person, he relied more on ad hoc arrangements for coordination of agency information and counsel. In crises, decision making tended to be ad hoc.

Directing the Executive Branch

White House assistance to the president in directing departments and agencies reflected the diversity of such activities. The structure of presidential assistance was different for three basic resources for presidential influence: for executive appointments a unit of organization was created within the White House, for administrative reorganization a two-tiered operation of Bureau of the Budget (BOB) and White House assistance existed after mid 1965, and for budgeting and managerial guidance and control the BOB continued its traditional activities. On the uses of presidential influence on policy and its application, guidance to the staff was two-pronged: on the one hand, the president imposed or accepted certain constraints on his own involvement; on the other, the staff was expected to maintain general surveillance and alertness to matters of presidential interest and to be prepared for whatever type of assistance the president desired. Although the proximity of staff members to the president gave them opportunities for influence that sometimes annoyed Cabinet officials, the president's grip on the reins and his relationships and direct contacts with Cabinet members circumscribed the aides' participation.

The Representational Function

A large amount of staff time and energy was devoted to representing the president before various constituencies. Congressional liaison and media contact were clearly defined operations, each headed by a single top White House assistant who had the support of at least one other top aide as well as the support of second-level aides who were exclusively involved with the more regularized and routine features of these activities. Speechwriting was initially more dispersed, but by the end of the Johnson administration it was systematized under unified staff direction. No similarly unified operation existed within the White House for representing the president's program to local and state governments or outside organizations.

The representational activities of White House staff inevitably included active participation and leadership roles in the campaign of 1964. While party positions were left to others, White House aides planned and coordinated the president's campaign schedules, wrote the president's speeches, and substantially directed the campaign.

The processes of policy making are so intertwined that all of the top assistants participated in representational activity. Presidential involvement and staff awareness of others' activities served to coordinate representational functions with policy.

That the representational staff has received slight attention or recognition from presidential scholars is surprising, not only because such a large number of assistants is involved partially or exclusively in this activity, but because effective performance on their part is critical to successful presidential governance. They are an important element in the shifting balance of power between the president on the one hand and Congress, the press, political parties, and interest groups on the other. During the Johnson administration these staffs performed with varying degrees of effectiveness. Partly because of presidential experience, skill, and attention, the Johnson congressional liaison staff performed very effectively, at least on most domestic policy issues. His media staff, on the other hand, was beset with frequent turnover, conflict between Johnson and two of his press secretaries, and overinvolvement of the president in detail. These difficulties clearly contributed to Johnson's steadily deteriorating relations with the media. In short, differences in the effectiveness of the various representational staffs had important consequences for Johnson's relations with key external groups.

Quality of Service

President Johnson accepted the Brownlow Committee's doctrine of anonymity for White House aides and the correlative guide of secrecy for White House deliberations. He wanted no threat to his programs by premature publicity or revelations of policy differences within his administration and stringently protected his own advantages in official position and personal responsibility. He expected complete dedication and willingness to work overtime as needed. Beyond these things, he demanded loyalty to himself and his policies, which in the later days included acceptance of his Vietnam policy. He required total commitment. He achieved these things and was saved from some problems, such as staff dissension before the public and aggrandizement of staff, that gave trouble in later administrations.

While the prestige of the presidency, Johnson's dominant personality, and his demand for loyalty on the Vietnam issue undoubtedly inhibited frankness among some associates and impeded reexamination of policy within the government, the president encountered candor, openness, and even confrontation by some staff members. The staff in general believed strongly in his policies and hence had his confidence. Johnson's assistants suggested that deficiencies in White House aid were attributable to possible inaccuracies in analysis, bias in personal viewpoint, or work pressures that prevented deliberation.

Judged by the standards of education and government experience, the Johnson White House, including both carryovers from the Kennedy administration and new appointees, was capable of efficient presidential service. As for substantive consequences, there were obviously some successes and some failures. Notably successful was service in legislative liaison; by contrast, Johnson experienced difficulty in obtaining fully satisfactory service in press relationships until roughly the last half of his administration. The ultimate tests of White House service are varied, including among other things the supply of adequate information, clarification and accurate weighing of alternatives for policy, and service to presidential objectives, but with warnings of hazards to be avoided. The overall performance of staff aides, measured by such tests, is usually not clearly distinguishable from the president's own exercise of his responsibility and the contributions of other persons and institutions in policy deliberations.

The Future of the White House

We began this book with the concept of the subpresidency, meaning that the presidency includes at a given time, in addition to a person, all those who help him in the discharge of his responsibilities. We noted the existence within the subpresidency of an inner circle of White House aides and central themes in contemporary concerns about the role of the White House staff in the subpresidency and presidential strategies in its use: declining reliance on the Cabinet, inadequate development of the institutional structure of the executive office, interposition of White House assistants between the president and the executive departments and agencies, the abuse of power in the White House, and excessive size and centralization within the White House.

The Johnson presidency was intermediary between the emergence of the contemporary presidential staff system under Franklin D. Roosevelt and the later extension of that system during the 1970s. The expansion of the White House, as of the executive office and the departmental and agency structure, had followed the New Deal and World War II. Specific White House functions evolved prior to Johnson, including the coordination of program planning by Roosevelt and Truman, of legislative liaison by Eisenhower, of national security advice by Eisenhower and Kennedy, of science advice by Eisenhower and Kennedy, and of assistance to the president in his political functions by all of these.

Johnson added no new White House functions, but enlarged roles and activities and problems of management were evident. One was the volume and centralization of legislative programming and attendant activities in the White House. Another was lack of an explicit strategy for managing White House affairs. Of smaller significance were some instances of White House penetration into administrative operations, notably in administration of wage-price guidelines.

Increased concern about White House operations has been expressed as subsequent manifestations of these appeared. The Richard M. Nixon administration brought an enormous increase in White House staff size, a concentration of power in White House aides, lack of presidential control over staff aides, and misconduct of these, in which the president himself became involved. President

Gerald R. Ford's problems in command of his staff have been detailed,[1] and President Jimmy Carter's White House was characterized by continuation of large staffing and expansion of representation of interests. The Ronald Reagan administration has generated comment on the lack of cohesion and effectiveness of White House coordination. All of these developments have contributed to apprehensions about the role of the White House and methods of presidential management and emphasize the relevance of experience in the Johnson presidency.

The Role of the White House

In chapter 1 we sampled some literature from distinguished sources that expressed concern about the lofty and powerful—and potentially effective or ineffective, beneficent or dangerous—American presidency. The anxiety in this literature is over the capabilities and proprieties of a total presidency, including the role of White House assistance to the president.

The official advisory system of the presidency will include the chief officers of the executive departments and agencies, institutionalized executive offices, and more personalized White House staff aid. The roots of the concerns are centralization and personalization of presidential assistance. This results in proposals for institutional change in the balances among elements of the subpresidency.

To correct perceived imbalances in the advisory system, one suggestion calls for strengthening the position of the Cabinet. Stephen Hess of the Brookings Institution has concluded that "the centralization of responsibilities in the person of the President has lessened his ability to perform the duties of the office" and advocates "a more collegial government" in which "the Cabinet must become the focal point of the White House machinery." The recommendation is based on the premises that the Cabinet would be constituted "to reflect the president's need for advice" and that its size would be "strictly limited." Its effectiveness would be dependent upon certain practices and structural arrangements. A first requirement would be to increase "the frequency and the regularity of cabinet meetings." There would need to be a "skillful cabinet secretariat" whose director "should be the highest ranking member of the White House staff" but who "should not be in the business of advising presidents." In addition, "most White House advisory systems should be subgroups of the cabinet." For example, the National Security Council would become a Cabinet subcommittee.[2]

The proposal aims toward a radical transformation of the presidential system and is not likely to be adopted by any president. Hess admits that "There is little in American history to create a sense of optimism about the cabinet becoming a viable collective body that presidents can rely on as the prime supplier of advice."[3] Indeed, the proposal is contrary to the evolution of the executive branch. The Constitution opted for a single executive and gave the president "the executive power" and the important legislative powers of recommendation and veto. The popularization of the electoral process has further elevated and personalized the office. All recent presidents have used a staff system that was oriented to a single rather than a collegial executive.

The practical problems of grafting a collegial advisory system onto a personal presidency are many and likely to be frustrating or inhibiting to a president. Even if it could be assumed that a president would appoint executives with the sole objective of providing competent advice to him, the departmental executives would develop attachments to their own departments and supporting interests that could qualify the uncompromising loyalty expected often in presidential advice. Also, heavy burdens of leadership for the legal duties imposed on departments consume the time of departmental executives and limit their ability to be prepared for advice in areas foreign to their delegated responsibilities. A cabinet system with cabinet subcommittees and staffs would provide a less intimate system than the president would seek. Moreover, it could rob him of the flexibility provided in the present system where he can balance as he desires in variant situations the advantages of White House, executive office, and departmental help. Finally, a cabinet system of advice could fail to provide the help needed by the presidency for balancing intergovernmental policy advice with the political and personal considerations that a president responsible to or dealing with external constituencies would consider important.

Any president will place great value on the advice that can be given by Cabinet and other government executives selected by him. The nation will have more assurance of wisdom and probity in presidential decisions if the president consults regularly with officials whose stature, character, and qualifications have been tested in the gauntlet of public attention and Senate confirmation. Yet both the practical difficulties and the inherent constraints on a personal, democratically responsible president may be expected to lead presidents to rely on diverse sources of assistance, including White House aides.

As noted at the end of chapter 5, presidents since Johnson have initiated efforts to structure participation of Cabinet members in the development of presidential policy. President Ronald Reagan has moved in this direction through the use of Cabinet subcommittees. Yet White House staff and the Office of Management and Budget remain coordinators and independent sources of policy advice. Cabinet participation is strengthened, but the president is served and the personal presidency preserved by the continuing triadic subpresidency that arose with Roosevelt and his successors.

A second of the studies in our sample concentrates attention on the executive office. A prestigious panel under the auspices of the National Academy of Public Administration wanted to assure that a president would "inherit" from the executive office the help needed for a "more effective presidency." Their report particularly emphasized the need of a president for "a reliable base of non-partisan, unbiased advice. The institutional staffs reporting to the president should have a highly professional ability to supply objective and factual information." They "should not mirror special interests represented elsewhere." Operating responsibilities should be in executive departments, and the "immediate staff of the president should be small." Perhaps the central recommendation of the report was for three policy staffs within the executive office, each headed by "a senior White House assistant." There would be an international affairs staff, an economic affairs staff, and a domestic affairs staff. The essence of their recommendations was summarized as follows:

> In our recommendations we have proposed four Senior Assistants to the President: three to head the policy coordinating staffs and one to head the Secretariat. We have also optionally proposed a director for long-range policy studies. These assistants, plus the Director of the Office of Management and Budget, would be responsible for what we have called the core process of policy coordination, policy advice, information flow, and management. These senior aides would constitute an informal "management committee" for the Executive Office as a whole, meeting as frequently as necessary to ensure that communications and the division of labor are working effectively on behalf of the President. A chief of staff, if one were chosen by the President, would be the natural chairman of this committee.[4]

While the recommendations have basic consistency, some variations and flexibilities are present. The NSC staff would be replaced by the international affairs staff, but the CEA would be retained as one of the four instruments (with Treasury, Federal Reserve Board, and OMB) transmitting information to the economic affairs staff. The director of OMB would not be a White House assistant but would be a member of the "management committee." The panel does not take a position on whether there should be a chief of staff or reach a conclusion on the exact status of a possible new executive office unit for "long-range policy studies."

The support of the panel for strengthening the professional arm of the subpresidency conforms with trends since the creation of the executive office in 1939. Indeed, its purpose was consistent with that of the Johnson-appointed Heineman Commission, which recommended in 1968 two new units in executive office structure: an Office of Program Development in BOB "to provide year-round professional support to the president's personal staff in the vital task of constructing a domestic legislative program"; and an independent Office of Program Coordination to deal with problems of program administration, particularly those requiring cooperation among federal departments and with governors and mayors.[5]

The first of these recommendations would presumably have facilitated considerable decentralization of one function from White House to executive office; the second addressed a need demonstrated in administration of Great Society programs and would probably have led to some accompanying White House expansion. The differences in the specific recommendations in the two studies suggest difficulties in judgment on precise prescriptions for the executive office and indeed that these may reflect variances in perceived needs in different periods and therefore for adaptations over time.

The recommendation by the panel of linkage between professional and personal assistance for the president through designation of White House aides as directors of certain executive office staffs is consistent with the structural arrangements in the Johnson presidency for national security and science and technology and with actual behavior of BOB and CEA in service to the president in economic policy and budgeting. Since the panel made the recommendation without discussing the possibility of compromise of either or both types of assistance resulting from their linkage, our study should contribute to discussion on this issue and lends support to the panel's recommendation.

Yet the panel's report did not provide a full analysis of the needs for a presidency of the future. It focused on one of the three components of the official subpresidency. It did not address the role of departmental and agency executives in the subpresidency. More significant to the purpose of our study, it did not include analysis of the requirements of the president for White House assistance for his representational functions. It is desirable to have perspective not only on what can be done outside the White House but also on what the president may find desirable and necessary to do within it. In this respect, this study supplements the academy's report.

A study by another panel for the National Academy of Public Administration sought for institutional safeguards against the recurrence of abuses that occurred during the Nixon presidency. The tone and substance of the panel's report were censorious of past conduct, and numerous positive recommendations related to the presidential advisory system were made.

The panel affirmed "its belief in the wisdom and essentiality of a strong institutional presidency." A theme running through a major section of the report was "the essential difference between staff serving the President and staff serving the presidency." The staff serving the president personally should not be interposed, as in the Nixon administration, between the president and the departments of government. Also, the institutional quality of the service of the departments and the executive office should be protected. Two-hat arrangements, such as the recent statutory designation of the director of OMB as assistant to the president or appointment of Cabinet officers to other offices, should be avoided. "To increase the options now available to the president, he should be authorized by law to create a limited number of temporary offices of secretarial rank outside the Executive Office of the president to whom he could delegate ad hoc assignments, including coordination of programs involving a high degree of interdepartmental collaboration." The OMB should be restored to its pristine institutional and professional service, and executive office units should have no nonstaff functions. The "decline of the institutional agencies in the Executive Office" and the "proliferation of agencies within the Executive Office" were condemned.

The report sought also for means of depoliticizing the presidency. "As a political candidate, a president should look outside the White House and the government for legitimate campaign assistance." Also, "generally the president, his staff, the Executive Office, and the heads of executive agencies [should] refrain from participating in cases involving individuals or specific institutions. . . ." Further, there should be "complete professionalization and depoliticization" of the attorney general's office, with statute precluding the attorney general "from advising the president in his political or individual capacities" and the Justice Department removed "from the process whereby federal judges are promoted and selected."

The thrust of the various suggestions was confinement of the role of the White House staff. The report never discusses what is needed, in contrast to what should be excluded, in that role. Yet it confidently asserts with unusual drift into unexplained arithmetic that the White House "should be limited to not more than 15 top aides" and "50 supporting professional employees." Remarkably, this corresponds closely with our tabulation of the number of aides serving at any time in the Johnson White House.[6]

Many of the conclusions of the report would receive general approval. Keeping White House aides in a staff position, avoiding location of operating responsibilities in the executive office, and maintaining strong professionalized institutional assistance for the president are accepted ideas among commentators on the presidency. Keeping political influence out of action on individual cases is a sound general objective, though not attainable in all instances. But whether the attorney general or some other official should be the president's adviser on judicial appointments is an appropriate matter for presidential discretion. And the appropriate and unavoidable, as contrasted with the undesirable use of White House assistants in political campaigns, need recognition.

The goal of separating "staff serving the president and staff serving the presidency" is not achievable at the level of directorship of executive office agencies where obligation to serve presidential goals merges with assimilation of professional assistance. There is an obligation of service to the president in those appointed by him to institutional positions. Whatever position a president or Congress might take with respect to opposed perspectives reflected in the two Academy studies (one that certain executive offices be directed by White House assistants, the other that the law making the head of OMB a White House assistant be repealed), we believe that the behavior of top officials of the executive branch, both in departments and agencies of the executive offices, will reflect assistance both to the president and to the presidency. The distinction between serving the president and serving the presidency is certainly not an absolute one. While standards of legal, institutional, or personal ethics should limit loyalty and assistance to a president (or even under our system of divided powers to the president alone), service to the president's policy goals and to his political purposes will supplement and bias the direction of institutional service. Indeed, this personal service may provide necessary breadth of perspective in a government of divided institutional loyalties.

This discussion of three reports that emphasize the needs for assistance to the president (or presidency) external to the White House and the exposition in this book of roles within the White House during one presidency enable us to make general observations about elements of the presidential advisory system and the White House role within it that can be expected in the future.

1. The Constitution, popular election, and the history of the nation provide a presidential system, and it is not likely that the instruments of coordination and leadership developed for that system will be transferred to a cabinet system of any form.
2. The president will inherit an ongoing structure of departments and agencies, an executive office, and interdepartmental arrangements and will require their help. Their organization may be imperfect and their services limited for presidential purposes, but the bureaucracies within them and the presidentially appointed leadership at their summits will provide the basic resources of intelligence and advice within the subpresidency.
3. A large continuing role for a sizable White House operation, at least as large as that in the Johnson presidency, is indicated by various compulsions operating on the presidency.
   a. The chief among these is the political character of the office. A large service bureaucracy is required to handle the people's communication to the president and to support his continuous effort to reach the people. More significant is the president's need for top-level assistance in representing and winning support for his policies in the several forums in which such support is needed. While limitations on campaign activity of White House assistants may be developed in the future, and while departments and executive offices will assist in representing the president, it may be expected that there will be integration and coordination of representational functions in the White House. In a democracy more than any other system of governance and in a government of "separated institutions sharing powers," policy decisions must ultimately be based on the political consideration of what others will support. The president will find this a part of the compulsions for White House staff assistance.
   b. A second compulsion is the crosscutting nature of decisions at the presidential level and the necessity for a staff with a government-wide perspective. Increasingly, policy consideration must stretch across the jurisdictional boundaries set by the historical evolution of government structure; yet the competence, indeed the interest, of each of the agency or executive office structures is materially restricted to a portion of the total presidential policy realm. Whatever structure

exists in departments and agencies and the executive office, the input of more than one of these, indeed several, is likely to be needed. In some instances, a single agency or executive office may be able to exert a chairmanship, priority, or leadership influence that integrates the various inputs and resolves differences. Yet a White House staff may often, and quite regularly, be the convenient, even necessary, and effective instrument to ferret out information from diverse places, to search for and construct elements of consensus, and to supply information for the president. It may also be needed to ensure that decisions and directives of the president are implemented.

c. A further compulsion lies in the specific qualities of the aid that may be given by White House assistants. The Johnson presidency reveals the distinctive qualities of their service: availability, flexibility, comprehensiveness, loyalty, and intimacy. They are available to him for everything from errand service to counsel and for time and energy beyond normalcy in employment. They can be assigned duties as circumstances require and capability exists. Their perspectives and activities reach across institutional boundaries. Their loyalty is uncompromised generally by institutional allegiances or associations. Their proximity, continuous service, and loyalty assure access to the president and perception of the nuances of his purpose and will.

d. Finally, presidents may be influenced to expand White House help at least temporarily and intermittently because of special objectives or special problems. This is strongly illustrated by Johnson's use of White House staff to build his annual legislative program. In other presidencies particular presidential objectives and responsibilities will undoubtedly affect size of White House staff.

We conclude that numerous proposals to reform the presidency are incomplete because they are not based upon a full, realistic approach to what White House aides actually do or an adequate consideration of the political character of the modern presidency. Our detailed examination of the Johnson White House staff and how it related to other elements of the subpresidency provides a useful empirical foundation for future recommendations. We have found that a responsive White House staff intimately in contact with the president's policy preferences and closely identified with his political fortunes played an important part in bringing leadership and cohesion to a fragmented governmental system. We conclude that effective executive leadership is dependent upon the balanced use of various elements of the subpresidency.

There are hazards in the position and service of White House assistants: aggrandizement of their position, lack of loyalty to service ideals consistent with American traditions, diversion into institutional direction, attachment to particular interests, lack of competence or of time for thoughtful analysis of issues.

Yet the genius of the American constitutional system is its balances against excesses. It also places power in the president and must depend heavily on his judgment in balancing parts of his advisory system. Although excessive growth of White House staff can complicate his task of management, he will need to provide for orderly direction and supervision of a staff adequate for very extensive and diversified functions.

Strategies for White House Operation

The models for White House operation discussed in our introduction must be regarded as ideal types. We are confident that no future presidential management system for the White House will ever conform exactly with the ascribed Roosevelt or Eisenhower models and that no system will be exclusively ad hoc, centralized, or decentralized. To extrapolate future possibilities from experience under President Johnson, comments follow on structure, decision process, and personalization.

There was no evidence of deliberate planning of White House structure generally or of consideration of standard guidelines for organization planning during Johnson's presidency. Structure evolved with consideration of White House functions, but also by personal development of capabilities. The structure was relatively flat and allowed personal access to the president to many staff aides.

It is doubtful whether future presidents will earnestly try or, if trying, succeed in establishing a chief of staff for the diverse types of aid—foreign and domestic, managerial and policy and representational—that a president needs from his White House staff. Yet future presidents will probably seek more order and hierarchy in White House arrangements than prevailed under Johnson. Those arrangements contributed to flexibility, fostered multiple access and assistance to the president and preservation of his choices, and may have contributed to staff effort and enthusiasm. On the other hand, they probably contributed to internal confusions and tensions, depended for effectiveness and avoidance of outside exploitation of differences on cohesiveness in purpose, and placed a heavy burden of oversight and control directly on the president.

It is not likely that any president will avoid through his term both functional and policy area specializations or avoid some personal specializations. They are likely to see different needs and ways of aggregating duties. As in the Johnson presidency, science and technology, the arts, legislative programming, civil rights, and health and education had structural identification, so in the future, presidential priorities, congressional legislation, or special needs may dictate elaboration of structure. Possibilities that readily come to mind for special presidential attention are intergovernmental relations, party liaison, or unique policy areas that rank high in a president's priorities. While presidents will be well advised to attempt meeting special needs through established structures, some and perhaps all will have particular reasons for improvising White House structure.

Johnson had no consistent pattern of decision strategy. He did not regularly chair staff meetings for use as decision forums. His occasional efforts, as through Robert E. Kintner's service, to use staff meetings for operational coordination had little effect. He more generally allowed or encouraged regular staff meetings for specific types of staff activity. More broadly, he made no general choices among decision-making strategies, and indeed almost certainly never analyzed the characteristics and merits of different strategies. His decision processes exhibited a mixture of the models described by Roger B. Porter in chapter 1: adhocracy, centralization, multiple advocacy (decentralization). Decision strategy by Johnson's time was affected by the development that supplied the president with the triadic subpresidency. Gaps in and lack of unification of structure and policy issues crisscrossing its parts sometimes require adhocracy in decision making. The president's orientation to issues, rather than structure or process, and his habit of reaching impromptu for information also fostered adhocracy. In general, however, his decision-making process incorporated related institutional elements but with variations in their combination.

His system was centralized in that he did not delegate or allow presidential decisions to pass to others, but decentralized in the access of multiple advisers. He did not centralize his advisory system either by a chief of staff or excessive reliance on filtering of information and counsel through White House staff. Yet he did not create a system of multiple advocacy in which the viewpoints of elements of the subpresidency were conveyed to him by White House staff acting only as honest brokers. The White House assistants had a more positive role: they actively sought additional channels of information, independently defined options, and were often advocates both to and for the president.

In the area where he wanted large achievement—legislation for the Great Society—he centralized through the White House staff. In national security affairs he developed a conciliar structure, formalized in the Tuesday Lunch and backed by similarly informal consultation with the principals. In contrast, a chief of staff position on domestic policy was substantially achieved. In this area, particularly in development of legislative programs, staff resources were used to mediate conflicts in the advisory system and to bring to the president positions of consensus. The presidential strategy in general encompassed canvass of departmental and agency information and advice, heavy reliance but with much variation on executive office chiefs, and use of whatever White House aid was available and useful to the president. Overarching these processes of staff aid were the features of presidential decision: Johnson's deliberateness and even delay of decision in difficult situations, his continuous involvement through stages and frequently in details that other presidents might have left to others, his reach for more information across and beyond regular lines, and his adherence to policy once decision was made.

In the multiple policy/political situations in which they must act presidents undoubtedly will use various decision and structural arrangements. Johnson's pattern of operations was one of minimum hierarchy and loose integration that distributed counsel for the president through a triadic subpresidency composed of White House, executive offices, and departments and agencies. It exhibited definite features: multiple points of integration within the White House; fusion of personal and institutional aid in executive office directorships; habitual use of specialized, coordinative, and generalist service from the three divisions of the subpresidency; and special crosscutting arrangements for particular policy areas or instances of policy decision and implementation. The constitutional and political responsibility of the president was maintained, but with the burden of that responsibility heavily concentrated on him personally.

The personal qualities of presidents will strongly affect White House operations. Operating styles reflect work habits, purposes, and various dispositions of a president. Let us look again at this personalization as it affected White House operations during the Johnson presidency. First, he personally was active in details as well as broad directions of policy. There was little opportunity for behavior deviating in any particular from his purposes. He was able to dominate because of his knowledge of government and because he devoted his energy completely to his task. Second, he wanted much.

He was driven by an insatiable desire for large accomplishment, especially in a legislative record. Third, he led the White House staff in a fast-paced operation that fully consumed their time and energy. For the burdens imposed he had a staff whose time was his, whose dedication to his policies was strong, and whose competence had been tested by him. These qualities of service were not likely to be adequately supplied by any source except the White House staff.

In the inherently personalized office of the president, Johnson's personal qualities heightened the personalization. In sum, the fluid triadic subpresidency was capped by personal presidential centralization.

For White House activity, the yield was loyalty to the president's purposes and personal integrity, drive toward "coonskins on the wall," and work on a fast-moving treadmill. For substantive results, whether from chance or presidential imprint, the consequences were enormous success for the president's legislative program and a divided nation and a weakened presidency in foreign policy. As a model of presidential management it offers the advantage of flexibility and adaptability to presidential purpose with hazardous dependence on personal exercise of power.

It cannot be expected that future presidents will possess the same combination of governmental experience and work involvement that enabled Johnson to personally command the White House. Assessment of their own potentials and habits and of the magnitude of presidential responsibility will probably lead them to more dependence upon structural integrations and less on personal direction and coordination than characterized the Johnson White House. But they are likely to find, as Johnson did, that an extensive White House role and varying combinations of institutional and personal assistance are intrinsic to the personal nature of presidential responsibility.

Final Comment

The extensive roles performed by the president's proximate aides discussed in the foregoing pages and anticipated for the future give significance to issues of structure, decision process, and personalization. Wise choices within and among these elements are vital to the welfare, even security, of the nation. They are too important to be labeled presidential "style" or to be dealt with only ad hoc or anecdotally. A new president's freedom with respect to them may be limited by his own capability and work habits and by circumstance, including perhaps his advance to the office from the vice presidency. In the last event, questions of continuity and duality or change of staff are unavoidable. In other instances transition papers and thought should concentrate attention on a system for presidential management.

Whatever predispositions future presidents may have toward systematization or personalization and centralization versus decentralization through White House operations, they will need to be informed by previous thought or transition planning on a broad list of problems. What balances in decision making between integrated and multiple channels of advice will be sought? What balances and structural arrangements among department, executive office, and White House aid will be emphasized? What types of assistance will be needed from White House aides? What structure will make their contribution most effective? What size staff is needed to insure adequate deliberation, weighing of facts and alternatives correctly, expedition of decision, and performance of diverse functions for the president? What standards of competence, personal and program loyalty, and public ethics will govern in choice of White House personnel? A president may even ask what inadequacies of presidential experience will need to be compensated and what propulsions of his personality will contribute to or hazard the success of his incumbency. While precise answers to all of these questions are not necessary or possible, relatively prompt and satisfactory judgments on these and other questions of White House management may have as much bearing on his success as planning on policies to be pursued.

Appendix. The White House: Comments on Size and Service Functions

The Total Operation

Despite the frequent use of the term "White House" or infrequently "White House office" to describe an institution or persons assisting the president in distinction from the other use of the term to describe the official residence of the president, it is difficult, if not impossible, to define precisely what is included at any particular time. While budget and personnel registers reveal total numbers for the White House office, these figures will not reflect a vastly larger number of persons who support the operation or the lesser number who assist the president in the important policy and administrative tasks of the presidency.

The total number of persons serving the presidency officially and exclusively had by the Johnson administration become quite large. The executive office of the president, not including 3,110 employees in the Office of Economic Opportunity (OEO)—an operating agency anomalously located in the executive office—had, on 18 June 1968, 1,442 employees, which compared with 630.3 in 1939 when the office was created.[1] This included 250 employees in the White House office, compared with 45 in 1939. The figures for the White House do not include those on detail from departments and agencies,[2] those engaged on various kinds of special projects, and vast support and service operations from outside the executive office. When President Johnson was surprised by the number of persons who attended a function for staff and employees serving the White House soon after he became president, a report was prepared from the social secretary's list of persons to be invited.[3] The report listed a total of 1,757 persons, broken down as follows: military, 743; White House office, 396; special projects, 162; Secret Service detail and White House police, 328 (the accompanying summary showing 100 Secret Service and 213 police); executive mansion, 128. In the case of the White House office and the military these figures probably included some persons who had only part-time, occasional, or even social functions related to the White House.[4]

Appropriations figures are the starting point for analyzing the cost and size of the White House office. Costs were quite stable in the fiscal years 1962 to 1968, varying in approximate figures from $2.5 to $2.8 million.[5] Also, a special projects appropriation of $1.5 million, regularly made but usually only partially expended, could be used at the president's discretion for such diverse activities as the Food for Peace program, the Science Advisory Committee, the poverty task force initially, and recruitment of key personnel. Up to 10 percent of the appropriation could be used to reimburse "Salaries and Expenses of the White House Office."[6]

Also stable was the average number of employees carried on White House rolls for budget reporting. In the budget summaries this ranged from 250 in 1966 to 263 in 1963 and 1964. The average civil service classification during the Johnson presidency ranged from 7.4 to 7.7. The number carried on the rolls for special projects varied at least between 67 and 162.[7]

Use of the special projects appropriation, detail of numerous persons from departments and agencies, and various other special factors clouded function as well as number in actual White House operations. Thus, the White House office included the director of the Office of Science and Technology (OST) because he was special assistant to the president, but did not include the directors of such other executive offices as the Bureau of the Budget (BOB) and the Council of Economic Advisers (CEA). It included several assistants for Joseph A. Califano, Jr., Johnson's chief domestic aide after 1965, but not at least one assistant for a considerable time because he was on detail from the Department of Justice. Califano's staff assistants and other advisers on domestic affairs were included, but not the staff assistants of the special assistants for national security affairs, since these were on the rolls of the National Security Council (NSC), an executive office unit. Also included were several persons who assisted the president in choosing appointees to executive positions, but not the person vested with the primary responsibility for assistance on this function in the post-1964 period, who was officially listed in another position.

The Service Operations

White House operations included large security, support, and facilitative segments. The president is protected and supported by several different units or groups that are attached to the White House or included within it. In large part these are institutionalized to an extent that they can serve any president without a significant drain on his time or attention.

The mansion, as already noted, is separately financed and staffed but provides support for the social functions of the president and the First Lady. Noted already are the large operations of the military, Secret Service, and White House police. Among other things, the military provides transportation support, including during Johnson's administration about seventy-five persons for the garage and sometimes a hundred or more for transportation on a single trip out of Washington. The military also managed the physical facilities for communication and the White House Mess.

Within the White House office itself a separate division for routine service functions included approximately 60 percent of the personnel (150 of 250). Its duty was "to assist in providing for the orderly handling of documents and correspondence within the White House Office, and also assist in the organization and supervision of the clerical services and procedures."[8] This routine service operation consisted "basically of a file room, a mail room, a correspondence section, telegraph and transportation services, a telephone room, an administrative office, a messenger and duplicating section." The volume of work was large. During the Herbert Hoover administration there were "maybe four or five hundred letters a day." Under Franklin D. Roosevelt the number jumped to around three thousand a day and remained at that level until John F. Kennedy, when the volume rose to about two and one-half times that number, to remain at that level during the Johnson presidency.[9]

Much continuity of personnel marked this division, though many came initially to it on detail from other parts of the government. The director of the division, Hopkins, had been in the Civil Service since 1929, had come to the White House on detail in 1931, had become head of the unit in 1948, and on 15 July 1966 President Johnson gave him the title of executive assistant. It was in all respects an institutionalized segment of the White House office.

In addition to the approximately 60 percent of White House personnel serving under Hopkins, many others performed service functions that were largely routine. They were secretaries or other assistants who answered letters under instructions as to content and form and aided in a variety of activities related to travel or social functions.

Notes

1. Introduction

1. The President's Committee on Administrative Management, *Report of the Committee with Studies of Administrative Management in the Federal Government* (Washington, D.C.: Superintendent of Documents, 1937), p. 5.

2. The term was set forth and explained in Emmette S. Redford and Marlan Blissett, *Organizing the Executive Branch: The Johnson Presidency* (Chicago: University of Chicago Press, 1981), p. 11.

3. President's Committee, *Report*, p. 5.

4. Two bills to designate by statute the position of assistant to the president for national security affairs and to require senatorial confirmation of appointments to the position were considered in Senate committee hearings in 1980. Expert testimony emphasized that this would interfere with the right of the president to have a confidential adviser and would also hazard the creation of a position that would be in competition with the secretary of state. "The National Security Adviser: Role and Accountability," Hearing before the Committee on Foreign Relations, U.S. Senate, 96th Cong., 2nd sess., 17 April 1980, particularly pp. 1–45.

5. *United States Code*, pp. 301–323.

6. Executive Order no. 8248, 8 September 1939.

7. On limitations on the president's claim, see U.S. v. Nixon, 418 U.S. 638 (1974). For a sharp critique of arguments, see Raoul Berger, *Executive Privilege: A Constitutional Myth* (Cambridge, Mass.: Harvard University Press, 1974).

8. See the discussion of the position of White House assistants in a publication of the National Academy of Public Administration, *Watergate: Its Implications for Responsible Government* (Washington, D.C., March 1974), chap. 2.

9. Stephen Hess, *Organizing the Presidency* (Washington, D.C.: Brookings Institution, 1976), p. 150.

10. *A Presidency for the 1980s*, a Report by a Panel of the National Academy of Public Administration (Washington, D.C., 1980), p. 17. Italics in original.

11. National Academy, *Watergate*, p. 38.

12. Hess, *Organizing the Presidency*, p. 151.

13. Ibid., p. 154.

14. See *A Presidency for the 1980s*, pp. 3, 15.

15. For an example of concern with the growth of the "Executive Establishment," see Thomas E. Cronin, "The Swelling of the Presidency," *Saturday Review* 1 (February 1973): 30–36.

16. National Academy, *Watergate*, quotations from pp. 27, viii, 40, 38.

17. Richard E. Neustadt, interview with one of the authors, 2 July 1984. See also Richard E. Neustadt, "Approaches to Staffing the Presidency: Notes on FDR and JFK," *American Political Science Review* 57 (December 1963): 855–864; and *Presidential Power: The Politics of Leadership with Reflections on Johnson and Nixon* (New York: Wiley, 1976). Neustadt's most distinctive contribution to staff roles has been his articles on legislative programming: "Presidency and Legislation: Planning the President's Program," *American Political Science Review* 49 (1955): 980–1021; and "Presidency and Legislation: The Growth of Central Clearance," *American Political Science Review* 48 (September 1954): 641–671. The articles are cited in chapter 5.

18. Norman C. Thomas, "Presidential Advice and Information: Policy and Program Formulation," in *The Institutionalized Presidency*, ed. Norman C. Thomas and Hans W. Baade (Dobbs Ferry, N.Y.: Oceana, 1972), p. 118.

19. Hess, *Organizing the Presidency*, p. 99.

20. Richard Tanner Johnson, *Managing the White House: An Intimate Study of the Presidency* (New York: Harper and Row, 1974), p. 235.

21. Roger B. Porter, *Presidential Decision Making: The Economic Policy Board* (Cambridge: Cambridge University Press, 1980), particularly the appendix, pp. 229–252. The arguments on multiple advocacy in presidential decision making have been analyzed in detail in Alexander L. George, "The Case for Multiple Advocacy in Making Foreign Policy"; I. M. Destler, "Comment: Multiple Advocacy, Some 'Limits and Costs'"; Alexander L. George, "Rejoinder to 'Comment' by I. M. Destler," all in *American Political Science Review* 66 (September 1972): 751–795.

22. Ibid., p. 252.

23. Ibid.

24. Hugh Heclo, "Studying the Presidency: Results, Needs, and Resources," Report to the Ford Foundation (Brookings, October 1976), p. 20.

25. Ibid., p. 15.

26. Ibid., p. 23.

27. Thomas E. Cronin, "Political Science and Executive Advisory Systems," in *The Presidential Advisory System*, ed. Thomas E. Cronin and Sanford D. Greenberg (New York: Harper & Row, 1969), pp. 321–335.

28. Fred I. Greenstein, *The Hidden-Hand Presidency: Eisenhower as Leader* (New York: Basic Books, 1982).

29. For examples of recent concern on these matters, see Barbara Tuchman, "Should We Abolish the Presidency?" *New York Times*, 13 February 1973; and Arthur M. Schlesinger, Jr., *The Imperial Presidency* (Boston: Houghton Mifflin Co., 1973).

30. Patrick Anderson, *The President's Men: White House Assistants of Franklin D. Roosevelt, Harry S. Truman, Dwight D. Eisenhower, John F.*

Kennedy and Lyndon B. Johnson (New York: Doubleday and Company, 1968), pp. 299, 395.

31. Eric F. Goldman, *The Tragedy of Lyndon Johnson* (New York: Alfred A. Knopf, 1969), p. 275.

32. George E. Reedy, *The Twilight of the Presidency* (New York: New American Library, 1970), pp. xi–xii.

33. Ibid.

2. Duality, Change, and Stabilization

1. When impeachment charges against President Richard M. Nixon were voted, a student from Afghanistan asked one of the authors if the military might maintain Nixon in power if he were convicted. The confident answer to the class was, "It is inconceivable." This heritage meant that for Johnson the only security needed was protection against assassination by an individual.

2. "Remarks to Governors after President Kennedy's Funeral" (25 November 1963), in *Public Papers of the Presidents of the United States: Lyndon B. Johnson, 1963–64* (Washington, D.C.: U.S. Government Printing Office, 1970), vol. 1, p. 4, hereafter cited as *Public Papers.*

3. "Address before a Joint Session of Congress" (27 November 1963), in *Public Papers, 1963–64,* vol. 1, p. 9.

4. Interview, Richard L. Schott with Bill D. Moyers, 20 June 1978, Austin, Texas, hereafter cited as Schott interview with Moyers. Harry C. McPherson, Jr., thought that even when he came to the White House in 1965 "one could still feel John Kennedy's presence in the White House." Harry C. McPherson, Jr., *A Political Education* (Boston and Toronto: Little, Brown, 1971), p. 245.

5. George E. Reedy, *Lyndon B. Johnson, a Memoir* (New York: Andrews and McMeel, 1982), p. 146.

6. Lyndon Baines Johnson, *The Vantage Point: Perspectives of the Presidency: 1963–1969* (New York: Holt, Rinehart and Winston, 1971), p. 18.

7. Transcript, Donald F. Hornig Oral History Interview, 4 December 1968, p. 23, LBJ Library, hereafter cited as Hornig Oral History.

8. As quoted in Doris Kearns, *Lyndon Johnson and the American Dream* (New York: Harper and Row, 1976), pp. 177–178.

9. Schott interview with Moyers.

10. President's Daily Diary, 22 November 1963, "November 1963" folder, LBJ Library, hereafter cited as Diary.

11. Transcript, Jack J. Valenti Oral History Interview, 4 June 1969, pp. 1ff., LBJ Library, hereafter cited as Valenti Oral History.

12. Diary, 22 November 1963.

13. A sixth, Clifton Carter, was Johnson's liaison to the Democratic party structure but was never on the White House rolls. According to Walter W. Jenkins, he was paid by Johnson himself. Interview, Emmette S. Redford and Richard T. McCulley with Walter W. Jenkins, 12 November 1980, hereafter cited as Redford and McCulley interview with Jenkins.

14. 2 December 1963, Box 39, Files of Bill D. Moyers, LBJ Library.

15. The title of special counsel was given by President Franklin D. Roosevelt in 1944 to Samuel I. Rosenman, a former judge, and a broad bundle of duties assigned to him. A similar arrangement was made for Clark M. Clifford and Charles S. Murphy in the Harry S. Truman administration. The duties were dispersed under Dwight D. Eisenhower but reassembled for Sorensen by Kennedy. After Sorensen left, Johnson did not designate anyone as special counsel until McPherson was appointed in February 1966.

16. For a full account of his continuance, see Lawrence F. O'Brien, *No Final Victories* (Garden City, N.Y.: Doubleday, 1974), chap. 8. The quotation in the text is at p. 163.

17. Daily Diary worksheet and memo, Lee White to president, 29 November 1963, "November 29, 1963" folder, Appointment file (diary backup), LBJ Library.

18. Transcript, Ralph A. Dungan Oral History Interview, 18 April 1969, p. 8, LBJ Library, hereafter cited as Dungan Oral History; also Richard L. Schott interview with Dungan, 10 June 1978.

19. Daily Diary worksheet, 27 November 1963, "November 27, 1963" folder, Appointment file (Diary Backup), LBJ Library.

20. For an account of Richard N. Goodwin's initial service to Johnson, see Rowland Evans and Robert Novak, *Lyndon B. Johnson: The Exercise of Power* (New York: New American Library, 1966), pp. 424–447.

21. Redford and McCulley interview with Jenkins.

22. Ibid.

23. Transcript, Lee C. White Oral History Interview, 29 September 1970, pp. 29–30, LBJ Library, hereafter cited as White Oral History.

24. The president's diary records telephone calls and personal conferences.

25. Transcript, S. Douglass Cater, Jr., Oral History Interview, 29 April 1969, pp. 1–9, LBJ Library, hereafter cited as Cater Oral History.

26. Theodore White, *The Making of the President—1964* (New York: Atheneum Publishers, 1965), pp. 348–350.

27. See as illustration O'Brien, *No Final Victories*, pp. 167–169, and also the comments of White in White Oral History, 28 September 1970, p. 29.

28. See, for example, George E. Christian, *The President Steps Down: A Personal Memo of the Transition of Power* (New York: Macmillan, 1970), p. 10. Jenkins said only P. Kenneth O'Donnell of the Kennedy group could walk into the president's office at any time, but in reply to questions he affirmed that McGeorge Bundy and O'Brien had access in a way that denied a two-tiered situation. Redford and McCulley interview with Jenkins.

29. For discussion on the change from Dungan to Macy, see Richard L. Schott and Dagmar S. Hamilton, *People, Position and Power: Executive Appointments of Lyndon Johnson* (Chicago: University of Chicago Press, 1983), pp. 9–14.

30. Transcript, George E. Reedy Oral History Interview, 20 December 1968, pp. 7, 6, LBJ Library, hereafter cited as Reedy Oral History.

31. Transcript, Jake Jacobsen Oral History Interview, 27 January 1969,

tape 1, pp. 4–5, 22, 28, tape 2, pp. 12–15, LBJ Library, hereafter cited as Jacobsen Oral History.

32. For more details of the O'Brien appointment as postmaster general, see Schott and Hamilton, *People, Position and Power*, pp. 76–79.

33. Walt W. Rostow was one of two Johnson White House staff members who had served on the Kennedy staff before being transferred to the State Department. The other was Richard Goodwin, who was a Kennedy aide before he became deputy assistant secretary of state for Inter-American Affairs in November 1961.

34. McPherson, *A Political Education*, chap. 9. McPherson's speechwriting responsibilities grew following the departure of Goodwin in September 1965 and Moyers in December 1966.

35. Reedy Oral History, 20 December 1968, p. 16.

36. Transcript, Harry C. McPherson Oral History Interview, 16 January 1969, p. 1, LBJ Library, hereafter cited as McPherson Oral History.

37. Joseph A. Califano, Jr., *Governing America: An Insider's Report from the White House* (New York: Simon and Schuster, 1981), p. 411.

38. Hugh Heclo's figures in *A Government of Strangers* (Washington: Brookings Institution, 1977) are for all "political executives" and are not relevant to our narrower sample of top White House assistants.

3. The Johnson White House: An Overview

1. Walt W. Rostow, *The Diffusion of Power: An Essay in Recent History* (New York: Macmillan, 1972), p. 365.

2. Ibid., p. 364.

3. As quoted in Lawrence C. Pierce, *The Politics of Fiscal Policy Formation* (Pacific Palisades, Calif.: Goodyear Publishers, 1971), p. 99.

4. Ibid.

5. Rostow, *Diffusion*, p. 366.

6. The role of the White House assistant as substantive policy adviser will be considered in more detail in chapter 6.

7. Rostow, *Diffusion*, p. 365.

8. Pierce, *Fiscal Policy*, p. 99.

9. Stafford Warren resigned on 30 June 1965.

10. Memo, William J. Hopkins to W. Marvin Watson, 19 October 1967. The difficulty of preciseness is evidenced by the accompanying list of thirty-one sent by John W. Macy, Jr., to Hopkins. Ex FG 8-11, WHCF, LBJ Library.

11. Memo, "Current List of Employees by Office as of 10/21/67," 21 October 1967, "Johnson White House Staff" folder, LBJ Library.

12. The lists we refer to include all "professionals" working in the office whether in the manual or not or whether on the White House rolls or detailed to it. To our knowledge no studies of the presidency have built similar data. These lists of White House assistants cited in the text are typical of those assembled in a special file on the White House staff by the LBJ archivists. In addition to the indirect support noted by Hopkins in the text, we

had two former Johnson White House staff members and the most knowledgeable archivists review this section. They agreed with both our methodology and our conclusions.

13. See another volume in this series: Schott and Hamilton, *People, Position and Power*, pp. 203–204.

14. Transcript, E. Ernest Goldstein Oral History Interview, 9 December 1968, p. 15, LBJ Library, hereafter cited as Goldstein Oral History.

15. Our compilation of biographic data in Table 1 for the top White House assistants was based primarily upon research in the Office Files of John W. Macy, Jr. This file was extremely valuable, although not sufficient for our purposes. We supplemented data from the Macy files with information gathered from widely scattered published documents, oral histories, and written communication with practically all of the aides in our sample. No researcher should expect complete and uniform data on all the entries in the Macy files.

16. Memo, Horace Busby, Jr., to Macy, 7 April 1967, Office Files of John W. Macy, Jr., LBJ Library.

17. Transcript, George E. Christian, Oral History, 11 November 1968, pp. 1–7, LBJ Library, hereafter cited as Christian Oral History.

18. Transcript, Larry E. Temple Oral History Interview, 12 June 1970, pp. 1–6, LBJ Library, hereafter cited as Temple Oral History.

19. See, for comments, Christian Oral History, 27 February 1970, pp. 2–3; and Christian's book, *The President Steps Down*, pp. 9ff.

20. Transcript, W. DeVier Pierson Oral History Interview, 20 March 1969, p. 16, LBJ Library, hereafter cited as Pierson Oral History.

21. Clifford L. Alexander, Jr., Robert F. Fleming, Robert W. Komer, Esther Peterson, Hobart Taylor, Jr., and W. Marvin Watson.

22. Walter W. Jenkins, George E. Reedy, and Robert E. Kintner.

23. Jack J. Valenti, McGeorge Bundy, and Bill D. Moyers.

24. Jake Jacobsen and Horace Busby, Jr.

25. John P. Roche.

26. S. Douglass Cater, Jr.

4. Johnson's Management Style

1. McPherson Oral History, 5 December 1968, tape 2, p. 28.

2. Transcript, James C. Gaither Oral History Interview, 17 January 1969, p. 11, LBJ Library, hereafter cited as Gaither Oral History.

3. "Washington: Johnson's Administrative Monstrosity," *New York Times*, 23 November 1966.

4. Reedy Oral History, 20 December 1968, tape 4, p. 26.

5. McPherson Oral History, 5 December 1968, tape 1, p. 15.

6. Gaither Oral History, 15 January 1969, p. 12.

7. George E. Reedy, *The Presidency in Flux* (New York: Columbia University Press, 1973), p. 93.

8. Conversation with Emmette S. Redford, Senator Lyndon B. Johnson's office. Jack J. Valenti said that it was Johnson's judgment that the key to all

the Negroes' problems was the right to vote. Valenti Oral History, 14 June 1969, tape 1, p. 26.

9. Willard Deason, conversation with one of the authors, 1957.

10. Cater Oral History, 8 May 1969, p. 31.

11. Joseph A. Califano, Jr., *A Presidential Nation* (New York: W. W. Norton, 1975), p. 242.

12. McPherson Oral History, 5 December 1968, tape 1, p. 39.

13. Jacobsen Oral History, 27 May 1969, tape 3, p. 16.

14. Transcript, Robert L. Hardesty Oral History Interview, 26 March 1969, p. 20, LBJ Library, hereafter cited as Hardesty Oral History.

15. Memo, Bill D. Moyers to Robert E. Kintner, 5 May 1966, Box 10, Files of Bill D. Moyers, LBJ Library.

16. The special counsel's office did not become a center of general policy integration, as under presidents Roosevelt, Harry S. Truman, and John F. Kennedy, though legal duties and advice to the president on enrolled bills placed them in a general advisory role on presidential signature of bills. For discussion of the special counsel's function on enrolled bills in the Johnson presidency, see McPherson, *A Political Education*, pp. 273–281. On the special counsel's role in earlier presidencies, see Richard E. Neustadt, "Presidency and Legislation: The Growth of Central Clearance," *American Political Science Review* 48 (September 1954): 641–671, *passim*; and "Approaches to Staffing the Presidency: Notes on FDR and JFK," *American Political Science Review* 57 (December 1963): 841–863, *passim*.

17. Christian, *The President Steps Down*, p. 12.

18. See, for examples, memos, W. Marvin Watson to president, 6 July 1965, on reduction of number of newspapers, and Richard N. Goodwin to Watson, 18 August 1965, Ex FG 11-8-1, sarcastically referring to Watson's disallowing expenditure for two books; Watson to Califano and others, 29 January 1966, Ex WH 14-2, reporting infractions of rules on use of White House cars; Watson to president, 12 January 1966, Ex WH 14-2, on reduction of garage staff from 103 to 66. The president often showed interest in such details, thus requesting a check on the number of long distance calls, Watson to president, 27 June 1966, Ex WH 1; and passing personally on expenditures for the vice president's service, Watson to president, 30 June 1965, "Humphrey, Senator Hubert H." folder from Famous Names Files, Dorothy Territo's Files, LBJ Library; and expenditures for furniture for the social secretary in the mansion, Watson to president, undated, Ex FG 11-8-1, WHCF, LBJ Library.

19. Cater Oral History, 29 April 1969, tape 1, p. 9.

20. Ibid., pp. 10–31.

21. Goldstein Oral History, 10 and 19 December 1968, *passim*.

22. Temple Oral History, 11 June 1970, pp. 41–42, 12 June 1970, pp. 10.

23. McPherson, *A Political Education*, p. 250.

24. For a survey of his duties in the White House and the kinds of function of four successive Special Counsels, see McPherson Oral History, 19 December 1968, pp. 19–22.

25. Ibid., p. 34.

26. Transcript, Sherwin J. Markham Oral History Interview, pp. 24–28, 21 May 1969, LBJ Library, hereafter cited as Markham Oral History.

27. Letter to Miss Mary Hensel, 22 April 1964, Gen FG 11-8-1, WHCF, LBJ Library. Feldman described the office under his predecessors: "The office of the Special Counsel cannot be described in very precise terms. The duties of the office depend largely upon the particular talents of the incumbent and the manner in which the president wishes to utilize those talents."

28. See a document entitled "Staff Interest in Correspondence and Substantive Matters," dated 2 June 1964, Ex FG 11-8, WHCF, LBJ Library, and a memo from Myer Feldman to Moyers on reassignment at his departure of his conglomerate specific duties, 25 January 1965, Ex FG 11-8, WHCF, LBJ Library.

29. Ex 11-8-1, WHCF, LBJ Library. For the Cabinet assignments, see attachment to a letter from William J. Hopkins to Watson, 19 February 1968, Ex FE 14, WHCF, LBJ Library.

30. Memo, Hopkins to Watson, with reply, 19 February 1968, Ex FE 14, WHCF, LBJ Library.

31. Temple Oral History, 11 June 1970, p. 5.

32. Memo to president, 21 September 1965, Ex FG 11-8-1, WHCF, LBJ Library.

33. McPherson Oral History, 12 December 1968, pp. 3–4.

34. Ibid., 9 April 1969, tape 3, p. 34. McPherson noted the significance of proximity and readiness in giving opportunities to seize activities. He noted that Valenti and Moyers were with the president early and late, and they could thus seize activities or become tip-in men for others on the team. At least one person apparently declined White House duty because the duties were indefinite, and Valenti remarked, "It is the nature of the beast that White House staff work is very difficult to delineate and specify. . . ." Memos, Valenti to president, 21 and 22 December 1964, Ex FG 11-8-1, WHCF, LBJ Library.

35. Gaither Oral History, 17 January 1969, p. 9.

36. Christian Oral History, 27 February 1970, p. 4.

37. Gaither Oral History, 17 January 1969, p. 12.

38. Cater Oral History, 8 May 1968, pp. 22, 22a.

39. Transcript, Matthew Nimetz Oral History Interview, 7 January 1969, tape 1, p. 5, LBJ Library, hereafter cited as Nimetz Oral History.

40. Ibid., pp. 5–6.

41. Cater Oral History, 8 May 1969, p. 22.

42. Memo, Moyers to McGeorge Bundy, Horace Busby, Jr., S. Douglass Cater, Jr., Goodwin, John W. Macy, Jr., Lawrence F. O'Brien, Reedy, Watson, Lee C. White, and Valenti, EX WH 10, WHCF, LBJ Library.

43. See comment of White in White Oral History, 2 March 1971, p. 1.

44. Memo, Moyers to Watson, 3 May 1966, Ex WH 10, WHCF, LBJ Library.

45. Memo, Semer to Kintner, 20 May 1966, Ex WH 10, WHCF, LBJ Library.

46. Copy of agenda, Ex WH 10, WHCF, LBJ Library.

47. Memo, Kintner to staff members, 30 January 1967, "White House Staff Meetings" folder, Box 32, Files of Frederick Panzer, LBJ Library.

48. Memo, Kintner to president, Ex WH 10, WHCF, LBJ Library.

49. For a time at least Kintner, on the direction of the president, held regular meetings with a smaller group: Califano, Cater, Christian, McPherson, and Rostow. See memo, Kintner to this group, 12 January 1967, WHCF, LBJ Library.

50. Memo, James R. Jones to Watson, 17 May 1967, Ex WH 10, WHCF, LBJ Library.

51. Memo, Sanders to Watson, 9 August 1967, Ex WH 10, WHCF, LBJ Library.

52. Memo, Charles M. Maguire to staff, 16 June 1967, Ex WH 10, WHCF, LBJ Library, announcing institution of the meetings.

53. For examples, see memos, Maguire to a group, 12 August 1967, Sanders to a group, 11 October 1967, Ex WH 10, WHCF, LBJ Library.

54. Reedy, *The Twilight of the Presidency*, p. xiv. The same views are stated in the oral history interviews with Reedy located in the LBJ Library.

55. Ibid., chap. 1.

56. Reedy Oral History, 20 December 1968, p. 7.

57. Hardesty Oral History, 26 March 1965, p. 21.

58. Christian Oral History, 26 March 1969, p. 21.

59. The several comments by Christian are from Christian Oral History.

60. White Oral History, 18 February 1971, p. 31.

61. Jacobsen Oral History, 27 May 1969, tape 3, p. 33, 35.

62. Among the most severe are those of Reedy, in Reedy Oral History, 20 December 1968, tape 4, pp. 9, 11–13, tape 5, pp. 40–42.

63. Cater Oral History, 8 May 1969, p. 21.

64. McPherson Oral History, 24 March 1969, tape 5, p. 38.

65. See the pointed comments in a memo from Maguire to Kintner on the signing of the Foreign Assistance Act of 1966, Ex FG 11-8-1, WHCF, LBJ Library.

66. The quotation is included at p. 7 in Christian, *The President Steps Down*, pp. 5–9, where a vivid description of the early morning events is given.

67. Temple Oral History, 11 June 1970.

68. McPherson Oral History, 19 December 1968, tape 3, pp. 18–19.

69. Transcript, Mike N. Manatos Oral History Interview, 25 August 1969, p. 38, LBJ Library, hereafter cited as Manatos Oral History. Manatos commented, ". . . sometimes I wished he wouldn't carry them around with him."

70. For further discussion of the effort to obtain public support, see chapter 8.

71. Cater Oral History, 29 April 1969, p. 11.

72. Markham Oral History, 21 May 1969, p. 11.

73. See the revealing story of a White House aide's operations in McPherson Oral History, 24 March 1969, tape 1, pp. 11–28.

74. Harvey C. Mansfield, *President Johnson and His Cost Reduction Campaign: Methods and Limitations of Presidential Leadership in Administrative Management*, an as yet unpublished case study in this series.

75. Valenti Oral History, 3 March 1971, p. 25. This, however, overlooked staff ingenuity in getting late memos on the day's stack.

76. Ibid., 19 February 1971, p. 5.

77. Ibid., 3 March 1971, pp. 22–25.

78. Temple Oral History, 12 June 1970, tape 2, pp. 40ff.

79. Goldstein Oral History, 17 December 1968, p. 3.

80. McPherson Oral History, 16 January 1969, tape 4, p. 27.

81. Cater Oral History, 8 May 1969, p. 25.

82. Goldstein Oral History, 17 December 1968, p. 3.

83. Reedy Oral History, 20 December 1968, tape 4, p. 27.

84. Jacobsen Oral History, 27 May 1969, p. 21.

85. Transcript, Peter B. Benchley Oral History Interview, 20 November 1968, p. 5, LBJ Library, hereafter cited as Benchley Oral History.

86. Gaither Oral History, 15 January 1969, p. 10.

87. Manatos Oral History, 25 August 1969, p. 51.

88. Transcript, John P. Roche Oral History Interview, 16 July 1970, pp. 49–50, LBJ Library, hereafter cited as Roche Oral History.

89. Christian, *The President Steps Down*, pp. 22–23, 36–37, 41–42.

90. Interview with Bill D. Moyers, "A Look at the Inner Workings of the White House," *U.S. News and World Report*, 13 June 1966, pp. 78–79.

91. Goldstein Oral History, 17 December 1968, pp. 4–5.

92. On a memorandum from Cater to president, 2 February 1965, with respect to a letter to Congress supporting the Truth in Lending and Truth in Packaging legislation, Johnson wrote at the bottom: "Who committed me to send letter and why? This looks like blackmail." "Memos to the President, November 1964–February 1965" folder, Box 13, Office Files of S. Douglass Cater, Jr., 2 February 1965, LBJ Library.

93. McPherson, *A Political Education*, p. 285.

94. Christian, *The President Steps Down*, p. 19.

95. See Redford and Blissett, *Organizing the Executive Branch*, p. 120. In the case of the proposal for a Department of Commerce and Labor the president's action was not as precipitate as Reedy has reported. See Reedy, *Twilight of the Presidency*, p. 13. See the Redford and Blissett discussion.

96. Reedy, *Twilight of the Presidency*, foreword and chap. 1, quotation at p. xiii.

97. White Oral History, 18 February 1971, p. 22.

98. Califano, *A Presidential Nation*, p. 43.

99. Goldstein Oral History, 9 December 1968, p. 15.

100. McPherson Oral History, 19 December 1968, tape 3, pp. 22–28.

101. Ibid., 24 March 1969, tape 5, pp. 24–25.

102. Roche Oral History, 16 July 1970, p. 54.

103. Interview with Joseph A. Califano, Jr., by Robert Hawkinson, Washington, D.C., 11 June 1973, LBJ Library.

104. Transcript, interview, James E. Anderson, Jared Hazleton, and Emmette S. Redford with Joseph A. Califano, Jr., Austin, Texas, 17 May 1980, hereafter cited as Anderson, Hazleton, and Redford interview with Califano. Robert T. Hartman, staff aide to President Gerald Ford, has echoed Reedy's

concern: "No matter how extroverted his disposition, no matter how curious his mind, a President invariably finds himself hearing mostly what people believe he wants to hear." "Every American President, even one who toasts his own English muffins or totes his own suitcases, needs one or more close associates who can and will remind him when he is full of baloney." *An Inside Account of the Ford Years* (New York: McGraw-Hill, 1980), p. 208.

105. Memo, Cater to president, 18 November 1965, "Memos to the President, November 1965" folder, Box 14, Office Files of S. Douglass Cater, Jr., LBJ Library.

106. Memo, Cater to president, 20 August 1964, "Memos to the President, August 1964" folder, Box 14, Office Files of S. Douglass Cater, Jr., LBJ Library.

107. Reedy Oral History, 20 December 1968, tape 4, p. 8; and George E. Reedy, *Lyndon B. Johnson: A Memoir* (New York: Andrews and McMeel, 1982), pp. xiv, 5, 66–67, 139.

108. Califano, *Presidential Nation*, p. 48.

109. McPherson Oral History, 24 March 1969, tape 5, p. 8.

110. Ibid., p. 9.

111. Cater Oral History, 8 May 1969.

112. Califano, *Presidential Nation*, p. 48.

113. McPherson Oral History, 16 January 1969, tape 4, p. 30.

114. Hardesty Oral History, 26 March 1969, p. 29.

115. Conversations with one of the authors, Austin, Texas, summer 1980.

116. Anderson, Hazleton, and Redford interview with Califano.

117. Christian Oral History, 16 January 1969, tape 4, p. 31.

118. Gaither Oral History, 24 March 1970, p. 18.

119. Califano, *A Presidential Nation*, p. 48.

120. McPherson, *A Political Education*, p. 292.

121. McPherson Oral History, 9 April 1969, tape 9, p. 7.

122. McPherson, *A Political Education*, p. 292.

123. White Oral History, 2 March 1971, p. 6.

5. Developing the Legislative Program

1. No separate chapter is needed on the functions of management service and legal counsel, these having been treated sufficiently in the previous chapters. See the listings of personnel in Table 3.

2. For the record of the complementary influences of the president and congressional members and committees in New Deal legislation, see Lawrence H. Chamberlain, *The President, Congress and Legislation* (New York: Columbia University Press, 1946).

3. For a description of the process, see Richard Neustadt, "Presidency and Legislation: The Growth of Central Clearance," *American Political Science Review* 48, no. 3 (September 1954): 641–671; and "Presidency and Legislation: Planning the President's Program," *American Political Science Review* 49, no. 4 (December 1955): 980–1021.

4. For a meticulous summary of legislative programming from Roosevelt

to Carter, see Stephen J. Wayne, *The Legislative Presidency* (New York: Harper and Row, 1978). After experimentation with task forces in the pre-convention period of Kennedy's campaign, at least twenty-nine were constituted in the post-election and pre-inaugural period. Arthur M. Schlesinger, Jr., *A Thousand Days: John F. Kennedy in the White House* (New York: Fawcett World Library, 1967), pp. 155–161.

5. A participant proudly asserted the process was "one of the most significant institutional changes in the government made by the president." Gaither Oral History, 19 November 1968, tape 1, p. 3. It would have been if it had been preserved in later presidencies; as it was, it remains as one model for presidential leadership. For a description of four models in the evolution of presidential domestic policy apparatus, see Lester M. Salamon, "The Presidency and Domestic Policy Formulation," chap. 6 in *The Illusion of Presidential Government*, ed. Hugh Heclo and Lester M. Salamon (Boulder, Colo.: Westview Press, 1981).

6. "Remarks at the University of Michigan," (22 May 1964), in *Public Papers*, 1963–64, vol. 1, pp. 704–707, quotations from pp. 704, 705.

7. Ibid.

8. Johnson, *The Vantage Point*, p. 327.

9. See, for illustration, memos from Bill D. Moyers to the White House group on 22 June 1964, Ex FG 600, and from Moyers to the total group of collaborators on 6 July 1964, Ex FG 600, WHCF, LBJ Library.

10. Memo, 30 May 1964, Ex LE, WHCF, LBJ Library.

11. Memo, Moyers to Gardner Ackley and others, 6 July 1964, Ex FG 600, WHCF, LBJ Library.

12. The president's remarks are attached to a memorandum from Moyers to the twelve collaborators, 6 July 1964, Ex FG 600, WHCF, LBJ Library. Emphasis is in the copy of the president's remarks. This and the following statements by the president are from this attachment.

13 Memo, S. Douglass Cater to president, 10 July 1964, LBJ Library.

14. Memo, Moyers to All Task Force Liaison Officers, 21 July 1964, Ex FG 600, WHCF, LBJ Library.

15. Nimetz Oral History, 7 January 1969, tape 1, p. 27.

16. Califano, *A Presidential Nation*, p. 39.

17. Ibid.

18. Ibid., p. 36.

19. Memo, Califano to president, 14 July 1966, Ex FG 11-8, WHCF, LBJ Library.

20. Anderson, Hazleton, and Redford interview with Califano.

21. Califano, *A Presidential Nation*, p. 41.

22. See Gaither Oral History, 15 January 1969, pp. 1ff., for comments on staff leanness and the contributions made in policy construction after Nimetz and Frederick M. Bohen were added.

23. In 1967 the Office of Science and Technology (OST) assigned a staff member to Califano for several weeks and Walt W. Rostow assigned one for a shorter period. See memo, Gaither to Califano, and Califano's penned notation, 16 May 1967, unclassified document, LBJ Library.

24. Memo, Cater to president, 11 July 1965, "Memos to the President, July 1965" folder, Box 13, Office Files of S. Douglass Cater, Jr., LBJ Library.

25. Transcript, Interview, Robert Hawkinson with Joseph A. Califano, Jr., Washington, D.C., 11 July 1973, p. 6, LBJ Library, hereafter cited as Hawkinson interview with Califano.

26. Johnson, *The Vantage Point*, pp. 326–327.

27. Ibid., p. 35.

28. Memo, Charles L. Schultze to Califano, 7 January 1966, Ex FG 600, WHCF, LBJ Library.

29. Norman C. Thomas and Harold L. Wolman, "Policy Formulation in the Institutionalized Presidency: The Johnson Task Forces," in *The Presidential Advisory System*, ed. Thomas C. Cronin and Sanford D. Greenberg (New York: Harper and Row, 1969), p. 140. The Thomas/Wolman chapter is an excellent discussion of the task force experience in the Johnson presidency. A somewhat revised version is their "The Presidency and Policy Formulation: The Task Force Device," *Public Administration Review* 29 (September/October 1969): 459–471. Thomas and Cronin assert that "it is, of course impossible to measure directly the impact" of task forces on policy. The difficulty can be illustrated. Rowland Evans and Robert Novak in *Lyndon B. Johnson: The Exercise of Power* (New York: New American Library, 1966), p. 492 state, "The second great accomplishment of Johnson's Task Force on Education was a scheme to give Catholic schools access to books and educational centers for special instruction under the new program." But Wilbur J. Cohen, who was then an assistant secretary in HEW, has stated to the authors that the idea that broke the Gordian knot was concurrently developed within the department. Liaisons with task forces ensured their knowledge of ideas within the government that may have been adopted without task force proposal. See also Nancy Kegan Smith, "Presidential Task Force Operation during the Johnson Administration," *Presidential Studies Quarterly* 15 (1985): 320–329.

30. Memo, Cater to president, 11 July 1965, Office Files of S. Douglass Cater, Jr., LBJ Library.

31. Memo, Califano to the White House staff, 28 August 1965, Ex FG 600, WHCF, LBJ Library.

32. For total numbers of commissions, statement on their influence, and the analysis of commission proposals in Johnson's presidency (as given in the text), see Thomas R. Wolanin, *Presidential Advisory Commissions: Truman to Nixon* (Madison: University of Wisconsin Press, 1975), pp. 124, 142, 229–239. See also on presidential commissions Alan L. Dean, "Ad Hoc Commissions for Policy Formulation?" and Daniel Bell, "Government by Commission," in *The Presidential Advisory System*, ed. Cronin and Greenberg, pp. 101–116, 117–123.

33. Hawkinson interview with Califano, p. 4.

34. Ibid.

35. Memo, Schultze to Moyers, 6 July 1965, Ex LE, WHCF, LBJ Library.

36. Memo, Califano to president, 11 August 1965, Ex LE, WHCF, LBJ Library.

37. Memo, Califano to the White House staff, 28 August 1965, Ex FG 600, WHCF, LBJ Library; memo, the president to department and agencies, 15 November 1965, Ex LE, WHCF, LBJ Library.

38. See Nimetz Oral History, 7 January 1969, tape 1, pp. 29–30; and Schultze Oral History, 20 January 1969, p. 36. Schultze believed, however, that the task force use "got overdone" in that the attempt to be comprehensive each year led to "exploring the same ground in many cases." Ibid., p. 35.

39. Califano has said that from the end of 1966 his office devoted less time to devising new programs than to the problems of implementation. *A Presidential Nation*, pp. 31–32.

40. This factor is noted in copies in the LBJ Library of an undelivered speech on task force development prepared by Gaither for the president, undated.

41. Califano, *A Presidential Nation*, p. 239.

42. Gaither Oral History, 19 November 1968, tape 1, p. 9.

43. Memo, Califano to president, 2 August 1967, Ex WE, WHCF, LBJ Library.

44. Hawkinson interview with Califano, pp. 17–21.

45. Memo, Califano to aides and Mrs. Johnson's secretary, 16 May 1967, Ex LE, WHCF, LBJ Library; memo, Califano to seventeen White House Fellows, 18 May 1967, "Misc. on 1968 Legislative Program" folder, Box 305, Files of James C. Gaither, LBJ Library.

46. Memo, Califano to Heads of Departments and Agencies, 15 May 1967, "Misc. on 1968 Legislative Program" folder, Box 305, Files of James C. Gaither, LBJ Library.

47. These steps may be seen in two memos: Gaither to Edward E. Hamilton, 6 June 1967, and Gaither to Califano, 10 July 1967, "Misc. on 1968 Legislative Program" folder, Box 305, Files of James C. Gaither, LBJ Library.

48. See memos in "Misc. on 1968 Legislative Program" folder, Box 305, Files of James C. Gaither, LBJ Library. The meetings at this stage were numerous. Califano in 1967 held them in mid August with at least ten groups. Gaither held them with smaller groups (e.g., with Hamilton, Francis M. Bator, and Nimetz on foreign aid and trade).

49. See, for example, a listing of the numerous studies that were current, 8 November 1968, Ex FG 600/Task Forces, WHCF, LBJ Library.

50. Gaither Oral History, 19 November 1968, tape 1, pp. 8–9.

51. Ibid., tape 2, p. 13.

52. When departmental historians from the Department of Transportation (DOT) and the Office of Economic Opportunity (OEO) asked to read task force reports so that they could accurately include White House impacts in their histories, Johnson approved with the comment to Califano, "If you personally watch it." Memo, Califano to president, 12 August 1968, Ex FE 12/Johnson, L.B./2-3-1, WHCF, LBJ Library. And he refused on 7 October 1968 to allow BOB to include references to task force reports in transition reports to the new administration or to retain copies for future reference. Memo, Califano to president, 7 October 1968, Ex FG 1-8, WHCF, LBJ Library.

When Charles S. Murphy, Johnson's transition coordinator, inquired of Johnson whether he should forward the requested copies of the Heineman task force reports, in which he had candidly affirmed defects in administration of Great Society programs, to President-Elect Richard Nixon's transition representative, Johnson checked "no" on the approval sheet and added, "Hell no. And tell him I'm not going to publish my wife's love letters either." Memo, Charles S. Murphy to president, 22 November 1968, Ex FG 11-18, WHCF, LBJ Library.

53. Gaither Oral History, 19 November 1968, tape 2, p. 3.

54. Memo, "Planning the Legislative Program for 1968 and Beyond," 25 April 1967, "Misc. on 1968 Legislative Program" folder, Box 305, Files of James C. Gaither, LBJ Library.

55. Gaither Oral History, 19 November 1968, pp. 3–5.

56. Ibid., p. 2.

57. Hawkinson interview with Califano, p. 21.

58. Gaither Oral History, 19 November 1968, tape 1, pp. 31–32.

59. Memo, Charles M. Maguire to Robert E. Kintner, 11 March 1967, CF LE, WHCF, LBJ Library.

60. Hawkinson interview with Califano, p. 34.

61. Memo, Gaither to Califano, 1 December 1968, "Message Schedules" folder, Box 305, Files of James C. Gaither, LBJ Library.

62. Hawkinson interview with Califano, p. 13.

63. Ibid., p. 22.

64. Ibid., p. 33.

65. Johnson, *The Vantage Point*, p. 447.

66. Doris Kearns, *Lyndon Johnson and the American Dream* (New York: Harper and Row), p. 222.

67. See the list of "Landmark Laws of the Lyndon B. Johnson Administration" in Johnson, *The Vantage Point*.

68. Report on "The Organization and Management of Great Society Programs," 15 June 1967, LBJ Library.

69. *The Work of the Steering Group on Evaluation of the Bureau of the Budget*, July 1967, BOB Files, LBJ Library.

70. On program development during the Reagan administration, see Dick Kirschten, "Decision Making in the White House: How Well Does It Serve the President?" *National Journal*, 3 April 1982, vol. 14, pp. 584–589. For a compact summary of the structure for domestic policy development under presidents since Johnson, see Erwin C. Hargrave and Michael Nelson, *Presidents, Politics, and Policy* (Baltimore and London: Johns Hopkins University Press, 1984), pp. 181–185, 257–263. For a detailed summary for presidents from Roosevelt to Carter, see also Wayne, *The Legislative Presidency*.

71. For an insightful analysis of the problem, see Lester M. Salamon. "The Presidency and Domestic Policy Formulation," in *The Illusion of Presidential Government*, ed. Hugh Heclo and Lester M. Salamon (Washington, D.C.: National Academy of Public Administration, 1981), chap. 6.

6. Developing Executive Policy

1. Some of the major studies that examine the role of the special assistant for national security affairs are Keith C. Clark and Lawrence J. Legere, eds., *The President and the Management of National Security: A Report by the Institute for Defense Analysis* (New York, 1969); R. Gordon Hoxie, *Command Decisions and the Presidency: A Study in National Security Policy and Organization* (New York, 1977); I. M. Destler, *Presidents, Bureaucrats and Foreign Policy: The Politics of Organizational Reform* (Princeton, N.J.: Princeton University Press, 1972). See also I. M. Destler, "A Job that Doesn't Work," *Foreign Policy* 38 (Spring 1980): 80–88; and "National Security Management: What Presidents Have Wrought," *Political Science Quarterly* (Winter 1980–81): 573–588.

2. Destler, *Presidents, Bureaucrats and Foreign Policy*, pp. 99–100; Margaret Jane Wyszomirski, "The De-Institutionalization of Presidential Staff Agencies," *Public Administration Review* 42 (September–October 1982): 452–453. Wyszomirski believes this change in the relation of the president to the NSC staff to be part of a much larger trend away from reliance on professional staff support in the tradition of "neutral competence" to a more personalized staff responsive to presidents' political requirements.

3. Transcript, Bromley K. Smith Oral History Interview, 29 June 1969, pp. 14–15, LBJ Library, hereafter cited as Smith Oral History.

4. As quoted in Clark and Legere, *Management of National Security*, p. 72.

5. Ibid., pp. 31–32.

6. "Komer, Robert W." folder, Box 312, Files of John W. Macy, Jr., LBJ Library.

7. "Bator, Francis M." folder, Box 30, Files of John W. Macy, Jr., LBJ Library.

8. Transcript, Edward R. Fried Oral History Interview, 22 April 1969, tape 1, p. 2, LBJ Library, hereafter cited as Fried Oral History.

9. Smith Oral History, pp. 1–4.

10. Memo, "Personnel under the Supervision of the Special Assistant to the President for National Security Affairs," 12 March 1966, filed with memo, Smith to president, 16 March 1966, Ex FG600/S, WHCF, LBJ Library.

11. Ibid.

12. Memo, McGeorge Bundy to president, 1 March 1964, "Memos to the President" folder, Box 1, Files of McGeorge Bundy, National Security Files, LBJ Library.

13. Memo, Bundy to president, 6 March 1964, "Memos to the President" folder, Box 1, Files of McGeorge Bundy, National Security Files, LBJ Library.

14. Ibid.

15. Memo, "Statement on Air Surveillance over Cuba," undated, filed with Dean Rusk to president, 15 March 1964, "Memos to the President" folder, Box 1, Files of McGeorge Bundy, National Security Files, LBJ Library.

16. Memo, Bundy to president, 24 March 1964, "Memos to the President" folder, Box 1, Files of McGeorge Bundy, National Security Files, LBJ Library.

17. Transcript, Michael V. Forrestal Oral History Interview, 3 January 1969, p. 21, LBJ Library, hereafter cited as Forrestal Oral History.

18. Ibid.

19. Ibid., p. 22.

20. Memo, Bundy to president, 22 May 1964, "Memos to the President" folder, Box 1, Files of McGeorge Bundy, National Security Files, LBJ Library.

21. Memo, Bundy to president, 25 May 1964, "Memos to the President" folder, Box 1, Files of McGeorge Bundy, National Security Files, LBJ Library.

22. Memos, Bundy to president, 11 February 1964, 14 May 1964, "Memos to the President" folder, Box 1, Files of McGeorge Bundy, National Security Files, LBJ Library.

23. Smith Oral History, p. 21.

24. Testimony of Richard Neustadt, National Security Council, New Role and Structure, 7 February 1969, Subcommittee on National Security and International Operations pursuant to S. Res. 24, 91st Cong., 1969.

25. I. M. Destler, one of the eminent scholars of national security management, reviewed the roles of national security assistants from presidents Kennedy through Carter and concluded: "Time and again, national security advisers have become highly visible policy advocates, identified with particular viewpoints and involved in specific negotiations. They have jeopardized their own ability to manage the decision-making process and have intruded on the job of the secretary of state." Abuses under Nixon and Carter became so disruptive of national security policy that Destler concluded that "the most effective way to deal with the problem" was to abolish the post altogether. See Destler, "A Job that Doesn't Work," pp. 80, 87.

26. Smith Oral History, 29 July 1969, p. 35.

27. Memo, Bundy to president, 31 August 1964, "Memos to the President" folder, Box 1, Files of McGeorge Bundy, National Security Files, LBJ Library.

28. Memo, McGeorge Bundy to president, 27 January 1965, NSC History—Troop Deployment, National Security Files, LBJ Library.

29. As quoted in Bundy to president, 27 January 1965, NSC History—Troop Deployment, National Security Files, LBJ Library.

30. Cable, Maxwell Taylor to president, 6 January 1965, NSC History—Troop Deployment, National Security Files, LBJ Library.

31. Memo, McGeorge Bundy to president, 27 January 1965, NSC History—Troop Deployment, National Security Files, LBJ Library.

32. In this brief sketch of the roles of Johnson's national security assistant we cannot do justice to the complexity of the decision-making process involved in Vietnam decisions. While many assumed Johnson's Vietnam decisions to be the result of a faulty advisory process (see Alexander L. George, "The Case for Multiple Advocacy in Making Foreign Policy," *American Political Science Review* 66 ([September 1972]: 751–785), recent scholarship indicates that much more critical thought and dissent existed within the administration. See the elaborate studies of the advisory process in Leslie H. Gelb with Richard K. Betts, *The Irony of Vietnam: The System Worked* (Washington, D.C.: Brookings Institution, 1979); and Larry Berman, *Plan-*

ning a Tragedy: The Americanization of the War in Vietnam (New York: W. W. Norton, 1982).

33. Memo, McGeorge Bundy to Robert S. McNamara, 30 June 1965, NSC History—Troop Deployment, National Security Files, LBJ Library.

34. "The President's News Conference of March 31, 1966" (31 March 1966), in *Public Papers, 1966*, vol. 1, p. 385.

35. The lack of availability of material precludes full assessment of Rostow's role as policy adviser. While the Bundy files had been reviewed at the time of the writing of this book, none of Rostow's files were available. The Vietnam Country file had not been reviewed beyond 1965, and the two NSC histories on Vietnam—Gulf of Tonkin and Troop Deployment—do not concern events during Rostow's tenure as national security assistant.

36. Henry F. Graff, *The Tuesday Cabinet: Deliberation and Decision on Peace and War under Lyndon B. Johnson* (Englewood Cliffs, N.J.: Prentice-Hall, 1970).

37. Rostow, *Diffusion of Power*, p. 358.

38. Ibid., p. 359.

39. Ibid., p. 360.

40. Ibid., p. 362.

41. Clark and Legere, *Management of National Security*, p. 88.

42. Califano, *A Presidential Nation*, p. 40.

43. The concept of the economic subpresidency is elaborated in James E. Anderson and Jared E. Hazleton, *Managing Macroeconomic Policy: The Johnson Presidency* (Austin: University of Texas Press 1986).

44. See "Description of Robson-Ross Office Files," Guide to White House Aides Files, LBJ Library.

45. As quoted in Pierce, *Fiscal Policy*, p. 99.

46. Henry H. Fowler to president, 16 August 1966, "Califano: Taxes (3)" folder, Box 52, Files of Joseph A. Califano, Jr., LBJ Library.

47. Transcript, Arthur M. Okun Oral History Interview, 15 April 1969, tape 2, p. 17, LBJ Library, hereafter cited as Okun Oral History.

48. Ibid.

49. As quoted in Pierce, *Fiscal Policy*, p. 100.

50. Okun Oral History.

51. Califano, *Presidential Nation*, p. 40.

52. Memo, Walter W. Heller to president, 23 November 1963, Ex BE 5, WHCF, LBJ Library.

53. Memo, Heller to president, 1 December 1963, Ex FG 11-3, WHCF, LBJ Library.

54. Ibid.

55. Ibid.

56. Heller also played an important role in persuading Johnson to adopt the War on Poverty program. Memo, Heller to president, 6 January 1964, Ex WE, WHCF, LBJ Library.

57. Okun Oral History, 20 March 1969, p. 14.

58. Ibid., p. 20.

59. Memo, Heller to president, 3 December 1963, Ex FG 11-3, WHCF, LBJ Library.

60. Memo, Heller to president, 17 January 1964, Ex FG 11-3, WHCF, LBJ Library.

61. Memo, 14 December 1963, Ex FG 11-3, WHCF, LBJ Library.

62. Memo, president to Heller, 23 December 1963, Ex FG 11-3, WHCF, LBJ Library.

63. Transcript, Gardner Ackley Oral History Interview, 13 April 1963, p. 12, LBJ Library, hereafter cited as Ackley Oral History.

64. Ibid.

65. Ibid.

66. Ibid., p. 13.

67. As cited in James E. Anderson, "Managing the Economy: The Johnson Administration Experience," paper delivered at the 27–30 August 1980 meeting of the American Political Science Association, Washington, D.C., p. 8.

68. For a full discussion of the Quadriad and less formal relationships with the FRB during the Johnson presidency, see Anderson and Hazleton, *Managing Macroeconomic Policy.*

69. Ibid. Much of this discussion is based on the fuller analysis in chapter 5 of this book.

70. Ibid.

71. Ackley referred to this as the "greatest weakness." Memo, Ackley to president, 13 November 1968, Ex BE 5, WHCF, LBJ Library.

72. Memo, Califano to president, 16 November 1965, WHCF, BE/4 Aluminum, LBJ Library.

73. Memo, Okun to president, 25 May 1966, CEA Microfilm, Roll #68, LBJ Library.

74. Ackley Oral History, 7 March 1974, p. 44.

75. For elaboration of presidential use of advice on science and technology issues, see W. Henry Lambright, *Presidential Management of Science and Technology: The Johnson Presidency* (Austin: University of Texas Press, 1985).

76. Hornig Oral History, 4 December 1968, tape 1, p. 29.

77. Ibid., p. 30.

78. *Administrative History of the Office of Science and Technology during the Administration of President Johnson, Nov. 1963–Jan. 1969,* vol. 1, p. 19, LBJ Library, hereafter cited as *Administrative History of OST.*

79. Lambright, *Presidential Management of Science and Technology.*

80. Hornig Oral History, tape 1, pp. 26–27, 32.

81. Ibid., tape 2, pp. 4–5.

82. Ibid., p. 5.

83. Ibid., tape 1, pp. 30–31.

84. Ibid., p. 19.

85. Letter from Hornig to Richard T. McCulley, 29 June 1981.

86. Hornig Oral History, tape 1, p. 33.

87. On 11 August 1965. See committees to president, 27 May 1966, Ex UT4, WHCF, LBJ Library.

88. See memorandums, Lee C. White to president, 12 August 1965, 21 September 1965, 22 January 1966, Ex UT4, WHCF, LBJ Library.

89. Memo, Ex UT4, LBJ Library.

90. Memo, 31 July 1967, Ex UT4, WHCF, LBJ Library.

91. See, for example, memorandums, James E. Webb to Horace Busby, Jr., 23 March 1965, Box 27, and Busby to Edward C. Welsh, 13 May 1964, Box 28, Files of Horace Busby, Jr., LBJ Library.

92. Hornig to James C. Gaither, 8 November 1968, and Gaither to Califano, 29 November 1968, Box 27, Files of James C. Gaither, LBJ Library.

93. Memo, Charles L. Schultze to president, 20 January 1967.

94. See Bill D. Moyers to president, 15 May 1964.

95. Memo, Califano to president, 27 April 1966, Ex CA, WHCF, LBJ Library.

96. Memo, Myer Feldman to president, 26 March 1964, Ex CA, WHCF, LBJ Library.

97. Milton P. Semer to president, 1 April 1966.

98. Letter, Hornig to Robert S. McNamara, 11 September 1964, *Administrative History of OST*, vol. 2, pp. 26–30, LBJ Library.

99. Memo, Califano to president, 27 April 1966, Ex CA, WHCF, LBJ Library.

100. Memo, W. Marvin Watson to president, 15 March 1966, Ex CA, WHCF, LBJ Library.

101. Johnson, *The Vantage Point*, p. 168.

102. Ibid., pp. 167–168.

103. Memo, "The Detroit Riots Chronology," undated, filed with Lawrence E. Levinson to president, 29 July 1967, "Detroit Chronology: July 23–31 (1)" folder, Box 58, Files of Joseph A. Califano, Jr., LBJ Library.

104. Ibid.

105. McPherson Oral History, 9 April 1969, p. 22.

106. Ibid.

107. "Detroit (3)" folder, Box 44, Files of James C. Gaither, LBJ Library.

108. Telegram, George W. Romney to Ramsay Clark, 24 July 1967, filed with memo, Califano to president, 24 July 1967, "Detroit Chronology: July 23–31 (2)" folder, Box 58, and "Detroit Riots Chronology," Files of Joseph A. Califano, Jr., LBJ Library. Later in the morning Romney stated that he was hesitant to certify that a state of insurrection existed because he believed that such action would invalidate insurance policies in the state.

109. McPherson Oral History, 9 April 1969, p. 20.

110. Johnson, *The Vantage Point*, p. 170.

111. Transcript, Ramsay Clark Oral History Interview, 16 April 1969, LBJ Library, hereafter cited as Clark Oral History.

112. Memo, "Notes of the President's Activities during the Detroit Crisis," 24 July 1967, filed with W. Thomas Johnson, Jr., to president, 25 July 1967, "July 24, 1967" folder, Box 71, Diary Backup, LBJ Library; see also "Detroit Riots Chronology," Files of Joseph A. Califano, Jr., LBJ Library.

113. "Detroit Riots Chronology," Files of Joseph A. Califano, Jr., LBJ Library.

114. "Remarks to the Nation after Authorizing the Use of Federal Troops in Detroit" (24 July 1967), in *Public Papers, 1967*, vol. 2, p. 716.

115. McPherson Oral History, 9 April 1969, p. 21.

116. Ibid.

117. Ibid., p. 22.

118. "Detroit Riots Chronology," Files of Joseph A. Califano, Jr., LBJ Library.

119. Memo, "Notes of the President's Activities during the Detroit Crisis," 24 July 1967, filed with Thomas Johnson to president, 25 July 1967, "July 24, 1967" folder, Box 721, Diary Backup, LBJ Library.

120. Memo, H. Barefoot Sanders to Watson, 26 July 1967, "Detroit" folder, Box 1, Files of George E. Christian, LBJ Library; Sanders to president, 27 July 1967, "Detroit Chronology: July 23–31 (2)" folder, Box 58, Files of Joseph A. Califano, Jr., LBJ Library.

121. "Detroit Riots Chronology," Files of Joseph A. Califano, Jr., LBJ Library.

122. Memo, Califano to president, 27 July 1967, "Detroit Chronology: July 23–31 (1)" folder, Box 58, Files of Joseph A. Califano, Jr., LBJ Library.

123. Memo, Califano to president, 28 July 1967, "Detroit Chronology: July 23–31 (2)" folder, Box 58, Files of Joseph A. Califano, Jr., LBJ Library; memo, Paul C. Warnke to Califano, 27 July 1967, memo, Matthew Nimetz to Califano, 9 August 1967, "Detroit Chronology: July 23–31 (1)" folder, Box 58, Files of Joseph A. Califano, Jr., LBJ Library.

124. See "Final Report of Cyrus R. Vance, Special Assistant to the Secretary of Defense Concerning the Detroit Riots, July 23 through August 2, 1967," pp. 33–40, appended to transcript, Cyrus R. Vance Oral History Interview, LBJ Library.

125. Memo, Farris Bryant to Califano, 27 July 1967, memo, Califano to president, 10 August 1967, "Detroit Chronology: July 23–31 (1)" folder; memo, Califano to president, undated, "Detroit Chronology: July 23–31 (2)" folder, Box 58, Files of Joseph A. Califano, Jr.; memo, Califano to Bryant, 2 August 1967, CF FG 11-6; memo, Califano to president, 28 July 1967, "July 29, 1967" folder, Box 72, diary backup, LBJ Library.

126. Memo, Califano to president, 10 August 1967, "Detroit Chronology: July 23–31 (1)" folder, memo, Califano to president, undated, "Detroit Chronology: July 23–31 (2)" folder, Box 58, Files of Joseph A. Califano, Jr., LBJ Library.

127. Memo, Califano to president, 28 July 1967, "Detroit (2)" folder, Box 44, Files of James C. Gaither, LBJ Library.

128. Memo, "Funding and Administrative Arrangements for the Special Advisory Commission on Civil Disorders," 29 July 1967, "Detroit (2)" folder, Box 44, Files of James C. Gaither, LBJ Library.

129. "Talking Points to the Commission on Civil Disorders," 29 July 1967, "Detroit (2)" folder, Box 44, Files of James C. Gaither, LBJ Library.

130. See chapter 8.

7. Directing the Executive Branch

1. Transcript, Nicholas De B. Katzenbach Oral History Interview, 23 November 1968, p. 5, LBJ Library, hereafter cited as Katzenbach Oral History.

2. Redford and McCulley interview with Jenkins.

3. Transcript, Richard L. Schott interview with Ralph A. Dungan, Washington, D.C., 20 June 1978.

4. See Schott and Hamilton, *People, Position and Power*, chap. 2.

5. Transcript, Emmette S. Redford and Richard L. Schott interview with John W. Macy, Jr., Washington, D.C., 9 November 1976. When Robert E. Kintner came to the White House he was told that one of the things Johnson wanted him to do was to give advice on presidential appointments; during his short period as White House aide he supplemented the Macy search for talent and, in Macy's words, became a kind of "internal critic" of his operation.

6. The Macy operation has been fully described elsewhere. In addition to the Schott/Hamilton exposition already cited, see John W. Macy, Jr., *Public Service: The Human Side of Government* (New York: Harper and Row, 1971), pp. 226–231; Joseph Kraft, "Johnson's Talent Hunt," *Harper's Magazine* (March 1965): 40–46; John Macy and Matthew Coffey, "Executive Recruiting and Management Information in the White House," *Advanced Management Journal* 35 (January 1970): 5–13.

7. For a full account, see Redford and Blissett, *Organizing the Executive Branch*. Most of the data for this section are drawn from that book and its sources.

8. Ibid., pp. 80–83.

9. Ibid., p. 222.

10. See, on these particulars, ibid., pp. 114, 120, 124, 132, 143–144, 189. Horsky was White House adviser on national capital affairs; Taylor was at this time special consultant to the president.

11. For summary and discussion of the Price and Heineman reports, see ibid., pp. 187–189, 195–209.

12. Redford and Blissett, *Organizing the Executive Branch*, p. 222. After analysis of Johnson's varied relations with BOB, Larry Berman concluded that "by 1968 it was hard to distinguish personal from institutional staff services in the Executive Office." *Office of Management and Budget and the Presidency 1921–1979* (Princeton, N.J.: Princeton University Press, 1979), p. 74.

13. The reader may note the very illuminating title, *The Illusion of Presidential Government*, of a book edited by Hugh Heclo and Lester M. Salamon (Boulder, Colo.: Westview Press, 1981). Introducing the discussion, Heclo wrote (p. 1) that "presidential government is the idea that the president, backed by the people, is or can be in charge of governing the country." It would be an illusion also to view the president as governing the executive branch, for as Heclo further wrote, "the vast bulk of ultimate administrative power rests with the Congress, not the President" (p. 15).

14. Califano, *A Presidential Nation*, p. 50.

15. Ibid., p. 215.

16. "Statement by the President on Cost Reduction by the Government during the First Three Months of 1965" (24 May 1965), in *Public Papers, 1965*, pp. 573–574.

17. Memo, Califano to principal staff, 22 June 1967, Ex FG/RS, WHCF, LBJ Library.

18. Ex WH 5-1, WHCF, LBJ Library.

19. Transcript, Stewart L. Udall Oral History Interview, 19 May 1969, p. 5, LBJ Library, hereafter cited as Udall Oral History.

20. Memo, Califano to president, 21 November 1965, Ex FG 11-8-1, WHCF, LBJ Library.

21. Udall Oral History, 19 May 1969, pp. 7–8.

22. Larry E. Temple reports that when he came to the White House he went over to meet the people in the Department of Justice and that the attorney general asked him to weekly luncheons of the top people in the department. Temple Oral History, 12 June 1970, p. 2.

23. "Statement by the President to Cabinet Members and Agency Heads on the New Government-Wide Planning and Budgeting System," and "The President's News Conference of August 25, 1965" (25 August 1965), in *Public Papers, 1965*, pp. 16–19. Also, the president appointed on 3 March 1967 a Commission on Budget Concepts.

24. Most of the information in the paragraph is from Harvey C. Mansfield, Sr., *President Johnson and His Cost Reduction Campaign: Methods and Limits of Presidential Leadership in Administrative Management*, as yet unpublished manuscript in the series of which this book is a part.

25. On Watson's role, see chapters 2 and 3.

26. For discussion of these in a period that included the Johnson administration, see Macy, *Public Service.*

27. As a consultant in the Department of Agriculture during the summers of 1967 and 1968, one of the authors attended Secretary Orville L. Freeman's morning staff meetings in the coffee room. He recalls that repeatedly the secretary told the staff that in the last Cabinet meeting the president had again urged stronger effort to eliminate racial discrimination in the public service.

28. For illustration, one may note the letter to Secretary of Defense Robert S. McNamara urging continued efforts and particularly cooperation with the governors with respect to the National Guard, 26 December 1964, and one to the Department of Agriculture asking for a report on "actual progress" in each unit of the department, 18 April 1965, in *Public Papers, 1963–64*, vol. 1, p. 433, vol. 2, p. 816.

29. Memo, Harry C. McPherson, Jr., to president, 28 February 1966, "Memoranda to the President (1966)" folder, Box 52, Files of Harry C. McPherson, Jr., LBJ Library.

30. Califano, *Presidential Nation*, p. 241.

31. Transcript, David S. Black Oral History Interview, 12 November 1968, LBJ Library, hereafter cited as Black Oral History.

32. Udall Oral History, 18 April 1969, pp. 21–22.

33. "Appointments to the Regulatory Agencies: The Federal Communications Commission and the Federal Trade Commission (1949–1974)," Committee Print, Senate Committee on Commerce, 94th Cong., 2nd sess., April 1976, p. 240.

34. Goldstein Oral History, 10 December 1968, tape 2, pp. 3, 4.

35. Udall Oral History, 29 July 1969, pp. 33ff.

36. David Welborn, *Executive Leadership in the Administration of Economic Programs: The Johnson Presidency,* forthcoming publication in the series of which this book is part.

37. See Francis E. Rourke, "The Presidency and the Bureaucracy," in *The Presidency and the Political System,* ed. Michael Nelson (Washington, D.C.: Congressional Quarterly Press, 1984), pp. 339–362.

38. Letter, Johnson to McNamara, 25 November 1963, Ex FG 11-8-1, WHCF, LBJ Library.

39. Lyndon B. Johnson School of Public Affairs Policy Research Project Interview with Walter W. Jenkins, 14 December 1976, Austin, Texas.

40. Califano, *Presidential Nation,* p. 241.

41. *Washington Post,* 11 March 1965.

42. Johnson revised prescribed standards of ethical conduct for executive officers and employees and extended them for presidential appointees and certain other officials to include filing of statements of financial holdings. Executive Order 11222, 11 May 1965, 30 Federal Register 6469.

43. His statement was in a letter from W. Marvin Watson, Jr., to George F. Galland, 7 June 1965, Gen. CA/7 Island Airlines, WHCF, LBJ Library.

44. Memo, McPherson to president, 1 April 1966, "Memos to the President (1966)" folder, Box 52, Files of Harry C. McPherson, Jr., LBJ Library. And when George Meany came to the White House to protest government dealings with a firm condemned by the National Labor Relations Board, Johnson said to Temple, "What did you let that guy in here for anyway?" Temple Oral History, pp. 6–7.

45. The matters discussed in the paragraph in the text are fully examined in the previously cited volume in this series, Welborn, *Executive Leadership,* chap. 3.

46. As quoted in ibid.

47. Temple Oral History, pp. 7–10. Full analysis of the participation of the president and White House staff with respect to antitrust will be presented in another volume in this series, Welborn, *Executive Leadership.*

48. Note on memo from Califano to president, Ex TW 4, WHCF, LBJ Library.

49. The summary in the text is based on a telephone interview of Emmette S. Redford with F. Peter Libassi on 25 May 1982. The strong presidential support of Johnson in the conference with governors was corroborated by Cohen and also the freedom from intervention by Johnson.

50. "Remarks to Members of Congress at a Reception Marking the Enactment of the Education Bill" (13 April 1965), in *Public Papers,* p. 416.

51. See, for summary of that event, Edward S. Corwin, *The President:*

Office and Powers, 1787–1957, 4th ed. (New York: New York University Press, 1957), pp. 83–84.

52. See Redford and Blissett, *Organizing the Executive Branch*, pp. 180–183 for details.

53. For details, see transcript, Wilbur J. Cohen Oral History Interview, 10 May 1969, pp. 8ff., LBJ Library, hereafter cited as Cohen Oral History.

54. See report, "Presidential Involvement," "Economic Opportunity Act Amendment of 1967" folder 1739, Box 34, p. 1, Files of Joseph A. Califano, Jr., LBJ Library.

55. Ibid.

56. For a full discussion, see Redford and Blissett, *Organizing the Executive Branch*, pp. 99–104.

57. Memo, Cater to president, 30 March 1965, Cater Aide Files, LBJ Library.

58. While the Civil Rights Act of 1964 was signed on 2 July, memos began to circulate within the White House and between it and agencies as early as 15 June. Both flexibility and insulation of the president were achieved by a decision to allow agencies to issue guidelines on compliance with regulations. The president was informed on their content but did not sign them.

59. See Redford and Blissett, *Organizing the Executive Branch*, pp. 115–118.

60. See "The Secretary of State and the Problems of Coordination: New Duties and Procedures of March 4, 1966," Committee Print, Committee on Government Operations, U.S. Senate, 89th Cong., 2nd sess.

61. "Letter to Thomas C. Mann upon His Assuming New Responsibilities for Latin American Affairs" (15 December 1963), in *Public Papers, 1963–64*, p. 56.

62. "Letter to Secretary Dillon on the Need for Coordinating Federal Actions in the Field of Bank Regulation" (18 March 1964), in *Public Papers, 1965*, p. 393.

63. Respectively, Executive Orders 11247, 24 September 1965, 11297, 11 August 1966, 11307, 30 September 1966, 11269, 14 February 1966. Such orders sometimes supplemented congressional directives for coordination. For vivid discussion of the use of coordinators and the inadequacies of coordination, see James L. Sundquist, with the collaboration of David W. Davis, *Making Federalism Work: A Study of Program Coordination at the Community Level* (Washington, D.C.: Brookings Institution, 1969), especially the discussion of coordination in Washington in chap. 1; see also Redford and Blissett, *Organizing the Executive Branch*, especially chap. 4 on the Office of Economic Opportunity (OEO), chap. 8 on executive guidance and control, and pp. 228–229 in the conclusion.

64. 26 August 1965, in *Public Papers, 1965*, vol. 2, pp. 453–454.

65. "Memorandum Concerning the Power Failure in Northeastern United States" (9 November 1965), in *Public Papers, 1965*, p. 1109.

66. White Oral History, 28 September 1970, p. 11.

67. The Cabinet met nine times in 1964, thirteen in 1965, sixteen in 1966,

twenty-one in 1967, and sixteen by September 1968. "Cabinet Meetings," no date, Cabinet Papers, Box 19, LBJ Library.

68. Maguire Oral History, 19 August 1969, p. 60.

69. Ibid.

70. Memo, Robert E. Kintner to president, 16 June 1966, CF, FG 100/MC, LBJ Library.

71. Cronin does not argue that tensions are unavoidable or undesirable, but he suggests that presidents need to give more consideration to the need for skilled management mediators on their staff. "Everybody Believes in Democracy until He Gets to the White House . . ." and "An Examination of White House–Departmental Relations," in *The Institutionalized Presidency*, ed. Norman C. Thomas and Hans W. Baade (Dobbs Ferry, N.Y.: Oceana Publications, 1972), pp. 147–199, quotations from p. 149. Another author sees tensions as creators of "opportunities as well as constraints. A president with some self-awareness can use this cat's cradle of tensions to see that he is at the center of things when he wants to be and 'out of it' when he needs to be." Hugh Heclo, "The Changing Presidential Office," in *Politics and the Oval Office*, ed. Arnold J. Meltsner (San Francisco, Calif.: Institute for Contemporary Studies, 1981), p. 183.

72. Conflicting attitudes can exist. Thus, DeVier Pierson thought Udall sometimes felt his staff position "insulated" Udall from the president, but also thought Udall would think Pierson helped him with access to the president. Pierson Oral History, 19 March 1969, pp. 13, 14.

73. See chapter 4.

74. President Johnson's relations with top executive officials will be further illuminated by the LBJ Library's future release of some of the president's telephone conversations that were preserved on dictaphone belt recording and tapes of meetings in the Cabinet room recorded in 1968.

75. Pierson Oral History, 19 March 1969, pp. 11–12.

76. Transcript, Robert C. Weaver Oral History Interview, 19 November 1968, pp. 19–20, LBJ Library.

77. Katzenbach Oral History, 23 November 1968, p. 10.

78. Temple Oral History, 12 June 1970, p. 3.

79. Transcript, Orville L. Freeman Oral History Interview, 14 February 1969, p. 16, LBJ Library.

80. Cohen Oral History, 2 March 1969, pp. 12, 19–24.

8. Representing the President

1. *A Presidency for the 1980s*, A Report on Presidential Management by a Panel of the National Academy of Public Administration (Washington, D.C., 1980), p. 17.

2. Richard E. Neustadt, *Presidential Power: The Politics of Leadership*, 2nd ed. (New York: John Wiley and Sons, 1976).

3. In a comparative study, Stephen J. Wayne, *The Legislative Presidency* (New York: Harper & Row, 1978), pp. 168–172, discusses the difficulty of objectively measuring presidential influence in Congress. The evidence he

presents, however, indicates that in the period between the administrations of Dwight D. Eisenhower and Gerald R. Ford, Johnson annually presented more legislative proposals than any other president, a total of 1,685 between 1965 and 1968. Moreover, of all the presidents in Wayne's sample, Johnson had the highest percentage of submitted proposals enacted into law by Congress, over 57 percent.

4. Johnson, *The Vantage Point*, p. 448.

5. Lawrence F. O'Brien, *No Final Victories, a Life in Politics—From John F. Kennedy to Watergate* (New York: Doubleday and Company, 1974), p. 170.

6. Memo, Joseph A. Califano, Jr., to president, 18 February 1966, Ex FG 165 6-3, WHCF, LBJ Library.

7. The staff at the end of 1967 included H. Barefoot Sanders, Jr., Mike N. Manatos, John P. Roche, John Gonella, Irvine H. Sprague, James R. Jones, William M. Blackburn, Jr., Sherwin J. Markham, W. DeVier Pierson, and Robert L. Hardesty.

8. Manatos Oral History, 25 August 1969, p. 9.

9. Ibid., p. 15.

10. McPherson, *A Political Education*, p. 267.

11. Manatos Oral History, 25 August 1969, pp. 25, 36.

12. Markham Oral History, 21 May 1969, p. 22.

13. See a memo on follow-up on such a suggestion from Lawrence F. O'Brien to George E. Reedy, 2 April 1965, Ex FG 400, WHCF, LBJ Library.

14. "Statement by the President at a Cabinet Meeting: Personnel Appointments" (19 November 1964), in *Public Papers, 1963–64*, vol. 2, pp. 1605–1606.

15. Ralph K. Huitt, "White House Channels to the Hill," in *Congress against the President*, ed. Harvey C. Mansfield, Sr. (New York: Academy of Political Science, 1975), p. 77. The account in the remainder of the paragraph in the text is based on Huitt's discussions, pp. 77ff.

16. Ibid.

17. See, for example, a memorandum from O'Brien to White House staff reminding of procedures, 21 January 1965, Ex 400, WHCF, LBJ Library.

18. The Diary and Diary Backup of the president contain notations of speechwriting activity in the early days of the Johnson presidency.

19. Theodore H. White, *The Making of the President, 1964* (New York: Atheneum Publishers, 1965), p. 348.

20. Maguire Oral History, 8 July 1969, p. 36. See also Benchley Oral History, 20 November 1968, p. 8.

21. Ibid.

22. Benchley Oral History, 20 November 1966, p. 8.

23. Maguire Oral History, 29 July 1969, pp. 1–53, has a meaty discussion of the processes during the post–Robert E. Kintner period. The speechwriting process is also extensively discussed in Benchley Oral History, pp. 6–18.

24. Benchley Oral History, 20 November 1968, pp. 12–13.

25. McPherson, *A Political Education*, pp. 297–298.

26. Benchley Oral History, 11 November 1968, p. 14.

27. McPherson, *A Political Education*, p. 320.

28. Benchley Oral History, 11 November 1968, p. 17.
29. Maguire Oral History, 8 July 1969, pp. 16–17.
30. McPherson, *A Political Education*, p. 327.
31. Ibid., pp. 299–303.
32. The best general, interpretive discussion of presidential-media relations is Michael B. Grossman and Martha Kumar, *Portraying the President: The White House and the News Media* (Baltimore: Johns Hopkins University Press, 1981). See also David Culbert, "Johnson and the Media," in *Exploring the Johnson Years*, ed. Robert A. Divine (Austin: University of Texas Press, 1981), pp. 214–248.
33. For illustration, see George E. Christian's notes on interviews for early 1968, Box 1, Office Files of George E. Christian, LBJ Library.
34. Memo, S. Douglass Cater to Califano, Kintner, McPherson, Manatos, and Henry Hall Wilson, 1 March 1967, Ex WH 10, WHCF, LBJ Library.
35. Memo, Cater to president, June 1965, LBJ Library.
36. Transcript, interview with George E. Reedy, 7 June 1976, Interview III, tape 1, p. 6, LBJ Library, hereafter cited as Reedy interview.
37. Reedy Oral History, 19 December 1968.
38. Ibid., p. 29.
39. Ibid., p. 33.
40. Ibid., p. 30.
41. George E. Reedy, *Lyndon B. Johnson, A Memoir* (New York: Andrews and McMeel, 1972), p. 141.
42. McPherson Oral History, 16 January 1969, p. 1.
43. Christian Oral History, 11 November 1968, pp. 7–8.
44. Ibid., p. 7.
45. McPherson, *A Political Education*, p. 265.
46. Ibid.
47. Robert H. Fleming, deputy press secretary under both Moyers and Christian, reported: "So when I first went, I would go to the bedroom each morning because Moyers wanted to get out of that. Then I would come back and sit with Moyers along about nine o'clock and tell him whatever happened up there. . . . When Christian replaced Moyers he took over going to the bedroom. . . . So I would then thereafter handle things George wanted done." Transcript, Robert H. Fleming Oral History Interview, 8 November 1969, pp. 13–14, LBJ Library.
48. Ibid., p. 14.
49. Memo, Kintner to Moyers, 30 April 1966, CR/PR 18, LBJ Library.
50. Memorandums, Kintner to president, 6 November 1966, Ex PR 18, 1 March 1967, Ex WH 10, WHCF, LBJ Library.
51. Memo, Kintner to president, 1 March 1967, Ex WH 10, WHCF, LBJ Library.
52. See a memo from Moyers to Kintner, 30 April 1966, WHCF, LBJ Library.
53. As usual the president acted selectively with attention to detail. He disapproved a suggestion that some staff members go to New York on the

days of final editing of *Newsweek* and *Time*, saying, "OK if they request come here."

54. Memo, Cater to Califano, Kintner, McPherson, Manatos, and Wilson, 1 March 1967, Ex WH 10, WHCF, LBJ Library.

55. Memo, Ben Wattenberg to president, 17 January 1967, Ex FG 11-8, WHCF, LBJ Library.

56. Memo, Kintner to president, 9 February 1967, CF FG 1, WHCF, LBJ Library.

57. Memo from president's office to McPherson, 20 June 1966, WHCF, LBJ Library.

58. Memo, Carol Welch to the secretaries to the special assistants, 21 June 1966, WHCF, LBJ Library.

59. Christian Oral History, p. 12.

60. Memo, Cater to president, WHCF, LBJ Library.

61. Memo, Cater to president, 29 September 1965, "Sep. 1965" folder, Box 14, Files of S. Douglass Cater, LBJ Library.

62. Memo to president, 9 January 1967, WHCF, LBJ Library.

63. Memo, 30 November 1965, WHCF, LBJ Library.

64. Memo, Cater to president, 29 September 1965, "Sep. 1965" folder, Box 14, Files of S. Douglass Cater, LBJ Library.

65. Memo, McPherson to president, 30 November 1965, "McPherson, Harry" folder, Box 1, Office Files of the President, LBJ Library.

66. Memo, president to Califano, 6 December 1968, Ex FG 11-8-1/Califano, WHCF, LBJ Library.

67. Valenti Oral History, 19 February 1971, pp. 10–11.

68. Transcript, Clifton C. Carter Oral History Interview, 15 October 1968, tape 4, p. 14, LBJ Library, hereafter cited as Carter Oral History.

69. Memo, W. Marvin Watson to president, 18 April 1966, "DNC/Activities Reports" folder, Box 19, Files of W. Marvin Watson, LBJ Library.

70. Memos, Louis Martin to John Criswell, 17 April 1967, filed with Criswell to Watson, 19 April 1967, Martin to Criswell, 27 February 1967, filed with Criswell to Watson, 1 March 1967, "DNC/Activities Reports" folder, Box 19, Files of W. Marvin Watson, LBJ Library.

71. Memo, president to John Bailey, 31 May 1965, "DNC/Financial Reports" folder, Box 19, Files of W. Marvin Watson, LBJ Library.

72. Ibid.

73. Memo, Moyers to president, 2 May 1966, CF PL 2, WHCF, LBJ Library.

74. Ibid.

75. Memo, Watson to president, 7 September 1966, "DNC/Miscellaneous" folder, Box 19, Files of W. Marvin Watson, LBJ Library.

76. Unsigned, undated memo filed with Watson to president, 18 November 1965, "DNC/Miscellaneous" folder, Box 19, Files of W. Marvin Watson, LBJ Library.

77. Memo, Watson to president, 18 March 1966, "DNC/Activities Reports" folder, Box 19, Files of W. Marvin Watson, LBJ Library.

78. Redford and Blissett, *Organizing the Executive Branch*, chap. 4.

9. Conclusion

1. See Robert T. Hartmann, *An Inside Account of the Ford Years* (New York: McGraw Hill, 1980).

2. Hess, *Organizing the Presidency*, p. 150. Quotations in the text are from pp. 151, 154, 214, 208, 210, 212, 213, 214, 215, 216.

3. Ibid., p. 206.

4. *A Presidency for the 1980s.*

5. *The Organization and Management of Great Society Programs*, "1966 Task Force on Government Organization" folder, Box 4, Task Force Files, LBJ Library.

6. National Academy of Public Administration, *Watergate*, quotations appearing in the text are from pp. 25, 40, 37, 41, 38, 51, xii, 60, 61, 38.

Appendix 1. The White House: Comments on Size and Service Functions

1. Memo, William J. Hopkins to S. Douglass Cater, Jr., 18 June 1968, Ex WH 2, WHCF, LBJ Library.

2. "As you know, the only reason money is being turned back to the Treasury from the S & E appropriation is because of the fact that in numerous instances vacancies have been filled by detail from other departments leaving the detailee on the rolls there rather than bringing them on this roll." W. Marvin Watson, Jr., to president, 27 June 1966, Ex WH 1, WHCF, LBJ Library. On 31 October 1967 Hopkins reported to Watson that he had forty vacancies because of the detail of persons from departments and agencies. Memo, Hopkins to Watson, 31 October 1967, Ex WH 2, WHCF, LBJ Library. Robert W. Komer wrote as follows to Watson: "On personnel, I'll recruit as much as possible from other agencies on detail—they'll pay (as in the case of Ambassador Leonhart). I'll also use NSC services as much as possible. On travel, we'll satellite on State/AID/DOD to maximum extent." Memo, Komer to Watson, 12 April 1966, Ex WH 14-2, WHCF, LBJ Library. Harry C. McPherson, Jr., has said he stayed on detail from the State Department for a period to save cost for the White House. McPherson Oral History, 24 March 1969, tape 6, p. 3.

3. Memo, Hopkins to Walter W. Jenkins, 20 January 1964, with accompanying attachments, Ex FG 11-8-1, WHCF, LBJ Library.

4. A memo from James U. Cross to president, 19 August 1965, reports he had reduced military support for the Office of the President by 61 from 509 when he became armed forces aide. Ex FG 11-8, WHCF, LBJ Library. Figures on number of staff in White House memos are frequently inconsistent.

5. *The Budget of the United States Government, Fiscal Year 1965, Appendix* (Washington, D.C.: U.S. Government Printing Office, 1964), pp. 45–46, 972; and *The Budget of the United States Government, Fiscal Year 1970, Appendix* (Washington, D.C.: U.S. Government Printing Office, 1969), pp. 49, 1012.

6. Ibid.

7. Lists prepared by persons in the White House are often undependable.

Thus, in comparison with Bess Abell's 396, and the budgetary nucleus of about 250, a list of persons within the White House office distributed by James R. Jones included, with obviously inappropriate inclusions, about 600 names of persons and positions. Memo, Jones to Cross, sent to WHCF on 10 August 1966, LBJ Library.

8. Transcript, William J. Hopkins Oral History Interview, 6 June 1969, p. 2, LBJ Library.

9. Ibid., pp. 2–4.

Index